She Was Never the Same

Susan Glasier

SHE WAS NEVER THE SAME

This work is loosely based on the life of the author's grandmother. Because some of the details of that life are difficult to verify, many of the incidents and all of the dialogue are products of the author's imagination. While the persons depicted herein really existed, their names have been changed to protect the privacy of the living and the legacies of the dead.

Published by Susan Glasier, Red Deer, Canada

ISBN:
    Paperback   978-1-7387146-0-5

Publication assistance and digital printing in Canada by

PUBLISHING
PageMaster.ca

DEDICATION

Dedicated with love to my descendants
with the hope you might all gain some insight into this
family's intergenerational battle
with the trauma of tragedy.
I also hope it provides a ticket on the train
to peace and wholeness.
A cousin once asked me
why our shared grandmother didn't like her.
Perhaps this provides an answer to her question.

 **PROLOGUE**

My grandmother's given name was Olive Amelia. I think Amelia was what she liked to be called in her youth though the servants and her sisters called her Melia from time to time. She was old when I got to know her, so Granny is the name I think of when I think of my grandmother.

She lived with us on and off for most of my young life. I always looked up to her as she seemed so wise, so independent and so determined about everything that came across her path. There was a certain spirit about her that fascinated me. I always sensed, however, that there were underlying secrets that haunted her, and the older I got the more I felt a need to know what those secrets were. I always wanted to know what her life was like before I knew her. At times she displayed a profound sadness brought on by what appeared to be the most innocent of events. At other times she was completely selfish and insufferable. I've seen her anger rise like an entity unto itself and frighten the daylights out of me and anyone near her. The dichotomy of her strength versus sadness and anger presented me with questions over the years. What was the foundation for all these emotions? What happened to my grandmother in her life that made her so volatile?

I tried over the years to get some answers directly from her, but she always said I didn't need to know, or I was too young to know, or it wasn't my business to know. I could never push her too hard for answers for fear I would trigger the rage that lived beneath the thin surface of her psyche. I even tried to get some answers from my own mother but was always met with a shake of the head and a melancholy dismissal of my questions, "Don't ask questions. Some things are better off left unknown."

I thought any possibility for getting answers was over when she died on Christmas Eve of 1968, but in early 1969 while my mother was going through Granny's papers, she found a diary. It started on my grandmother's tenth birthday and recorded important events until she was well into her fifties. It was a treasure of timelines. The only thing it lacked was how Granny felt about any of these events.

This diary, however, provided answers to the many questions I wondered about for so long. It provided a map of her life but there was so much more to my grandmother than a series of events. There is so much about her that is like me. So in order to sort things out, I decided to put myself in her head and write between the lines of her diary. I have "filled in the blanks" with my own suppositions.

I can see my granny almost in the flesh now, rolling in her grave and muttering "I can't believe she wrote this in a book."

I can barely believe it myself.

 # Chapter 1

1906

Stifled rage bubbles up and explodes out of me. "Lucille gets everything!" I scream at my father. My fingers roll into tight fists and the need to strike out, to punch something, anything, overpowers me. "Lucille always gets everything! It's not fair!"

Father hates it when I scream.

In the momentary silence that follows, Father pulls himself off his leather chair and stretches to his full six-foot height, thundering back at me. "Listen young lady, life is not often fair. I can only take one of you and Lucille is older. Look at you, you're a nineteen-year-old woman and you behave like a child. Stop making everything so difficult for everybody all the time. Your sister is the best escort for me on this trip. At least she knows how to behave."

I hear what he says but the unfairness of it all defeats me, and I burst into tears.

Father hates it when I cry.

He stares at me frowning and waiting. I watch as he curls his lip under in a tight, angry scowl until my tears stop. I stare back at him, but I can't control the words that tumble out.

"But Father, you're going to see the president. The President! Lucille doesn't care about Teddy Roosevelt, but I do. He's, he's President of the United States! He...he's famous," I stammer. I search for something more profound to add but all that comes out is, "All Lucille cares about are clothes, parties and finding a fiancé."

"Olive Amelia Lange that will be enough from you." He's using his official Judge voice. It's the voice he uses on lawyers that annoy him at the courthouse, loud and intimidating. It's also the voice he uses when he's upset with me or one of my sisters.

I look up into his bushy bearded face. His color slides from its usual rosy pink to bright red. I know I've said the wrong thing. He uses my full name and his booming voice only when he's angry. Pausing momentarily, he turns his back on me and walks to his desk. The conversation is over. I know better than to push him. His decisions are always final and there's no going back. I feel tears, again. This time they are tears of frustration. I am too afraid to say anything else, so I bound from my chair and storm down the hall to my bedroom, slamming the door, hoping he hears through the slam how mad I am. I can never win with my father.

I pace. Here we go again. It was never like this when Mother was alive. She's been dead for two years, and I still cry at the thought of her. She was the only person that ever understood me. She's the only person that ever loved me. She always made me feel like I mattered.

As I pace, I catch a reflection of myself in the large carved gilded mirror that hangs over my dressing table. Mother gave me this mirror on my tenth birthday. I stare into it, somehow expecting to see her staring back at me, but instead I am met with my own sad, red-eyed face. Usually I like my perfectly set sky-blue eyes, but now they look grotesque, all bloodshot from crying. I feel ugly. I touch my long, wavy chestnut hair. Mother always said it is my best asset. I wonder if she would still say that if she could see me now. Staring into the mirror is like staring straight into my unhappiness.

What am I going to do with myself?

"Mama, I miss you," I call out loud. I wonder if she can hear me. You were the only one I could talk to. I don't know what to do. I fling myself onto my bed and sob.

The acrid smell of sickness sweeps into the room and I hear my mother call. I look up and I am floating somewhere in some ominous dark sky. Mother beckons to me, stretching out her emaciated hands and long fingers. I watch her lips form words, I struggle to understand, I feel a longing for her touch, just one more time, just one more time. I hold out my fingers to feel something, anything, but the fingers I reach for fade away into the blackness.

Someone is banging on my door and calling. "Breakfast is served, Melia. Come quickly, your sister has exciting news."

Breakfast? My mind is groggy. How can it be breakfast already? I'm still in yesterday's clothes.

"I'll be down in a minute," I grumble, still feeling half asleep.

I roll over and discover Dotty hovering over me. "Sorry, to bother you, but the Judge says to come in a hurry. Your sister has news and he's about to leave for Boston. He wants to share a meal with all you girls before he goes."

"Oh, Dotty, I'll be down in a minute," I mutter, as I half-heartedly swing my feet over the edge of the bed. "And don't call me Melia."

"As you wish," Dotty mumbles and dutifully backs out the door. For some reason Dotty always bows demurely and turns backwards to exit a room. I don't know where she got this habit. Mother spent years trying to change her but after Mother died, Dotty just kept on with her annoying backward exits. She also took up the habit of calling me Melia. I've told her a dozen times that's not my name, but she doesn't seem to hear. Maybe she just doesn't care.

I used to hate having servants, but now that Mother is gone, I'm not sure any of us could live without them. Mother had six before she died, but Father let four of them go the day after she passed. It seemed wrong at the time, and he kept saying over and over how sorry he was, but he couldn't look at them without thinking of Mother. Last time I counted there were four new ones: upstairs maid, downstairs maid, gardener and a cook. Funny thing is, he kept Manson and Dotty. Manson has always been our butler and he also is the keeper of our horses. Manson and Dotty were Mother's favorites, which is totally contrary to his reason for letting the others go.

I understand why Father kept Dotty. She was a servant in Mother's house before Mother married Father. My grandparents got her from an orphanage when she was ten and she's been a loyal servant ever since. I once asked Mother why her family didn't adopt her, but Mother said we don't make servants part of the family.

As I readjust my clothes and pull the hairbrush through my locks, I wonder what is going on that is so important they sent Dotty to get me. As I descend the stairs all I hear is the usual breakfast clatter of dishes and happy voices. If I hadn't been summoned with such urgency, it would have sounded like just a normal morning in the Lange household.

As I approach the table, Father's voice rises above the din. "Well, finally decided to wake up and join the world, have we?" he sings out. I can't help but think back on our conversation from last night. Why is he mocking me? Same old Father; nothing ever changes. Why does he always make me cry? I decide not to respond to him and turn my face away and sink into my chair.

In the silence that follows, I hear Ada's low-pitched, manly voice, "Hey, Melia can't talk? Cat got your tongue?"

There she goes again. My sister Ada makes it her daily ritual to think up some new and clever way to annoy me and Lucille. Sometimes she even manages to aggravate both of us at the same time. She seems to live for those moments. She has been doing this since she was twelve. Lucille and I manage to get back at her by simply ignoring her. Today I am in no mood to put up with her snarky comments. I stand up, reach out and slap her across her stupid sneering face.

I watch the redness gather on her cheek. I am shocked that I actually hit something. My hand hurts. I back off and, as I look to find my chair, out of the corner of my eye I see a fat, determined fist coming at me and connecting directly with my nose. My body slams up against the hard wall and I land sprawled across the floor. I see red dripping down the front of my dress and there's a blinding pain in my head. Then nothing.

I smell leather and tobacco. My head hurts. I open my eyes and I'm lying on the chesterfield in Father's library. Who put a quilt over me? I reach up and feel my face. My nose is stuffed with cotton and the pain radiates out and encompasses my entire head. Even my eyes hurt. Someone's in the room.

"The doctor says you're supposed to stay quiet and not move." I recognize the voice: Ada.

I try to raise my head off the pillow, but it hurts too much. "Oh God, why did you hit me?" I ask, even though I already know the answer.

"You hit me first," Ada snaps. "Why did you do that?"

I can't answer. The question is too hard. Talking is too hard. "Why are you here?" is all I can manage.

"Father and Lucille have left for Boston and Father is disgusted with us. Father said he wants us to settle whatever is going on before he gets back. Doc Parker came and gave you an injection and you slept a long time. I broke your nose. I didn't mean to, but I did and then you banged your head on the wall. You can't go around hitting people. Father said to tell you that. Father is mad. I've never seen him so mad in my whole life. He said if we weren't his own daughters, he'd see to it we were locked up. I think he's mad enough that if we don't stop, he just might do that. I wish

Mother were here to talk to. I don't think she would be very happy with us right now."

I try to listen. What she is saying makes sense, but her rants annoy me.

"Please," Ada pleads again, "please, please stop being so darn mad about everything."

I search her face and see tears welling up.

She's right. I am mad. I'm mad at everybody and everything. Sadness overtakes me and I reach out to hug my sister. "You're right," I whisper, "We have to change the way things are or we'll all go crazy."

Ada smiles at me and comes close to hold me. She sits next to me on the edge of the chesterfield. She's different in looks from me. Her eyes are much darker, and she's the heavy one of the family. Her hair is nearly black and long and straight as a board. Sometimes I hate my curly hair, but I don't envy her limp dark locks. She loves playing the piano and singing more than anything in the world, but her voice is so low that if you heard her without seeing her, you would swear she's a man with a lovely tenor voice. I shiver just thinking about it. It's just odd, just plain odd, just like my sister.

"You have a heck of a punch, Sister. Maybe you should take up boxing," I tell her, hoping the sarcasm I feel reaches her.

She frowns at me for a moment and then smiles and nods in agreement. "You're probably right," she sighs. "I quite surprised myself. Remember not to slap me anymore and I promise not to say ugly things to you anymore. Deal?"

"Deal," I tell her, but I wonder if we can ever really be friends. We are just too different.

A sudden pain flashes across my nose. "Ada, can you bring me my mirror? I want to look at my face. It really hurts."

Ada shakes her head and looks worried, "I don't think you should look yet, Melia. Your face is really swollen, and it looks kind of funny."

"Really? If I look that terrible, perhaps I should look."

"I don't think so. Just wait a couple more days, maybe the swelling will go down," she pleads.

"Okay," I tell her nodding. "Oh God, even just nodding hurts."

***

Father and Lucille have been gone for more than three weeks when I become aware of an emptiness inside me. I hate to admit it, but I even miss Lucille – spoiled, prissy and annoying as she can be. It's nothing like the utter loneliness I felt when Mother died, but I'm surprised at the intensity of this ache, nonetheless. Even with the busyness of garden parties and social events, I can't erase the feeling that part of my life is missing. I wonder if Ada feels the same.

"I wish they would come home," I tell her at the dinner table. "I really do miss them both. Life feels meaningless. Just me and you and the servants. Wouldn't it be nice to have a more exciting life? You could be an opera singer and I could go to England and be an actress. Or maybe I could own a business making clothes or something."

"You have such an imagination," Ada says, cutting me off. Laughing, she adds, "Women don't run businesses – and if you became an actress, Father would disown you. Anyway, I bet it's not Father or Lucille you miss. I bet it's the lack of somebody to fight with."

"Why would you say that?"

"Amelia, you know I'm right. When everybody is together, we can't even get through a single meal without some sort of outburst from you. I think you thrive on confrontation. You enjoy goading people."

"I don't enjoy it. Sometimes, I feel like Father and Lucille actually plot to make me mad. You also do a good job of that."

"And you have the broken nose to show for it," Ada chuckles.

We eat in silence for a few minutes. Our pact of not provoking each other has held for the past three weeks. I can look at Ada without feeling I need to fly into a rage to keep her from insulting me. It's probably the fear of Father and what he might do if we don't settle our differences.

"As far as I'm concerned," Ada adds, "whether Father and Lucille are here or not makes no difference to me. We can never carry on a conversation with Father anyway. All he's interested in is being a judge. Half the time he still thinks he's in court when he comes home." She waves her fork in the air. "In my opinion the only thing he wants from us is to find respectable husbands and move away." She glances at me and then back down at her plate. "At least that's how I see Father." She takes another piece of meat on her fork. "And Lucille. Well, Lucille... I hate listening to how wonderful she is and all the important things she does. She makes even me mad sometimes." She chews and swallows. "Frankly, neither of them adds much to my world right now."

"Gosh, Ada, I guess we've found something we agree on." I reach out and touch her arm. She forces a small, sad smile. I recognize the sadness that surrounds her. It mirrors mine when it comes to Lucille and Father. I've seen it before. But today, I sense a more profound sadness in her at a depth that surprises me. I wonder if she misses Mother as much as I do.

"I can't talk about this anymore," she announces, standing up. "I'm going to play the piano for a while and then go to bed." She lumbers into the sitting room and plays some sad dirge that adds to my own melancholy. I listen for a few more minutes and then go to my room.

***

It's another four weeks – the end of July – before Lucille and Father return home. They arrive in the middle of the night, but I'm too tired to get up and greet them. My laziness means I am forced to wait until just before dinner the following evening when they wake up.

I peek into Lucille's bedroom when I hear her stir. I watch as she pulls herself out of bed and stands. When she sees me, I take a step towards her with arms outstretched.

"Good grief, Amelia, don't even think of hugging me," she whines. "Give me a chance to wake up and get cleaned up before any hugs. I smell dreadful."

"Oh Lucille, I don't care if you smell. I'm just glad you're home," I blather, grabbing her and holding her tight. She smells slightly musty. " "I am so happy to see you," I mumble into her knotted hair.

She laughs and then gives me a proper hug. "I have to confess I missed you too, Sister. Now leave me be and I'll meet you at dinner. I have much to tell you about our trip."

I find myself surprised by my reaction to her home coming. I can't help thinking how odd it seems. I thought having her gone would be a welcome relief – and it was, but only for a while.

Later that night, I enter the dining room at the same time as Father. He smiles when he sees me. I smile back, though I'm embarrassed to remember our last meeting. He walks over and hugs me tight. I hug him back.

"I missed you, Daughter. I hope all went well while we were gone?" Before I can answer, he adds, "And I hope you made amends with Ada while we were gone."

"Well, we are both still alive and neither of us is suffering any grievous injuries. Except for my nose," I laugh. I might as well make a joke of it. "Doc says it will always be crooked, but maybe that will make my face more interesting."

"Well, I'm glad you can laugh about it," Father responds. He examines my nose. "Frankly, I don't see much of a difference."

I laugh. "I hope your trip was successful."

"Oh yes, very successful! But I suspect your sister thinks herself a better judge than I am on that subject." He laughs at his little joke and I sense he is happy, though resigned to letting Lucille tell us all about the journey.

He is right about Lucille. She is so full of stories about Washington that he gets very few words in all evening.

"Wait a minute, Minnie Lucille," Father interjects in the middle of one of her overly enthusiastic rants. "Let's not get carried away. Let's get this straight. Your fervor for my role as a judge is flattering but when you tell stories, dear Daughter, you must put things in perspective and give credit where credit is due. I wish I were as influential as you think I am."

My sister ignores his pleas and continues, "I don't care what you say, Father; you have to admit that every senator and gentleman we met shook your hand and highly praised your work."

Father, red with embarrassment, shakes his head and smiles. He realizes he is unable to stop Lucille's enthusiasm once she gets going. I note that he isn't trying very hard. I think he's wallowing in her compliments.

As Lucille winds down her "Father is god" chatter, Father jumps in with praise for Lucille. "Thank you, Lucille, for your overeager representation of my accomplishments." He looks at the three of us around the table and says, "I must add that you, Lucille, my dear young woman, turned out to be a delightful traveling companion. I am pleased to report to your sisters that you were an excellent choice as my escort." He smiles and nods toward her, and she blushes in response.

Turning toward Ada and me, he chatters on about Lucille's intelligence and beauty. I know his comments are directed straight at me. His words find their mark. I feel worthless.

I have to put a stop to this endless blessing of Lucille, so I interrupt. "So, what else happened on your trip?"

Lucille looks at me, frowning. She glances at Father, then down toward her plate, and then back at me. After a few seconds of silence, she smiles, and says, "Well, we ran into Earl during our stop in Boston on our way to Washington." She blushes and drops her eyes. "And then we met him again on our stop in Boston on our way home." She looks at Father.

"Tell them," says Father, putting down his knife and fork. "They should hear the news from you."

"You and Earl got engaged, didn't you?" Ada screeches, scaring the bejesus out of all of us.

Lucille stares at Ada, frowning for a moment and then, rather than yelling at Ada for spoiling her surprise announcement, she smiles. "Yes," she says. "Earl asked for me and I accepted."

What a weird statement: Earl asked for me and I accepted. It's something only Lucille would say. "He asked for you? What does that mean?" I ask.

Lucille turns towards Father. "See. I told you Amelia wouldn't be happy for me. Why should I even bother to talk to her?"

I feel my father's anger even before he says anything. His shoulders rise up and an exaggerated sigh escapes as he stands up. He stares down at me for a moment, and says, in a voice louder than it needs to be, "You need to give more thought to what you say to people, young lady, and more importantly, how you talk to people. You need to think about how you talk to your family. You turn everything into a problem for everyone. I am not home one day and you are at it again. I don't know what to do with you."

I try to defend myself, even as I realize that the being-nice-to-one-another pact Ada and I agreed to also included Lucille. "I just asked her a simple question. I didn't mean anything bad by it." By this time, the old anger rises in me. "Why do you take everything I say and turn it around – especially when it comes to Lucille? It's always Lucille. Lucille can do no wrong."

Father is just as angry as I am. He throws his napkin into his half-finished meal. "Keep your mouth shut, Amelia. That would settle most of it. I don't have time to listen to your nonsense about Lucille. I see nothing has changed since I left. You make me unhappy, you and your need to push everyone to the edge." He pauses and then snaps, "Sometimes you are just like your mother." With that, he walks out of the dining room and up the stairs.

The room goes quiet for a moment before Ada whispers, "What does Mother have to do with this?"

I know what Mother has to do with this. It's true, I am just like my mother. I'm strong, just like she was. I say a silent thank you to her. I know she's watching.

I sigh and turn to Lucille. "I didn't mean to offend you, Lucille. It's just that you've never told me much about Earl and now you're getting engaged. I guess I'm just surprised. I don't understand. How did all this come to be?"

Lucille glances at the stairs where Father has disappeared. Maybe she wants to complain about me again, but she sighs and asks, "So, what do you want to know?"

"I just wondered how it all came about," I say. I'm not interested in anything about Lucille right now, but I suppose I have to make peace with her. "Well, I wasn't aware that you got to know him well enough to decide you wanted to marry him. He seems nice enough," I add quickly. Even though I think there's something creepy about him.

Lucille looks at me. "I thought maybe you were just pretending to be interested. I know you do that."

I don't react.

Sighing, she continues, "Oh, all right. Earl has been coming to dinner often in the past few months – and he always sits next to me." She blushes. "Haven't you noticed that? I thought we were pretty obvious about our feelings for each other."

"I guess he has been with us quite a bit lately." I lie. I can barely remember Earl being at dinner at all. I thought he was a friend of Father's – and a strange one at that.

"I know you, Amelia. You never pay attention to what I do. I can see how you wouldn't notice."

"So how did it start?" I ask, ignoring her snarky comment.

She blushes again. I've never seen her face get red like that so often. "Well, Earl started talking to me one day at dinner. Then, a week or so later, he asked me to go for a walk with him and you know, I decided I really like him." She looks down at her hands, which have knotted her napkin into terrible twists. "I know he's kind of old, but sometimes that's a good thing," she says, and hurries on. "He has money and a large house. And I feel safe with him." She looks at me and then at Ada. She smiles and blushes and her eyes get shiny. "Besides, it pleases Father – and I am not getting any younger. We plan to be married next October." Lucille tries to smooth out her napkin, but it is hopelessly wrinkled.

"He's not old," Ada says. "He can't be more than thirty-five or forty."

I think thirty-five or forty is old. Even if Lucille is twenty-eight, Earl seems like an older man. But I don't say that. I don't say anything.

Ada keeps talking. "Besides he owns a whole lot of property here and more in Mexico. He even owns a real farm just outside the city. Father says he's so rich he put up the money to build that big hotel downtown."

I smile at both of them, not sure how to respond. I shake my head. I still can't understand why Lucille is interested in somebody like Earl. I'm trying not to be cruel, not even in my thoughts. But he seems old for her and besides, no matter what she says, I think he's creepy.

Lucille chatters on, saying that after their honeymoon in Europe, they will move into Earl's house on the eastern edge of Salt Lake City. It's a spectacular old home left to him by his parents. Earl no longer farms, of course. He rents out most of the thousand acres to other local farmers, though he keeps some chickens and a few goats so he has fresh eggs and milk. I have trouble picturing Lucille looking after chickens and goats, but perhaps she will have enough servants to do that.

CHAPTER 2

One evening in late August, not long before dinner, Manson, our butler, announces, "Your father will be bringing guests for supper and requests that you all be at your best."

"How many guests? Who are they?" asks Ada, always impatient to know everything.

"Three young men," Manson answers emphasizing the young. "Your father says he wants you girls to dress appropriately." His smile widens as he leaves to take up a position next to the main entry of the house, awaiting their arrival.

"What does that mean?" I ask no one in particular.

"I guess that's an order to change our clothes," Ada answers. She heads upstairs. Lucille and I follow her. We're used to having guests for dinner. Father is always entertaining lawyers and other business associates, old men stuffed into white shirts and coats that smell of tobacco and whiskey. Only Manson's smile hints that this dinner might be something different.

The men are seated in the drawing room and stand as we enter.

The first man is Lucille's fiancé, Earl. Lucille looks at him with surprise. Her face goes pink in an instant. Earl steps forward and, looking deep into her eyes, takes her hand in his and presses it to his lips. The whole performance makes me want to gag.

"Earl," Lucille stutters, "I didn't expect to see you today."

Earl smiles at her, "I didn't expect to see you either, but I had a meeting with your father, and he insisted I come for dinner. I couldn't refuse, knowing you would be here."

I look at Earl. A shiver slides down my back. I try to shake it off. The thought of this man becoming my brother-in-law doesn't sit right.

I hear my name. "Amelia." It's Father's voice. "This is Mr. Dwight Deschamps."

The man before me has dark hair streaked here and there with grey. His face could be handsome, except that I can barely see what's underneath his thick beard. It makes him look unkempt. Yet, there is something interesting about him, in an odd sort of way. Maybe it's his confidence.

"How do you do?" I say.

"Very happy to meet you." he says, and grins widely. Father goes on to introduce him to my sisters while I try to define what it is that is so interesting about him.

Father's voice catches my attention again, so I turn back to meet the last guest. This man takes my breath away. He has soft, wavy blond hair and tanned skin. I try not to stare but I can barely help myself. He must be the handsomest man I have ever seen.

Father introduces him to Lucille first. "Sam, this is my daughter Lucille." Sam extends his hand to Lucille. Father tells him that Lucille is his oldest daughter and he relies on her to help run the household. Then Father introduces Ada. He says that Ada is his second daughter and is known for her wonderful ability to play the piano

Then Father turns to me. "Sam, this is my youngest daughter, Amelia. She tends to be a little pushy and outspoken."

Father laughs, but I cringe.

Sam extends his hand to me, saying, "How do you do, lovely lady? My name is Sam. Sam Goutière." He's smiling, but I don't think it's because of Father's joke. His voice is deep. It doesn't have the boyish tenor I anticipated.

"How do you do, Sam?" I smile at him. I can't stop staring, can't think of anything to say.

Sam's smile continues. "Pushy can be quite delightful, George," he says.

I glance at Father. Surely, he'll be shocked at Sam's forwardness. But Father guides Sam on toward the dining room. I'm smiling long after they move away.

There's an air of celebration over dinner, with a hint of mystery to it. Father must want to make an impression on somebody. Wine, which isn't often served at the Lange house, has been brought out and glasses have been liberally filled.

Father has instructed Manson as to how he wants us to be seated, again something that is unusual since Mother's death. I say a small prayer for Sam to be seated next to me, but I end up as far away from him as possible. I am placed between Dwight and Father which will be about as much fun as watching Dotty dust.

Before the meal begins, Father lifts his glass and proclaims, "A toast to our upcoming Mexican adventure. The arrangements are complete, and we will be departing in three days. Our guide and co-leader, Clarence Logan, sends his regrets that he is unable to attend tonight, but he has assured me he will join us on our day of departure. Here's to my soon-to-be traveling companions." He tips his glass toward Earl, Dwight, and Sam.

I find the meal difficult. I'm not very interested in Father's upcoming trip. He's always leaving to go somewhere. When Father isn't asking Earl, Sam, or Dwight questions about the plans for the trip to Mexico, Dwight takes over with a running commentary on the wonders of Mexico and the dangers of the banditos that live there. Dwight has some intrigue to him, but he does yammer on. I'm glad when the meal is over.

The next morning Dotty shakes me awake. "Sorry to wake you," she says to my grumbling, "but the Judge says he wants to talk with you before he goes off to work. Hurry now or he'll be mad at both of us."

"Oh, good grief, what next?" I roll over and cover my head with the quilt. "Go away, Dotty. I'm tired. I need to sleep."

"Not today," Dotty pleads, "you have to get up or the Judge'll be yelling at both of us."

I hear desperation in Dotty's voice. "Okay, Dotty," I throw back the quilt. "Tell Father I'll be down in a few minutes." I hear her sigh with relief and shuffle backwards out the door.

It'll take too long to decide what to wear, so I throw on an old pink taffeta dressing gown that I love and tie its flowered sash twice around my waist. Seeing myself in the mirror makes me smile. This gown belonged to Mother.

Father is in the dining room reading the papers and drinking coffee. He looks up and smiles at me. I like it when he smiles. I want to throw my arms around him and give him a kiss. But the memory of our last tiff is still fresh in my mind.

Father watches me sit down, unfold my napkin and place it on my lap before he speaks. "I think we should declare a truce, Amelia," he says. "I have had enough bickering. Let's bury the hatchet and have a discussion like adults." He picks up his napkin and puts it on his knee. "I've considered your plethora of grievances over the past number of months trying to figure out precisely what your issues are. I have decided that you may be right with some of your complaints."

I can hardly believe what I am hearing. "Really, Father? Do you really understand what I have been saying about Lucille getting everything? Do you really see that?" I sink further into my chair. This is the discussion I've been waiting to have.

"I do see what you mean about Lucille going everywhere with me. It's true she has been travelling a lot with me lately and I think, seen from your point of view, it is quite unfair."

I exaggerate my nod hoping he will see how much I agree.

He frowns at my bobbing head for a moment and pauses to get my attention. "So, I've decided that I want you to come on this trip to Mexico."

All I hear is the word "Mexico." All I can remember of the dinner discussion about Mexico are the rumors about the banditos, strange language, a hot desert and countless poisonous snakes. I'm about to express my displeasure, but Father continues.

"As you know from last night's dinner, we'll be traveling with Earl, Dwight, Sam, and Clarence, whom you haven't met yet. We'll travel by train to the California border and then by horseback and carriage into Mexico. We'll be gone for approximately two months."

"Two months?" I ask, horrified. "That's a long time to be gone, isn't it? We won't be home until the end of October."

Father ignores my question and looks at his watch. "It won't be an easy journey. Earl and Dwight have decided to partner with me in a mining venture, which may prove quite lucrative. Clarence is coming along as an advisor. He's been to Mexico several times." Father pauses and looks at me. "So, what would you say to serving as our official clerk?"

He stops and looks at me. Clearly, he wants an immediate answer. Is he offering me a job? Maybe that wouldn't be such a bad thing. It could be the start of a career for me. I wonder if he intends to pay me. "I – I'm not sure what to say, Father. What does a clerk do? What does all this mean?"

"It means you will record in a journal everything we do every day and when we get into negotiations with the mining people, you will take notes. I know you're smart. Even your teachers used to comment about how well you were organized and how good you were with numbers. I think you might be interested in this kind of work. Especially when you get to know more of what it's about."

Father hands me a sheet of paper. "Here, Amelia dear, is the list of items you will require for the trip. I'm sure one of your sisters will be happy to help you shop. Get yourself some suitable clothing and boots – today. Oh, and pack light. We won't have space for much luggage. We leave in three days – the first of September." He smiles, swallows the rest of his coffee and gets up from the table.

"But Father –" I start.

"But what?" Father interrupts me. "We will talk later; right now I am off to the Court House." He reaches for his hat. Halfway out the door he turns back to me. "I'm serious about this, Amelia. Make sure you are ready to leave when I am. You wanted a trip with me. Well, now you have it." He steps out and closes the door.

Has he gone absolutely out of his mind? Mexico? Mexico isn't a place I want to go. I don't want to ride a stupid horse. I don't like the smelly creatures. I can't believe he picked Mexico as a place for me to go. Lucille, he takes to Washington on a train. Me, he takes to Mexico on a horse. How unfair.

I don't have time to think of anything else because two things happen at the same time. Lucille and Ada come down the stairs arm-in-arm and Father opens the door and puts his head in again. He grunts when he sees my sisters and says, "Lucille and Ada, I have made arrangements for you two to stay with Aunt Margaret in Ogden while Amelia and I are away in Mexico."

My sisters stare at Father in disbelief. I can't blame them. I'm not sure who has the worst part of the deal: me, going to Mexico with the banditos and the deserts and the snakes, or them, going to stay with Aunt Margaret.

"What is going on?" Ada and Lucille say at the same time.

"Are you taking Amelia to Mexico?" Ada asks.

"Yes," Father tells them, "and soon," he emphasizes. "You have two days to be ready."

"Two days?" Lucille blurts out. "Two days isn't enough time to get ready to go anywhere, Father. We have to shop and pack and make arrangements."

Father cuts her off. "Too bad, my dear. You have two days. Aunt Margaret will meet you at the Ogden station. It has already been decided." He emphasizes his point by slamming the door as he leaves.

"Oh no," complains Ada, "Auntie Margaret's house is boring. Father leaves us alone while he goes off to Washington for three months but thinks he can't when he goes to Mexico. I don't understand him."

"Nobody understands him," I carp. "At least you don't have to ride a horse."

"Since when do you have to ride a horse?" Ada asks.

"Since Father ordered it." I tell her. "He said I'd have to ride a horse in Mexico."

"I'd rather ride a horse," Lucille snaps. "Anything would be better than Aunt Margaret's house of doom and gloom. At least you get to ride with interesting people, Amelia, and I think Sam might be very interesting. I think he took a shine to you."

All Lucille ever thinks about is getting married but this time instead of arguing with her I will just wish that what she thinks about Sam is true.

I fill the next two days with shopping, packing and saying goodbye to friends. I purchase some of the items on Father's imposing list. But I'm totally mortified by one item in particular: thick woolen bloomers. What young woman in her right mind would purchase such an item of clothing? What possible motive could my father have for even suggesting such a thing?

On the day of departure, Manson and Dotty arrive at my bedroom door at sun-up just as I am shoving the last of my clothes into a large trunk. Manson offers to carry it to the waiting carriage. Father stops to see how we are doing and interrupts Manson as he is picking up the trunk. "Amelia," he says, "a trunk will never do. I told you to pack light." He disappears and returns carrying a large carpet bag. He ignores me and turns to Dotty.

"Select no more than three travelling dresses for my daughter. Put in a minimum of everything else that she needs." He pauses. "That she needs, mind you. If it doesn't fit in here, she doesn't need it." He looks at me only as he goes out of the room.

"You can't put a trunk on a horse," he calls back.

"Oh, Dotty," I complain, "How will I ever manage? Father is just mean."

Dotty just shakes her head but says nothing. I wait while she carefully packs my dresses and other items in the bag. It feels like she's taking forever. I feel my impatience grow and as she puts the last item in the bag, I grab it from her and stomp down the stairs. The only thing that appeals to me about this whole process is that the bag was once Mother's.

As I reach the front door, it swings open, seemingly by itself. Startled, I almost fall into Sam's outstretched arms. "Oh, so sorry," Sam says, a look of happy surprise on his face. "I didn't realize you were there." He smiles wider as I struggle to compose myself. His smile is just as enchanting as the evening I met him. He takes the carpet bag and offers his arm to me. I feel hypnotized into linking my arm with his. He escorts me to the carriage in a most gentlemanly way and helps me on board. His fingers linger on my elbow a few seconds longer than necessary and my heart beats faster. As he follows me into the carriage, I inhale his smell: tobacco and sandalwood. He sets our bags on the seat leaving himself just a small area next to me. As he lowers himself onto the seat his leg presses against mine and I'm suddenly warm. I'm sure I should move away to give him more room, but I also think I'd like to move closer. I resign myself to putting some proper distance between us but find that I am already up against the edge of the carriage. He turns to speak to me, and we are nose to nose.

At just that moment, the door opens, and the carriage groans and leans under Father's weight as he hoists himself up, followed by Dwight and another man whom I assume must be Clarence. As they struggle into the tight space and wedge into the seat across from us, Sam subtly lifts the bags from the far end of the seat and places them between himself and me. I'm disappointed at the separation, but I smile up at Father.

Father frowns at me. "We are on our way. I'm hoping for an uneventful trip for you, and a productive trip for the rest of us," he announces in a booming voice. He shouts to Earl who has climbed on top to sit with the carriage driver. "Okay, Earl, we're ready in here. We can go now."

With a sudden jolt, the carriage begins to move. The mundane conversation on the way to the train station relieves the tension I feel about Sam.

Father formally introduces me to Clarence and then tells us, "We will board the train and head west through Utah to Stockton, California. That trip will take about twenty hours. Then, we'll head south into Mexico on horseback. Someday, we'll be able to head straight south from Salt Lake to Mexico by train, but until they finish laying all that track, we'll go the Stockton route."

I don't care. I'm still angry at Father for taking away my trunk. All I do care about is that I don't have to ride a horse. Yet.

CHAPTER 3

Our little group makes the transfer from carriage to train and settles into a small compartment that will house all of us for the next day or more. "We are traveling first class because of you, I hope you realize," Father announces to me as we settle in. "Enjoy the luxury, my dear. The next leg of this trip will be much more difficult."

Luxury? I look around. There are two narrow and uncomfortable looking benches facing each other. I wonder how three of us can fit on each bench. Two large mirrors extend behind each bench and up to the ceiling. I suppose they are meant to make the compartment look larger than it is. As I sit down, my hand touches the ragged looking red velvet that lines the benches. I imagine this must be the railroad's attempt at luxury. I look up and notice matching velvet curtains hang at the windows. Father and Dwight come behind me and we sit in a line like fat sardines in a tiny little can. This image makes me smile which is a good thing in an otherwise awful situation. Clarence, Earl and Sam enter the compartment and sit across from us. Our knees are inches apart. This compartment is too small for five large men and me. I have the feeling it's going to be a very long ride to California.

The train jerks its way out of the station, and the conductor arrives to collect our tickets. He explains that lunch will be served in the dining car at 1:00 p.m. and that the men are free to use the smoker car at any time.

Sam stands up and excuses himself. "I'm in need of a walk-around," he announces. "Think I'll check the place out." Father nods in his direction and I watch as Sam disappears out the door.

I listen to the men chatter. I stare out the window and watch the countryside roll by. It's beautiful scenery, but the openness of it all makes me feel even more closed in.

Father's voice breaks into my thoughts. "So, what do you boys think? Shall we go find the smoker car and get ourselves some refreshment before lunch?"

"Good idea," Dwight responds. Earl and Clarence both nod in agreement and practically leap to their feet. They must feel as cooped up as I do.

I wish the invitation could include me, but according to Father, women aren't allowed in the smoker car. Another unfair thing in my life. I should have been born a man. They are free to do what they want.

As I turn back to watching the scenery roll by, something catches my eye in the reflection of the window. I turn towards the compartment doorway and find Sam standing there, staring at me.

Startled, I blurt, "What are you doing here? I thought you'd be with the others having a drink."

"I don't drink in the morning," he chuckles, stepping into the compartment and coming to sit beside me. "Well, at least I try not to drink in the morning. Besides, I was hoping you might like some company. I'm finding this trip a bit boring already and I think together we could make it much more interesting."

I can't help but smile. He has the deepest blue eyes I have ever seen. I turn towards him.

He reaches out to touch my face. "I hope you don't mind if I tell you that I find you very attractive, my dear. Perhaps we will start with that."

"And how would my being attractive make the trip more interesting?" I ask him.

"There are endless possibilities, my dear, endless possibilities," he answers as he moves his face closer to mine.

The door to the compartment slides open and Father appears. Sam and I leap apart.

"What the –again?" Father starts. "There's a drink awaiting you in the smoker, Sam. Get yourself to it." Sam snakes himself around Father and out the compartment door, offering me a brief glance of disappointment.

Father stands in the doorway for a moment after Sam passes through. I hold my breath. He steps in and sits down across from me. Oh no, not another lecture.

"Amelia, please don't be a foolish girl. Behave yourself or I will send you home. Do you understand?"

"I have no idea what you're talking about," I tell him in a firm voice. I stand up to face him with my hands on my hips with as much indignation as I can muster. "I wasn't doing anything. Sam was just talking to me. That's more than anyone else does. What am I supposed to do on this trip? Shut my mouth and stare at the scenery?"

"Under the circumstances, yes, perhaps, that would be best," Father scolds. He pauses and then continues, his voice more tentative. "In case you don't understand what I mean, then here it is as clear as I can make it. Be careful of the men on this trip, especially Sam. You need to understand your place. Some men in this world will take advantage of young girls. You need to be aware of that. You are on this trip with me to work, not to play."

I can't believe what my father is saying. "What?" I storm, "I wasn't doing anything with Sam. Why are you always telling me what to do? I'm not stupid."

Father says nothing, but I see disappointment in his eyes. He watches me fume. It takes a long time before he speaks. He clears his throat. "Amelia, I can't sit here until tomorrow while you wind down. I know you're angry, but from here on out just do what I say, and we can avoid all this drama."

As if he just remembers that he has something in his hand, he extends it toward me. It's wrapped in paper. "Here," he says, "I brought you a pastry. I thought you might be hungry."

I look at my father. Maybe he's using the pastry as a peace offering. I find it endearing but annoying. I want to stay angry at him. He says such awful things. "I am hungry," I concede, and unwrap the pastry. "I could also use a cup of tea if you don't mind."

He laughs. "You never cease to amaze me with your ability to manipulate things to your own interest, but this time I'll ignore it and succumb to your demands with a willing heart." He reaches over and pushes the bell to summon the porter.

Before I can respond to Father's dramatic little speech, a porter appears to take my tea order. When the porter leaves, Father continues. "You and I need to have a little discussion about what I expect from you on this trip, my dear. Perhaps then we won't have to spend all our time bickering with each other. What do you say?"

I nod. He's right about that. I do have to stop fighting with him if we are going to be together for two months.

At my nod, he reaches under the seat and pulls out his brown leather briefcase. He rummages around, pulls out a thick black book and plops it in my lap. "I suggest for the rest of the train trip, you put your mind to this reading material. It will prepare you to do the work we'll need you to do. We're going to look at a number of mine sites and you'll be our recorder. "Oh," he adds, pulling a second thinner book from the case, "You can begin by writing a daily journal for us. This is the notebook you'll need to record what we do, and what we find."

I am speechless. I look at the thick black book first, *Handbook of Rocks, Minerals and Mine Sites in the North American West and Mexico* by Thomas Kemp. The gold letters shine out at me and for some reason, that makes me smile. I put the book down and open the pages of the notebook. I see a hundred blank pages of soft white paper inviting me to write something.

"I'll do my best," I tell him. "I will try, Father. Honestly, I will try."

Father smiles at me and stands up to admit the porter who has returned with my tea. The porter puts the tray on the little table between the seats. There is a silver teapot, a small pitcher of cream, a bowl of sugar and a beautiful old china cup and saucer painted with pink rose petals and green leaves.

"Oh, look at this cup," Father exclaims. "This cup looks just like the cups you painted at school." The cups I painted were the only remnants from an unhappy year I spent at a finishing school with my sisters shortly after Mother died. I can't help but smile. Sometimes my father does remember things. Sometimes he can be sweet.

Father dismisses the porter and follows him out of the car. I open the large and cumbersome book about mining that Father insists I read and sip my tea. The pictures of large strange machines and hand drawn rocks capture me, as do the interesting explanations and odd instructions.

Partway through the second chapter, as I struggle to read a complicated chart about ore weights, I am interrupted by the return of the men. As they enter, the smell of whiskey instantly fills the compartment and I feel nauseous.

"I need to go for a walk," I tell them, standing up and moving towards the compartment door.

Father frowns. Oh no, is he going to insist that I sit prisoner-like in this stinky space for the next two days? His loud voice enforces his frown, "I'm not so sure that's a good idea."

I stare at him in disbelief. "Father, in case you didn't know, a woman does need to visit a commode once in a while." I hope I sound as disgusted as I feel.

Father's face drains of color. Embarrassed, he pauses and then says, "Just be careful if you go beyond this car. Crossing between cars is difficult. It's easy to lose your balance. In the front are third-class patrons. The car will be dirty and smelly, and not a place you even want to pass through. The dining car is at the back. Beyond the dining car is the smoker. Don't try to go there. They'll turn you back," he warns.

I can't help it. I roll my eyes and slide the compartment door shut with a bang. There he goes again, telling me it's okay to go for a walk, then warning me not to. Either direction I go, everything will be boring or forbidden, somewhat like my life. Nonetheless it feels good to stand and move around. I start my exploration by walking the length of the car. The last compartment I come to has a large green sign on the door, "Commode for Ladies, No Gentlemen Allowed." The "No Gentlemen Allowed" part of the sign makes me smile. Who would need a rule for that, anyway?

I open the door and find the walls are covered in a drab green paper, decorated with ugly pink flowers. The flowers are so large and out of shape that they appear to have been drawn by a child or an artist who sees the world through distorted eyes. I walk past the flower paintings and open the door to the toilet room. It stinks and all I find is a small porcelain chair with a hole in it. The hole is large enough that I can see through to the train tracks below. I struggle to pull my long dress and multiple petticoats out of the way in order to sit down without soiling myself. A sign on the wall announces "Please do not dump this hopper toilet while train sits in the station." Oh, good heavens! I shall have to remember this as a good reason not to walk along the train tracks near my home.

Disgusting is the only word I can find for this whole process. I pull up my dress and all the petticoats in one fell swoop, straddle the stupid device and finish my business. I think for the rest of the trip I should leave my petticoats off. My life would be much easier. I try to ignore the thought that Father could have been right about my packing.

As I leave the commode compartment, I decide to do a little exploring. After all, Father said the dining car was this way. The first thing I see is a lever on the large steel doors that separates the cars. A sign reads, "Pull to Open." I grab the lever, pulling on it as hard as I can. Nothing happens. I struggle with it again, but either the door is locked, or I don't have the strength to get the heavy doors open. I guess I am condemned to spend the rest of the trip in that stuffy compartment with too many men.

Before I have time to turn around, a pair of strong arms reach past me and pull the lever, opening the door. Startled, I turn to find Sam smiling at me. As I turn back, the door swings open, a warm wind hits my face and the loud sound of the train on the tracks and the bouncing platform cause me to lose my balance. Sam takes hold of my waist from behind, pulls me close and walks me through the door, onto the platform between cars and towards the next set of doors. As we approach these doors, he reaches out with one arm and pushes down on the lever, opening the doors and allowing us into the next car.

When he lets go, I turn to face him. "What? What are you doing here? Won't my father come looking for you?"

"I told him I was going to visit with some old friends I noticed in third class, so I doubt he'll follow me. Besides, I wanted to be sure you don't lose your balance changing cars," he adds, smiling a mischievous smile.

I look into his eyes and can't help but smile back. "If I didn't know better, I would think you are trying to get me in trouble with my father again."

He leans down and whispers in my ear loud enough to be heard over the train noise, "I'm just here to lend you a hand, my dear. Just lend you a hand. No trouble in that, is there? Besides you're headed towards the third-class section in case you didn't know. Not exactly where a lady should go alone. You never know who might accost you."

"Oh, Sam, nobody would do that. Would they?"

Sam leans closer. "You never know," he says in a lower than usual voice. A shiver travels up my backbone, just like when he sat close to me in the carriage. He steps back and smiles. He is trouble. I know that, but I like the way he makes me feel and I don't care.

The car is filled with rows and rows of straight wooden benches. There are no compartments. This must be the third-class section that Father warned me about, though it doesn't seem as ominous as he indicated. Most of the benches are filled with people or packages but the back two rows are empty.

"Come sit a few minutes before we both have to get back," I invite Sam. Can it hurt to just sit?

Sam laughs and grabs my hand, pulling me along behind him. "Not here," he insists. "Let's go on to the next car. Your father is less likely to look that far."

I allow him to lead me into the next car. It is another car with compartments rather than benches and so we move on to a third car. This one has bench seats like the first. Only the front row is occupied by what seems to be a large family. Sam picks a bench near the back and leads me to it. "Let's sit here," he says. "Nobody will bother us."

I'm nervous, but I sit down. Sam sits next to me, leaving enough room so that he can turn to face me. He takes my hand and holds it for a moment before placing it in my lap. I feel his hand on my face, caressing my cheek.

"Like I said before, Amelia, you are beautiful. I want to touch you."

I stare into his sea blue eyes. There is something ominous there.

I feel his kiss on my mouth and, with "ominous" still in my brain, I pull back. He smiles at my reluctance and reaches for my hand. "Are you afraid of me?"

I don't know what to say. He is still smiling and before I can answer his question, he presses my hand to his lips. A strange new longing sensation makes me want to reach out for him. But, at the same time, I hesitate, knowing that I shouldn't. I'm embarrassed, and I pull my hand away. For a second, he won't let it go and I feel a sharp pain as he grips it tighter. "Ow!" leaps out of me, and it seems to break his hold. He sighs and lets me go.

I'm conflicted. I want to stay with him but mixed in with the funny longing I feel when he touches me is a knowing I should leave. "I need to go back," I sputter, "before Father comes looking for me."

I move to leave but find I have to squeeze between the bench in front and Sam to get out. Raising his eyebrows but smiling at me he moves and lets me pass. I want to run out as fast as I can, but reality hits when I reach the door to the next car. I can't open the door.

Sam is behind me. "Before you go running away, my dear, you should be sure you can get away. Here, let me help you with the door." He reaches around me and pulls the lever.

I let him take my hand and help me through the corridor between the train cars. When we get to the door nearest our compartment, he tells me, "You go first, and I'll come later. That way your father won't think anything of our absence." He smiles at me. "I apologize for upsetting you, Amelia; I didn't mean to. Was I wrong to think you like me?"

I turn away from him, embarrassed. "I do like you, Sam," I answer before walking away. "Really I do." But, I wonder. How can I feel so confused? I like him, that's true, but he makes me uncomfortable.

The only person in the compartment when I open the door is Dwight and he's sound asleep, draped over the entire bench, and snoring. His eyes open when I enter, and he turns over, banging his head on the table between the seats. The bang seems to complete the awakening process and he swings to a sitting position. "Oh darn," he grumbles, "I guess I fell asleep. Where is everybody?"

"Don't know," I shoot back. "Just went for a walk."

"Long walk," he chuckles. "Meet anyone interesting along the way?"

"What do you mean by that? You're not my father," I snap. There's something about what he said that irritates me. I look at Dwight's dejected face and feel guilty. "Sorry, I didn't mean to snap, but I get tired of my father always checking up on me, and right then you sounded just like him."

A frown crosses Dwight's face. "I didn't mean to imply anything by what I said. I was just making conversation." He pauses and then says, "If you want to know the truth, Amelia, I think your father is a bit nervous about having you along on this trip. I don't think he thought about the ramifications of bringing a young woman – you – on a trip like this. I think it's just dawning on him that maybe five men and a girl might be a problem over a long period of time."

I burst out laughing. "That's a funny statement, Dwight. What do you mean by 'the ramifications'? I thought my father has known all of you for a long time. Aren't you in business together?"

"Well, all of us have known your father for a long time except for Sam. I've known Sam for a few years. We've been to Mexico twice so far and he has a good knowledge of the country and the mining possibilities, but I don't think your father knew much of his character until now."

"What do you mean by 'until now'?" I ask.

"Just what I said," Dwight answers. "Sam is a lady's man and I think your father is not impressed by his attention to you."

"What attention? What are you talking about? Sam is nice to me, that's all. My father doesn't like it. He doesn't like anything I do if you want to know how it really is. Furthermore, calling Sam a lady's man isn't very nice of you either."

"Look, Amelia," Dwight argues, "I'm not in any position to judge and I don't want to get into a conversation about Sam or your father. This trip is going to be a long one. I think we should just call a truce. I promise not to say anything bad about Sam if you'll promise not to criticize your father. Is it a deal?"

I sigh. "It's a deal, Dwight. You're right. It's going to be a really long trip."

Another day I'll ask him why, if Sam is so bad, does my father have anything to do with him. But for today I'll let it rest.

"Want to play cards while we wait?" Dwight asks. "It's a good way to pass the time."

"I'd like to play, but I don't know how. I was never allowed to learn. Father always says playing cards is the work of the devil."

"Really?" responds Dwight. "That doesn't sound like something your father would object to. That surprises me."

"Why does it surprise you?" I ask, curious.

"Well, it makes your father sound like he's religious."

"I think he used to be when he was young. He used to tell us stories about how he couldn't play cards or dance growing up. His father was a Presbyterian minister and he was strict."

"That must have been tough for a kid," Dwight adds.

I feel sad talking to Dwight about my father's childhood but I keep talking. "My father witnessed a lot of death in his life. His parents died when he was ten and he had to go live with his aunt and uncle. Then he and Mother had three babies that all died one by one of whooping cough. I'm sure my mother was his greatest loss."

Dwight watches me. I'm not sure I should be talking so much, but the sadness makes my words flow even more. "Father made us follow some of these strict rules until Mother died when I was seventeen. I think he lost his heart for a lot of things when that happened."

After a pause, Dwight says, "I often wondered what happened to the Judge's wife. That's a tough thing to go through, especially having three girls to bring up and all."

"Yes, it is sad. Our family is different now." The conversation stops and we both look out the window. I get lost in my thoughts about the past.

"Well, how about I teach you to play cards today? Maybe it will cheer you up," says Dwight as he pulls out a worn deck of faded blue cards. "The first thing you do is deal the cards. I'll tell you the rules as we go along."

Our little game is interrupted partway through by the return of Father, Clarence and Earl. Father looks at me and asks, "So where is that Sam? We saved a drink for him, but he didn't show up."

"How would I know?" I snap. "I'm not his keeper."

Father shakes his head. "Amelia, Amelia, can you never just answer without rudeness?"

I ignore his question. He seems aching for a fight and I don't need another one. "I think it's time to eat," I tell him, faking sweetness. "I missed the mid-day meal and I'm starving."

"And put the cards away," Father adds. "I agree with the eating part. Let's go get supper. We won't be in Stockton until at least ten."

Sam shows up as we are being seated for dinner. He's disheveled and quite tipsy. "Well, it's about time," Father tells him. "Where have you been all afternoon? We were about to send the troops out to find you."

Sam slurs something I don't understand and then grumps back "And you're not my father." He smiles at me and winks in my direction.

I look at him, surprised. Surprised and mortified that he would take that tone with Father and surprised that Father says nothing. I don't want to believe it, but maybe what Dwight said is true.

The rest of the meal feels awkward. Earl spends most of it expounding on what Mexico is going to be like. I wonder about Earl. He is usually quiet, but when he gets on a subject he likes, he goes on and on. I wonder what he sees in Lucille. On second thought I wonder what my sister sees in him other than he's rich. No matter what, I will always have a difficult time thinking he will one day be my brother-in-law. He still feels creepy.

Then there's Clarence. He doesn't say anything throughout the entire meal. I'm not even sure he's said a word to anyone about anything the whole trip so far. He's another strange one.

The train pulls into the Stockton station at eleven pm. Due to the late hour there are no carriages available.

"We'll have to walk," Father says. "The hotel is a few blocks from here." The men nod in agreement except for me. I'm tired, and I don't want to lug the carpet bag any distance.

Dwight comes to my rescue. "I'll carry your bag, Amelia," he offers as if reading my mind.

But, before he can get to it, Sam scoops it up, smiles at me, and says, "I've got it." I smile back at him.

We reach the hotel just in time to catch the clerk getting ready to lock the door. He's a tall, thin man with a large ugly scar across his face and a disposition to match. "Don't have four rooms, only got two," he spouts when Father asks to rent four.

"I wired ahead," Father snaps back in his most judge-like voice. "I can't account for the lateness of the train. Surely you can accommodate a district court judge.

I have to smirk at how the clerk changes his demeanor when he hears father is a judge.

"So sorry, Your Honor. I didn't realize it was you. I have your telegram right here." He fidgets with his papers. "I can open up three rooms for you, sir, right away. You'll have to wait for the fourth as it needs cleaning." He hands father the keys and as we ascend the stairway, he adds, "I hope you find the rooms to your liking."

I find my room very much to my liking. The bed is huge and has a red and white satin coverlet topped with beautiful white pillows covered in lace. I change into my night clothes and lie down on the soft mattress.

***

I remember nothing until the city noises and the sunshine awaken me, and I'm faced with the first real hardship of the trip. I pull my remaining dresses out of the carpet bag. Both are horribly wrinkled. Living out of a carpet bag is going to be a chore. I choose the simple yellow summer dress and put it on. It's too hot for petticoats and I remember the commode. After washing up, I join the men for breakfast in the hotel restaurant.

The only one who acknowledges me when I arrive at the table is Dwight and then with only the nod of his head and a whispered "hello." They are all engaged in some deep conversation. I try to sneak a look at what they are doing. Maps are strewn across the table overlaying the dishes and Sam is busy drawing lines of what look like possible routes to places with odd names. I give up and seat myself and pick up the menu.

After five minutes of chatter Father looks up and explains. "We seem to be without transport south to the border. There's been a series of coach robberies between here and San Diego County and they are warning people not to travel for a few days, at least not without armed guards. We need to go east into the Arizona Territory and then south into the Hermosillo area."

I roll my eyes and ask with the impatience I feel, "Why didn't you figure this out before the trip?"

That gets his attention. Father looks up from his maps and frowns as he always does when he doesn't like what I say. He methodically folds the large papers into small squares and puts them in his traveling case. "We are not fools, as you seem to imply, dear daughter," he says. "Sometimes things just don't work out as planned. We will just stay here until we find the proper transport and the proper route. It could be days before we move on."

I open my mouth to defend myself, but the waiter approaches the table with a request for my breakfast order. Just as well. I don't need Father to chastise me in front of everyone again, but what am I going to do for days and days around here? This is so boring.

"I'll have an Arbuckle's Ariosa coffee please," I inform the waiter, "with a touch of cream." I chuckle to myself. It brings back a memory of how our Aunty Mary is always telling us girls that what we order at a restaurant is a sign of how well-bred we are. To her, Arbuckle's Ariosa coffee separates the poor people from the rich. I also order an oatcake and specify to the waiter it should be served with fresh butter.

Aunty Mary is our name for Mary Anne Connolly, Mother's best friend and confidant. They were friends from youth, having traveled together by covered wagon west from Pennsylvania to Utah many years ago. They were among some of the first non-Mormon families to settle in Utah. We were taught as children to call her Aunty. We've known her all our lives. When Mother was dying, she asked Aunty to help Father with us. Aunty is supposed to be the one we turn to when a woman's touch is needed. I used to see her often when I was a child, but lately I tend to stay away as I find her quite overbearing.

Father interrupts my reverie, "You're late, but you can eat while we talk. I was about to discuss our plans for the day."

Father has organized a long list of items. Leave it to him to be the king of organization. He turns back to the men. "First item on my list. I've rented three horses and Earl, Clarence, and I are off to make a quick trip to a little town called Clark's Corner. It's about ten miles to the south. We'll find an outfit that rents carriages. I'm not going to wait for the stage company to decide it's safe to travel. We need to get on our way."

Father checks that item off his list and proceeds. "Second, Dwight, you do a trip around town and find us two workers who might need some cash and want to travel as guards."

"Sure, Judge, I can do that," Dwight replies with a grin.

Father hands a paper to Sam. "Third, I need you to pick up the supplies on that list."

Sam glances at the list. "Uh, I guess I can do that," he responds, with mild enthusiasm.

"And last, Amelia," he adds, almost as an afterthought, "You stay in your room and read those books I gave you. Be ready to leave by tomorrow or the next day at the latest." With a flourish of his pen, Father checks off the rest of the items on his list.

An exaggerated sigh rushes out of me before I can contain it. Father frowns at me and says, "You wanted to come on a trip with me, so you'd better be prepared for what the trip brings. It's business, Amelia. Did you expect a constant party?"

Why is he so touchy? I want to grouch at him, but I don't. I sit for the next ten minutes trying to think of something appropriate to say while the men engage in further conversation about the trip. Just as I think it can't get any more boring, my breakfast arrives. What's the point of saying anything anyway? It'll just make trouble.

I'm hungry and the oatcake smells like brown sugar. I cover it with butter. The Arbuckle's another story. One sip and I know it's not Arbuckle's - at least not the Arbuckle's I know. "Yuk, this is just plain old coffee," I tell the men. "Why didn't that waiter tell me they don't have Arbuckle's? I would have ordered something else."

"Oh, for Pete's sake! What difference does it make?" Father grumbles.

He stands and the other men do the same. "Finish your breakfast, Amelia, and go back to your room. I'll come and get you when it's time for supper. We should be back by then." He heads for the door and the others follow.

Father is grumpy. I wonder if it's just because I'm along on this trip or if other things are bothering him. I wish I had never come. I kill as much time as possible before I climb the stairs to my room. I'm not that anxious to get at the job of reading books and trying to figure out what it is my father wants me to do on this trip.

I find Sam leaning on the wall next to my door. "What are you doing here?" I ask. I can already feel my heart beat a little faster. "I thought Father told you to do the shopping this morning."

"Oh, he did, but I waited until they were out of sight on their errands and then snuck back up here by the back stairway." He smiles. "I just couldn't leave you all by yourself for the day, now, could I?" His smile widens into a grin. "I am right. You are bored already," he taunts, laughing. "Why don't you come along with me? We can make a day of searching out supplies – or other things."

He's right. I am bored already. But I hesitate. Father said I was to stay in my room. I should tell Sam I can't go. I can stay in my room and be bored, or I can go with him. Yet, there is something about his boldness that makes me uneasy.

I look him straight in the eye and ask, "Don't you think my father might be just a little concerned if I go running around town with you?"

"Well, not if we don't tell him," Sam answers, bolder than ever. "I figure they won't be back till late tonight. We can get the supplies and maybe take a nice long walk. Anyway, I can use the help shopping." He grins again. "And I'll keep my hands to myself, so you don't go running off again."

His words sting and my face feels warm. He's right. He should keep his hands to himself but there's something I like about his touch. "I'm not sure I know what to say to that."

"Oh, Amelia," he answers, impatient with me. "I think you know exactly what to say and I think you know exactly what you want from me. You just like to tease." He hesitates and then adds in a softer voice, "But it's okay, I can wait."

Wait for what? I watch as he walks down the hall towards the stairs. I hear him mutter, "A little while anyway."

Still shocked at the bluntness of his words, I stand frozen. I expect he is leaving. But he stops and turns back smiling, "So, are you too afraid to come with me on a shopping adventure? Would you rather spend the rest of the day reading boring old account books in your boring old hotel room?"

I should go read, but the thought of stuffy old account books is outweighed by the excitement Sam promises, even if there is something a bit unsettling about him. "You win," I say, with more eagerness than I want to display. "You're more interesting than my books for sure."

"Aha!" he shouts with glee and strides back towards me. He grabs my hand and leans in, whispering, "I promise you'll have the best afternoon of your life."

Just before we reach the top of the staircase, Sam pulls me close and kisses me on my mouth. I want to stay where I am all day. I press against him and he feels warm and soft. He pulls away from me and smiles. "I almost forgot," he says, "I have something for you."

He fumbles around in his pocket until he finds a small silver ring. It is set with three tiny red gemstones and is on a beautiful silver chain. "I want you to have this," he says, his voice soft without a trace of boldness in it. "My mother gave it to me just before she died. My grandmother had it made for her when I was a baby." He holds the ring out to me and shows me where it's engraved with his name, Samuel. "I bought this chain so you can wear it around your neck where no one can see it. It'll be our little secret." He puts the ring and the chain in my hand. It's the prettiest little thing I've ever seen. My eyes brim with tears. Everything people say about Sam just can't be true. He's generous. I love this ring and its beautiful silver chain already. What can I say? What can this mean?

"Why are you crying?" Sam asks. "I thought this would make you happy."

"Oh, it does, it does!" I smile. "I – I just don't know what to say. It's beautiful. I'm just not sure I can accept it, Sam. I hardly know you. What does this mean? It's beautiful – it's beautiful."

Sam laughs. "Okay, I get that it's beautiful. Just accept it as a special friendship gift. It just means I think you're beautiful and I want to give you something. Turn around and I'll slip it around your neck. Let's see how it looks."

He fastens the chain around my neck. I turn back to face him. "Nice," he smiles. "The chain is just long enough to hide inside your dress. Wouldn't want anyone to ask questions, would we?"

He kisses me again and takes my hand, leading me out to the street and the beginning of our shopping spree. It doesn't matter what happens for the rest of the day. This is already the best day of my life.

In the first hour we rummage through three or four stores looking for the items on Father's list. My feet hurt. It's hot and uncomfortable in my long dress, even without my petticoats.

Sam complains endlessly. "We'll need a blooming team of horses to pack all this stuff," he tells me. "I thought your father would be more frugal than this. I don't know why he wants so much ammunition. We only have three guns.

Food I can understand, but ammunition? You'd think we were going elephant hunting or something."

"Maybe Father expects bandit trouble?" I offer.

"If he expects that much bandit trouble on the trail, I think we shouldn't go. Personally, I don't think it's that dangerous," Sam says. "Oh well, he's the boss." He shrugs.

I'm exhausted by the time we finish. Sam hires a swarthy man to haul our packages back to the hotel. I don't like the look of him, but Sam says not to worry. "At least he frees us from having to carry everything."

As we enter the hotel lobby, a familiar voice calls, "Hey, you two." It's Dwight.

"Well, you're back quick enough," Sam tells him, his voice sullen. "Thought finding guards would take longer than half a day."

Ignoring his tone, Dwight laughs, "Not in this town. Men seem anxious for some cash. I even lined up two extras in case the first two don't show. What's on your agenda for the rest of the afternoon?"

Sam looks at me. "Not sure, now," he mutters. "Guess we'll get something to eat."

"Good," says, Dwight, "I'll join you. I'm a bit peckish myself."

Sam and I exchange disappointed glances. "I need to check that our purchases are here," Sam says. "I'll meet you two in the restaurant."

Dwight and I walk into the restaurant and are offered a table near the door. It feels good to sit down and rest my feet. I wish I was having lunch with Sam alone but things never seem to turn out like I want them to. I smile at Dwight and he asks if we should wait for Sam to order.

"I guess so," I answer, not caring one way or another. Dwight seems as tired as I feel and offers no further conversation. Lucky for us, Sam arrives before many minutes pass. He orders whiskey for himself and a glass of ale for Dwight. He doesn't ask Dwight if he wants ale, he just orders it. I look to Dwight half expecting him to say something, but he just smiles. I find it strange that Dwight doesn't speak up for himself and I wonder how Sam knows what Dwight likes.

After lunch, Sam announces he is going to the saloon down the street for a glass of beer. He turns to me and suggests, "I'll see you to your room, before I leave, if you like."

"Yes," agrees Dwight. "Heck of a good idea, Sam. I'll come with you."

Sam looks at Dwight with disdain, followed by a sigh of resignation. "I guess. If you must," he mutters. He glances at me and then shrugs. It feels like he's giving up on spending any more time with me. I'm disappointed.

I walk between the men as they escort me to my door, and I feel like a prisoner being led to her cell. They watch as I unlock the door and step inside.

"Have a nice time, you two," I snap as I shut the door. The whole afternoon has been spoiled. Damn that Dwight. If he hadn't been around, I might have had a nice afternoon stroll with Sam. But then perhaps it's just as well. I should be the good daughter and get started on Father's books. I kick off my shoes, loosen my corset and climb onto the bed. I read and take notes but before too long, the pen gets heavy in my hand and the pillow is soft and inviting.

I waken to someone banging on my door and shouting my name "Amelia, it's Dwight. Are you in there?"

I scramble off the bed and find my way to the door, groggy and half awake. I look at the clock. Four hours have passed since I saw Dwight. I'm sure I worked on those boring books for at least two.

"I need to talk to you, Amelia. Can I come in for a minute?"

I unlatch the door and Dwight is standing in the hallway. At first he says nothing but he stretches above me, trying to see into my room. "Amelia, I apologize for disturbing you, but I was hoping your father and the boys were here. I thought they'd be back by now. It's getting late."

"No, Dwight, I fell asleep at some point after you went to the saloon and I just woke up. They aren't here. I'm sure they got delayed waiting for a carriage to be ready or something." It's all I can think of. He seems more distraught than he should be about the men being late.

Dwight looks at me but doesn't say anything more. Not sure how to respond to his silence, I ask, "So what do you intend to do?"

"Huh? Oh, not sure what I can do. The other thing is..." he hesitates. "I left Sam in the saloon hours ago, but I went back, and he isn't there. You haven't seen him, have you?"

"I told you I fell asleep and just woke up, so how can I know where Sam is?" Dwight is starting to sound like Father again. I bet he was looking to see if Sam was here with me. Before I can tell him what I think of his question, he nods his head at me and looking embarrassed says, "Please pardon me. I shouldn't have asked you that. It isn't unusual for Sam to disappear. We seem to spend half our time on these trips looking for him." He grins.

Why does Dwight always grin or snicker when he talks about Sam? I find it irritating but curious that if Dwight is that put off by Sam, he still seems to follow him around.

"I have an idea," I tell Dwight. "Why don't you join me for supper? Maybe Father, or at least Sam, will turn up by the time we're finished. Besides, I hate eating alone."

Dwight brightens up at my invitation. "That's a good idea," he says. "At least we can do something until they all turn up. I'm afraid I'm not very good at waiting."

As we are about to be seated in the restaurant, Dwight hesitates before sitting down. "I'll be right back," he tells me. "I'm going to have one more look in the saloon for Sam."

He walks away. An uncomfortable, anxious feeling seizes me. What if Dwight doesn't return? What if Sam is lost? What if bandits have killed all of them? What would I do if I'm left here alone? How would I get back home? I laugh out loud at myself. Amelia, sometimes you are just stupid. Of course, they will all come back. If they all died, you would get on the train and go back to Salt Lake. Somehow that thought doesn't make me feel any less anxious. But before I can scare myself any further, I see Dwight returning.

"Well, he's not there. When I left him earlier, he said he was going to have one more beer and then come back to the hotel. The bartender didn't seem to remember him, so he couldn't have been there long. I guess it's just us for supper. We might as well order."

Before the meal arrives, I ask, "Could Father, Earl and Clarence be in any real danger or are they just delayed? What do you think?"

Dwight pauses for a moment, then, looking worried, responds, "Uh, I don't know, Amelia. Maybe they just can't find the people who rent carriages or maybe they have to wait for the carriage. The only thing I don't understand is why your father wouldn't just send Earl or Clarence back to tell us why they are delayed. But who knows? I'll go look for them tomorrow if they don't get back by then. Frankly, I'm more worried about Sam than about your father. He's the scoundrel of our bunch. Sometimes, I think he likes getting himself into trouble."

"You've said that to me before, but I don't see him as that bad," I grump at Dwight. Why does he continue to say such awful things about Sam?

"Oh, he's that bad and probably worse," Dwight continues. "I could tell you stories, but then I suspect your ears are too delicate for such tales."

"If he's that bad, why is my father so involved with him?" I ask.

"That's an easy one. Sam is the son of a senator from Connecticut, well connected, and rich. Sam's father had influence over your father's appointment to the district court a couple of years ago and your father made an agreement with him then to take Sam on to teach him about the Mexican land development business. Although if you want my opinion, I think Sam now knows more than your father does. Sam and I have made a few more trips into Mexico than your father in the last couple of years and I think Sam learned a lot. Anyway, on this trip, I think Sam is more than your father bargained for in terms of his character, especially with you in the picture."

"I think my father worries about me too much. I can look after myself." I see the darkness cross Dwight's face and he frowns but says nothing.

After dinner, Dwight walks me to my room. "Make sure you lock your door, Amelia, and don't open it to anyone, okay?

"Of course not," I laugh. "You sound like my father."

Dwight looks thoughtful for a moment and then tips his hat. As he leaves, he adds, "Just be careful. You never know who's lurking around."

I find Dwight's words both ominous and curious. Maybe that's just the way men are with women. They want to protect us. Or, maybe they just like to scare us to death. I smile when Sam comes to mind. But Dwight's words churn around in my head, so I lock the door and look for something I can put against it. All I can find is a small wooden chair. It's not heavy enough to stop an intruder, but it makes me feel like I have done something. A shiver winds its way up my spine.

I change into my nightclothes and remove Sam's sweet gift from around my neck. I place it on the night table next to the bed. Touching it makes me feel close to him and just looking at the red jewels twinkling next to the silver chain makes me smile.

CHAPTER 4

It's been a confusing day and I'm tired. I wonder where Father is and what's going on with Sam. Just as I am about to fall asleep, street noises disturb me, and I lie for a while somewhere between awake and asleep. I hear something. It sounds like footsteps. No, it's a tapping sound, like someone knocking. I sit up. Why is someone knocking on my door? Oh, thank goodness, it must be Father returning. I stumble out of bed, move the chair out of the way and unlatch the door.

The light in the hallway blinds me. "Father?" I ask assuming it must be him but whoever it is, doesn't answer. I don't know who it is. Before I can push the door closed, he's inside. He kicks the door shut and slams his body hard against me. We crash to the floor. I try to get up, but I can't. His heavy weight pins me down. I don't see the blow coming. I just feel the pain that shoots across my face.

Scream. I try to scream but there is no sound. I struggle against the weight on me. Oh God. Oh, God. No. He tears at my clothes. His hands are all over me. A foul-smelling hand reaches up and covers my mouth and cuts off my breath. I struggle to bite his hand. He swears something

I can't understand and then he hits me again. The room spins and then nothing.

I open my eyes and my first thought is that the window curtains are strange. They are orange but the drapes in the hotel are red – heavy red velvet. Where am I? I try to raise my head but my whole face hurts. I lift my hand to touch it, but my fingers feel a thick bandage. I'm groggy but I remember something – something terrible. I struggle to get up. What has happened to me?

Strong, but gentle arms hold me down. "You're safe dear. Don't worry. You're safe. Stop grabbing your bandage, honey. I know it hurts but you'll pull out your stitches if you don't calm down. Try to stay still." I don't recognize the female voice.

The next thing I hear is men talking. Familiar voices. Is that Father? "Father," I call out as I open my eyes.

A woman dressed in white is sitting next to my bed. The window is still covered by orange curtains. She smiles and brushes the hair back from my brow. "It's all right," she says. Her voice is gentle and soft. "You've had a bad time of it, but you're all right."

"No, I'm not all right. Where am I?" I struggle to sit up. A wave of pain sweeps over me, and I lie back.

"Father," I call out. "Father. Where's my father?" My voice is weak and hoarse. None of this makes any sense.

The woman in white whispers, "Your father is just outside, dear. He'll visit you later. You must rest now."

I lie back on the pillow. "Where am I?" I ask again. I need to know why I went to bed in a room with red velvet drapes and woke up in a room with orange curtains. I feel too weary to ask where I am again. A flash of memory pierces my consciousness. I remember a foul-smelling hand across my mouth. My body slamming against the floor.

The hotel room ordeal comes back to me. It unfolds piece by piece. It's like a long journey and each piece is a footstep. I wonder who this evil man was and why he picked me. I push out with both hands, as if I still need to fight him off. The woman takes my hands in hers.

"You're at Doctor Talbot's house. I'm Mrs. Talbot," she says. Her eyes meet mine, slide away, and then come back to mine. "You were found –" she hesitates. "You were – " her voice stops again "– injured in your hotel room. Your father brought you here."

"Father?" I ask again. Thank heavens Father is safe. "Where's my father?" I struggle again to sit up. "Oh, it hurts," I tell her. A searing pain deep inside my body makes me catch my breath. It pushes me back down onto the hard mattress of the cot. "It hurts. I hurt." I close my eyes.

The next thing I hear is my name. "Amelia." Father's voice. "Amelia, I'm here." His voice is soft, softer than I've ever heard it before.

I open my eyes to find Father standing over me. "Father," I say. I reach out to him and he takes my hand and strokes it. I feel tears fill my eyes and slide down the sides of my face.

Father moves closer to me. "Oh, Amelia," he whispers "Oh Amelia, I am so sorry."

I touch his cheek. It's wet. Can this be my father? I haven't seen him cry since the night Mother died. Why is he sorry? I don't understand any of this.

I struggle to get up again but it's too painful, so I lie down again. Father sits down beside me. He brushes away his tears and straightens his vest. In a voice that is soft and comforting he asks, "Can you tell me anything, Amelia? Can you remember anything about what's happened?"

Remember? Remember what? My body hurts all over. I try to focus.

"I was almost asleep and someone knocked on my door," My voice stumbles as the memory comes back, but I force myself to continue. "I thought it was you, Father. I opened the door – and someone dressed in dark clothes pushed in. Pushed me down. Then he punched me in the face. He ripped my clothes and – Father, what happened to me?" The memories won't stop, and I feel the horror of it all. I don't want to remember, but what happened keeps playing out behind my eyes.

Father shakes his head and stands up. His eyes are wide and round. I know that expression. He is angry. Very angry. "I'll kill the bastard," he mutters. Then he is gone. The door closes behind him.

Mrs. Talbot takes my hand and brushes my hair away from my face. She takes a cloth and wipes my tears. "It will be all right, my dear," she says. "Try to get up now and let me help you to the lavatory. I'll help you get washed and cleaned up. Your father has brought you some clothes."

I struggle to sit up. Even with help, it hurts. I swing my legs over the edge of the cot. My nightclothes are spattered here and there with dried blood.

Mrs. Talbot pats my back and whispers, "We'll wash it all away. Don't worry, sweetie, we will wash it away."

My head throbs and my body aches, but the promise of washing it all away motivates me. I let Mrs. Talbot help me down the hall into the lavatory. She helps me undress and then guides me into a large porcelain washtub filled with warm soapy water. It comforts me. It would be nice to just sit here forever and let the clean water take away the pain and the blood. I wish it could also take away the shame.

Mrs. Talbot's voice pushes through my thoughts, "Dear, use this washcloth to clean yourself. If you keep drifting off, the water will get cold and you'll catch a chill."

I take the cloth, but my hands and arms are sore and stiff, and I can't seem to make them work very well. My breasts are covered in large red claw-like scratches. My belly is ribbed with dark blue bruises. The sight of them makes the tears start again. Mrs. Talbot takes the washcloth from me and washes my back.

"This will be a difficult time for you," she whispers as she washes me. "You will never be the same, my dear, but you will get through this. I promise."

I stay in the bath until the water is cold. She helps me into clean clothes. I glance in the mirror. My hair is tangled. There's a large bandage taped across my nose. Just like when Ada hit me. I almost smile and then I remember that this blow wasn't from my angry sister.

Mrs. Talbot tells me the doctor had to close the wound on my face with sutures. I touch the bandage with my fingers, even my soft touch makes my nose begin to hurt. My lips are bruised and twice the size of normal. My face is swollen, and my eyes are dark and sunken.

Mrs. Talbot appears behind me in the mirror. "All that will heal in time," she assures me. "At least, most of it will."

I frown at her. Even moving my face muscles hurts. "What do you mean?" I ask her.

"My dear," explains Mrs. Talbot. She moves close to me and takes me by the shoulders. I feel safe with her, and her touch is gentle, but I flinch even from that. "Some man has violated you with his body. Do you not understand that?"

No. I don't understand. At least, I didn't. Not until this moment. My legs go weak. Mrs. Talbot tightens her grip, but she is only able to break my fall. I slump against the lavatory wall and slide to the floor. There are no words for my pain.

Minutes later I hear Father's voice. I open my eyes. He pats my cheek. "It's okay. I'm back," he whispers. "I'll get you home soon and everything will be better."

His strong arms lift me, and the warmth of his body passes into mine, wiping away my shivers. He carries me back to my cot. He smiles at me, a sad smile, and moves away. Mrs. Talbot covers me with a blanket.

The last thing I hear is Father's soft voice. "I want to take her home as soon as possible. I never should have brought her on this trip."

Then in a louder voice, he says, "Ask Dr. Talbot to let me know how soon she can travel."

Somewhere I hear a door slam. Then, all is quiet except for the sounds of horses clip-clopping on the street outside. "Damn horses; they are annoying," I think, as I slide into sleep.

Mother appears through a thick mist on a black stallion. She dismounts and stands over me dressed in a long black toga with knives stuck in her head like misshapen combs. I reach out but she twirls away without touching me and reappears with charcoal black rings around her eyes, grey-skinned and naked.

I jerk myself awake, feeling as though I'm going to vomit. I retch over the bedside.

Mrs. Talbot brings me a bucket and wipes my face with a cool cloth. "It's okay," she murmurs.

No, it's not okay. Why does she keep saying it is? I struggle to sit up, to retch again, but nothing comes up. The picture of my naked mother floats back to me. I want to scream, but my head hurts too much, and I throb with pain inside. "I hurt," I cry to Mrs. Talbot. "Everything hurts." The bandage on my face pulls the skin tight on my cheek when I move. "I hurt," I tell Mrs. Talbot again.

"I know," she answers. "It takes time for the pain to go away. When the doctor returns, I'll get you something more to help the pain. Just try to rest dear girl, just try to rest."

I lie back down on the soft pillow, but I'm afraid to close my eyes. I'm afraid Mother will come again in all her nakedness and horror. I struggle to get out of the bed. I refuse to rest until Mrs. Talbot gets Father.

Father comes and sits down on my bed. He pushes the hair out of my eyes. "Rest a little bit more, Amelia, and try to sleep. We have to listen to Mrs. Talbot and wait for the doctor to return before we leave." He pats my hand.

"Stay with me," I whisper as I close my eyes.

When I wake up next, Father is still there. He's sitting in a chair close to my bed and it's his snoring that awakens me. I don't know how long I slept, but it must have been a while as the sun is no longer visible through the small slits in the curtains. I move my head to see him better, but my stirring awakens him, and he pulls himself up straight in the chair.

"We must have slept a while," I whisper.

He smiles. "Yes," he says, "I think we were both tired. How do you feel now?" he asks, looking hopeful.

"I need to go home," I say. "Do you think the doctor is back yet?"

"I don't know. I'll go find Mrs. Talbot. She'll know." He returns in a few minutes to say that Doctor Talbot says I can go home in the morning. Father gives me a kiss goodbye and says he'll go back to the hotel to sleep. I don't want to ever return to that place.

In the morning, both Doctor and Mrs. Talbot come to my bedside. He takes off my bandage and examines the wound. "Looks much better," he says to both of us. "I think we will leave it off. The air will help heal it."

It's good to get the bandage off.

"I will give you something to help your pain." he says. "It will make your train ride more comfortable." I nod in agreement and he fixes a syringe with yellow fluid. As soon as he injects it into my hip, I feel a warm sensation and the pain slides away.

"Amelia, do you think you can sit up now?" Mrs. Talbot asks. "I'll help you get dressed if you like." My legs are wobbly. "Here," she offers, "hold onto me and steady yourself. I can dress you. Just stand."

As Mrs. Talbot and I finish the task of getting me dressed, I remember that I left Sam's gift on the night table in my hotel room. Oh no. What if Father finds it? I can't go back there, not now, not ever. Where's Sam? He never came to see me, and no one has mentioned his name since I was hurt. But thinking about anything is too much. I need to get out of here.

Father returns just as I finish dressing and says, "I've collected your things from the hotel room and sent everything to the station. I hope I didn't leave anything behind."

I want to ask about the chain and ring but I'm afraid to. Maybe he found them and put them in my bag without looking at them.

The ride home by train is a blur. I sleep most of the way. Father rents a berth for me so I can lie down and be comfortable. From time to time, he comes to check on me. Towards the last few miles of the journey home, I feel more awake. I even feel better. I'm wide awake when the train stops at the Salt Lake station and Father helps me down the narrow steps and onto the station platform. I look around for Clarence, Earl and Sam, but only Dwight is here.

Father helps me up into the carriage. "I'm going ahead," he says, "I want to talk to our own Doc about a few things. Dwight will see that you get home."

Ah yes, turn me over to the care of others, as usual.

"Have you been with us on the train all the way home?" I ask Dwight once we are settled inside the carriage.

He looks at me. "Yes, Amelia, I was."

"Dwight, if you don't mind, I have a few questions about the night I got hurt."

"Are you sure you want to talk about this right now?" Dwight asks.

I nod. "I need to know a few things. I need to know what happened to Father and the others the night they went missing. Father hasn't said where they went or anything about that time. Why was he so late getting back?"

"He and the others showed up just after you went to bed. He had trouble arranging transport to Mexico. He went to check on you later." Dwight hesitates. "He found your door unlocked and you all –" he searches for a word – "hurt."

I look away and Dwight whispers, "I'm sorry. Are you sure it's not too soon to talk about this?"

I look at him again and shake my head. "Where are Clarence and Earl? Where's Sam?"

Dwight hesitates again. Just as I think he isn't going to answer, he says, "Your father sent Clarence and Earl on to Mexico to see a couple of potential clients he had arranged to meet some time back. He asked me to come back on the train in case he needed help with you."

I pause, hoping Dwight will tell me about Sam but he says nothing.

"And Sam?" I ask.

"And Sam," Dwight repeats. He looks at the floor and I can see his jaw clench. "Well, Sam never appeared again after I told you I was looking for him. I thought he might come out of a drunken stupor somewhere, but...." He spreads his hands and shakes his head. "But, after all this time, there's been no word of him."

"What do you mean no word of him? Doesn't that bother you? Did you look for him?" I ask.

"Oh, we looked for him, all right. I searched for a full day asking just about everybody in that town, but nobody knew anything. It seems he has vanished. Gone, and nobody knows where. Your father says he'll contact Sam's father now that we're back in Salt Lake. I'm sure his family will want to continue the search for him." Dwight sits back and is silent.

I want to believe Dwight's story, but I get the feeling he's leaving something out. I have to let it go. I'm too tired to hear anything more about that day.

Dwight changes the subject. "You didn't see much of me because your father thought it would be better if I stayed away until you felt better. I respected his wishes. I'm happy to see you looking better," he adds.

I smile at him and he looks back at me. "I hope I'm not distressing you, Amelia," he continues. "I don't want to upset you."

I don't know what to say so I just look at him and shake my head no. I'm not sure if he upsets me or not. He knows what happened to me. I hope he doesn't tell anyone.

I'm happy to get home. Dwight sees me to the door and deposits my carpet bag inside before wishing me a good night. I watch until he climbs back into the carriage and is carried away. The house is quiet. My sisters must be out, and Dotty must be in her room. Funny she didn't hear the door. Just as I start up the stairs to put my things away and undress for bed, I hear another carriage arrive at the door. I peer from the window and see Father. His business with Doc must not have taken much time. I'm surprised he is here.

"Ah good. You are still up," he tells me when he sees me standing on the stairs. "Doc will come see you in the morning, but he gave me something to give you. It'll help you sleep. Go on upstairs and get ready for bed and I'll bring it to you."

Just after I slip out of my travel clothes and into my nightgown, Father appears with a glass of water to help me swallow the pills that Doc has given him. I don't like pills but I'm too tired to fight with Father, so I dutifully swallow what he gives me. He takes the glass from my hand and kisses my cheek. "See you tomorrow," he says as he closes my door.

I slip beneath the red-and-blue checkered quilt of my own bed. Mother made me this quilt when I was twelve years old. She embroidered tiny birds on every other patch and even gave them tiny pearl eyes. She loved me very much. I rub the cloth between my fingers and the softness reminds me of her soft skin when she bent to kiss me at the end of the day. What would she say now? Would she tell me that I would "never be the same"?

CHAPTER 5

1906

The next time I open my eyes, birds are chirping outside my window and the sunshine is full in my face. Why didn't someone close the drapes last night? Two truths hit me at the same time. I'm back at home in my own bed – and why I'm back at home in my own bed.

I roll over and open my eyes to find Dotty standing near me with a breakfast tray. "'Good morning, Dear," she says. "Your father said I should bring you some breakfast. You can't imagine how good it is to have you back home."

I roll away from the food and cover my head with the quilt. "Dotty, go away and let me sleep. I can't eat." All I want is to be left alone. I can't face any of them.

After a few minutes of total silence, I poke my head out from under the quilt to find Dotty still standing next to my bed. "What are you doing?" I ask, making my voice as grumpy as I can.

"I'm standing here until you at least try to eat a bit. You'll never heal if you don't eat. Besides, your father will be disappointed with me if I can't convince you to eat something."

This silly woman is making me mad. Doesn't she know what happened to me? No, she doesn't. She thinks I'm sick. "Dotty, go away. I don't care if Father is mad. Leave the tray and I will eat something later, but I don't need company right now. I just don't feel well."

Dotty's face turns red. She sets the tray on a chair and shuffles backwards out the door. I feel a twinge of guilt at having been rude to her, but I can't face anyone. I glance at the tray, but the sight of food makes me nauseous.

Just as I'm about to drift off again, I hear heavy footsteps near my door followed by a knock. "Excuse me, Amelia," Father says through the door. "Doc is here to see you."

Doc has been our family doctor since I was born. He helped Mother give birth to all of us and helped Father when Mother died. He's almost a part of our family. I try to sit up.

In a reassuring voice, Doc asks, "How are you feeling today, Amelia?"

All of what happened floods back into my mind. He isn't here because I have a cough. What will he think?

"My face still hurts. But I think I feel better than I did yesterday," I answer. Other things hurt but I don't know how to say it. I wonder how long I've been in this bed.

Doc puts his black bag down. He takes my chin in his hand, and peering over his funny silver-rimmed glasses, he says, "Let me see that wound. It looks like it's just about healed."

Then he is silent until I lift my head to meet his eyes. "I think I should examine you further, Amelia." he says, his voice softer than usual. He turns to my father and points to the door. Father nods and shuts the door as he exits.

"Amelia, your father explained how they found you and has passed on to me what Doctor Talbot found in his examination of you. My examination might be embarrassing for you, but it's necessary. We need to see how much damage was done." He stops, then adds, "I think enough time has passed that it won't hurt too much. I'll be quick."

I have no choice. I nod. It is humiliating, and it hurts. I cry throughout the whole thing. I can't help it.

Afterward, Doc helps me sit up. "I'm sorry, Amelia. I didn't mean to hurt you further. I know this is very difficult for you."

He looks at me. His eyes are sad. "Physically, you are nearly healed. I don't see any permanent damage and, thank heavens, you won't require surgery. I have seen much worse." He sighs, "I suspect you will need longer to heal your soul than your body."

Doc sits down on the bed. He takes his handkerchief out and wipes away my tears. But it doesn't stop them. They keep coming. He smiles at me and sighs. "Amelia, I'm afraid you are going to discover in the days and weeks to come that some people are most likely going to say some very unkind things to you and you're going to have to be strong. You have to get on with your life, despite what the insensitive people of the world might have to say."

His words explode in my mind. "Oh, Doc, if anyone knows – about this, about me – I would rather be dead! We can't tell anyone, not now, not ever." More tears slide out of my eyes and down my cheeks. I feel as if I'll cry forever.

"Secrets have a way of getting out so I want you to be prepared when they do. Just remember that none of this is your fault. Sometimes unfortunate things happen to good people. Just remember what I said: none of this is your fault." He pats my hand and stands up. "Now, I'll go talk to your father and tell him what's happening. I know you're in some pain, so I am going to keep coming by each day with something to help that and to check on you. How does that sound?"

I nod my compliance. I don't have much choice.

"That's a good girl," Doc tells me as he pats my arm again. "I'll give you something for pain right now so you can rest." He reaches into his bag and pulls out a syringe which he fills from a small vial of light liquid. "You'll feel better soon," he says as he injects it into my arm. The effects are like those of Dr. Talbot's injection and the pain slips away. He smiles at me one more time, packs up his bag and leaves, closing the door behind him.

I am back in that hotel, the one in Stockton. Someone is knocking on my door. I freeze but a man in black with a long knife steps through the closed door and pushes me to the floor. He raises his knife and cuts off my legs. The legs separate from my body and begin dancing to a strange tune: an Irish jig. I cry out to my legs to stop dancing. The music stops and the legs turn into mice that scurry across the floor and disappear into the walls of the room.

I wake to the sound of a loud scream. It's me. Father, Lucille and Ada are next to me. "What's wrong, Amelia?" Father asks. "What's wrong?"

"I – I had a terrible dream," I sob. "He cut off my legs. Oh, God, he cut off my legs."

Father gathers me up in his arms. "It's okay, Amelia. It's just a dream. You're safe. I'll keep you safe. I promise." I cling to him and sob into the softness of his shirt. Father pulls away after a few minutes.

Ada attempts to dry my tears with her handkerchief.

"Get a towel and bring her a glass of water," Father barks. "A handkerchief will never do." She brings a towel, and he presses it to my face.

Ada hands me the glass of water. I try to hold it in my hands, but I shake as though I have the palsy. Control yourself Amelia, I tell myself. I try with all my might to stop the shaking and the memory of the dream. Nothing works. I just want to cling to father but he moves farther away from me, pushing me gently down on the bed and covers me with the quilt.

"It'll get better with time, I promise," he tells me as he heads for the door leaving me with Ada. "I'll come back and check on you later."

"Father's right, you know." Ada tells me in a half whisper. "It will get better with time. I'll sit here for a while, until you sleep."

"I don't want to sleep, Ada," I tell her. "Please, maybe you could read to me." Anything to make her stay and me stop shaking.

Ada smiles and tells me she'll sing me a song she just learned. I used to hate her voice but today it soothes me.

**

Whatever the medication is that Doc gave Father is my godsend. I feel like I'm living in some faraway land where time means nothing. I sleep most of the day and often pace the hallway at night. I feel irritated by those around me when they come to visit but it's difficult to make out what they are trying to say to me.

One morning I wake up to find Father and my sisters all standing over me. "Amelia, I want you to come down and have breakfast with us. You'll feel much better if you get up and move around. You need to eat," Father tells me.

I shake my head. "I can't," I whimper. "I just can't." Nothing is normal. Nothing can be normal. Nothing will ever be the same.

"You can, Amelia. Lucille and Ada will help you get dressed. It's time for breakfast." He releases me and nods to my sisters to take over. He's not asking me to have breakfast, he's ordering me. "It'll be all right, dear girl, you'll see. It'll be all right," he says as he leaves the room."

Ada opens my closet. "What would you like to wear?" she asks.

"I hate this," I whimper as I struggle to sit up. "I don't know what to do."

"Aww. It's okay," Lucille coos, sitting on the edge of my bed. She puts her arm around my shoulders "Don't cry. We just want to see you back on your feet and joining us for breakfast. It's been too long."

What does she mean? I came home a few days ago.

"I, I haven't been gone that long," I say.

"Amelia," Lucille says, "You haven't been to breakfast with us for at least three weeks. It's time. Here, let me help you up."

"What do you mean weeks?" I ask, upset she would make up such a lie.

Lucille is firm. "I assure you it's been weeks. You've done nothing but sleep since you got home." She puts her hand under my elbow and tugs at me. "Put on your flowery dressing gown and come downstairs. Everybody is waiting for you, including Dwight." Lucille picks up my gown and holds it out to me.

Then I ask, "Why is Dwight here?"

"Dwight is always here. I think Father has adopted him."

If Lucille is right, I should try to get to the breakfast table. She brushes most of the tangles out of my hair and ties it back. I make my way down the stairs with Lucille on one side and Ada on the other.

They stay by my side as we go into the dining room and they help me lower myself onto the cushion padding my chair. I look up at my family and force my face into what I hope is a smile.

Dwight is at the table, sitting next to Father. He smiles at me and is the first to speak. "Hello, Amelia, nice to see you up and around. You must be feeling better."

I manage a weak smile. I'm relieved when Dotty sets a plate of food down in front of me. I drink a little coffee and nibble at a piece of hard toast.

The others chatter away about their day. Father's voice sounds as if it's in a tunnel. I don't understand much of what is being said. It takes too much energy to listen. Their voices go in and out, sometimes sounding like they are in a barrel, sometimes muffled as if their mouths are full of wool. I listen, but it feels like I'm only catching half of what they say.

"Well, it's time to get to work," Father announces. He comes and kisses me on the cheek, whispering, "You look much better, my daughter. I assure you everything will be all right. We just have to give it some time." He smiles at me, and then motions to Dwight to follow him out.

After they leave, I turn back to my food, but nothing is appetizing. It's cold and unpleasant. I put my fork down.

Ada comes and gives me an awkward quick hug as though she doesn't know quite how to touch me. "Oh, Amelia, I'm happy to see you back with us. I've missed you. We're sad for you –" she pauses "–and all you went through." She hugs me again. "I guess we are all quiet this morning. It's just that we're afraid if we say anything you might grouch at us like you always do – did – or that we'll hurt your feelings. If you want to talk about what happened, you can, but you don't have to." She looks at Lucille who frowns.

I can't believe Ada would bring up what happened. That's how I think of it now. "I don't ever want to talk about 'what happened,'" I state. "Not now and not ever. Is that clear? And I don't want anyone outside this family to ever know anything about this."

"Well, you're a little late with that idea. Dwight, Clarence and Earl were all there." Ada says. "And Sam." She covers her mouth, cutting off what she was going to say.

"What are you talking about? What about Sam?" I grab onto the name I want to hear.

Lucille clears her throat. "Dwight and Father brought you back from California, but Sam wasn't with them. When we asked what happened, all Father would say is that Sam left the job and disappeared. There was a big kerfuffle a couple of weeks ago when you first got home. Sam's father, the senator, showed up at the door, demanding to see Father. Father told him that Sam disappeared, and he and the boys had searched for him, but couldn't find him. When you had to come home, they abandoned the search and brought you back. Sam's father headed for California to look for him."

Ada adds, "I think Father thinks Sam is the one who hurt you. I'm not sure it would be good if they did find him."

Lucille cuts Ada off, "Shhh. Don't say that to her."

Ada looks at Lucille and then at me. "Why not? Why doesn't anyone ask Amelia if it was Sam? Then we could all get the answer."

Ada asks again. "Amelia, answer the question. Could it have been Sam?"

"What? Why would you even think that? I already told Father I don't know who it was. I would have known if it was Sam. Sam wouldn't do that anyway. I don't want to talk about it. There's nothing to say and I don't want to think about it anymore."

Ada points her finger at me. "You should tell Father again that it wasn't Sam, because he believes it was."

"You tell him," I beg. "You tell him yourself. I can't talk to Father about this. I just can't."

My sisters look at each other and after several moments of silence, Lucille agrees, "I'll talk to him."

Suddenly I'm exhausted. "I need to go to bed."

Lucille walks me up the stairs and pulls back the covers as I climb into bed. She watches until I close my eyes. I feel her put the quilt over me.

Doc arrives in the afternoon. He asks me how the pain is. "Are the injections giving you some relief?"

"They make me sleep," I tell him.

He nods. "That's what they're supposed to do. I hear you're having bad dreams. I'll cut the dosage down some and maybe that won't happen again. Sometimes opiates do that."

I sleep the rest of the day and most of the night. I dream about searching for something, but I don't remember the details. The only company I can tolerate is my sisters. They come and chatter on about some event they attended. Their chatter makes me sad. Why does everything make me cry?

From time-to-time Aunt Mary comes to visit me. She's a pretty woman with brown eyes and straight auburn hair that she wears in a large bun fastened low behind her head. The way she styles her bun is often a signal of how she's feeling. Sometimes, she pulls the hair so tight it stretches the skin on her cheeks. On those days you can be sure that Aunt Mary is upset about something. No one wants to make her upset. If they do, they are in for a lecture on "how young women should behave" or "the rules of etiquette that show you know your place in society." She is also a midwife, which seems a strange contradiction to the elegance that she cultivates in the rest of her life.

Today I just want her to leave. Today her bun is pulled extra tight and she has a lecture for me, something about how I've been in bed for too long and I need to move around. She says she doesn't understand what disease I could have that could cause me to stay in bed for such a long time. At least she doesn't know what happened. I tell her I will make a better effort to do as she says.

I know she's right. I want to leave my bed, but it's the only place I feel safe. The medicine Doc gives still makes me a bit drowsy and thick-headed, even though he lowered the dosage.

When Doc appears for his usual visit, he asks me how I am doing. I'm afraid to tell him I don't want any more medicine. Instead of preparing a syringe as he usually does, he comes to sit on the edge of my bed. He takes my hand in his and looks into my eyes. "Amelia, I have something to talk to you about." He sighs and his shoulders fall forward as if something is troubling him. It must be important.

After a pause, he says, "I feel I have done all I can do for you." He goes on to tell me that he and Father talked about arranging for me to go away to have a "rest." He says that it's normal for me to be sad, but if I stay cooped up in my room all day – if I'm not able to pull myself together – then maybe some time at Saint Agnes Asylum will be necessary.

I listen. I can't believe what I'm hearing. They are thinking of sending me away – to an asylum.

Doc's voice is firm. "It's time for you to get out of bed and restart your life. And, if you can't do that, then we have no other recourse but to send you away."

"But, but that's not right Doc." I tell him. "I couldn't stand that. I'd rather die." I cover my face with my hands. It's a terrible thought. When I look at Doc again I see a small smile cross his face.

"Then child, I highly recommend you surround yourself with friends and family. Staying cooped up in your room won't do anything for your health and it will just make you sad. The next time I visit you, and I will visit you again very soon, I want to see some progress in a positive direction. All right?"

I can only nod. An asylum? Would Father send me to an asylum?

"Further, these pills and injections I've been giving you are strong opiates. They have to be tapered off. We'll start with every other day and wean you off them over the next few weeks or so." He smiles at me as he leaves. "Don't forget what I said. It's time to restart your life and I'll be happy when I see you've done that."

Lucille knocks and enters. "I saw Doc leave. I thought you might want some company," she says.

Doc's words ring in my ears. I force myself to smile at her. I can't be angry forever. "Thanks, Lucille, that would be nice," I tell her, even though I'm not in the mood.

***

My sisters are right about Dwight. It is like Father has adopted him. He's at the table with us for breakfast every day, except for Sundays when he comes later in the morning after we have returned from church. Most days, he leaves with Father right after they eat. I get accustomed to having him around.

One morning Manson interrupts breakfast. He hands an envelope to Father. Father's frown grows deeper as he reads the note inside. He wipes his mouth and gets up from the table. "It appears I have to meet with one of our lawyers first thing this morning. An emergency of some sort," he says.

"You finish your breakfast," he says to Dwight. "I'll send the carriage back for you."

Lucille pipes up a moment later, announcing, "Ada and I are on our way to a dress-fitting. Amelia, you can come with us if you like."

"I'd rather not," I answer. "I've got a few things I need to do this morning."

As we finish breakfast, Dwight asks, "Do you really have something you need to do, Amelia? I have some time before the carriage returns to pick me up. Perhaps you'd like to go for a walk in the garden? Your sisters were saying earlier that your father's flowers are beautiful right now. I know you've been stuck inside for quite a while so maybe we could both go and explore."

I hesitate. "It's been a long time since I walked anywhere, Dwight. I feel like an old woman these days. I walk awfully slow."

The truth is that being outside is still scary. I tried it once, a while back but I made it only a few steps out the door before I froze. The world seemed big and the sky far away. I stood there shaking and crying until Manson appeared at my side. He put his arm around my shoulders, led me back to the house and sat me in a chair. He disappeared and returned with a cup of tea and a few biscuits. I'll never forget his kindness.

Dwight interrupts my memory. "That's okay," he says. "I don't mind slow. We'll have a better chance at seeing the flowers."

"Well, if you're okay with slow, I'll try."

Dwight nods. As we leave the house, I see Manson standing in the doorway to the servant's quarters, watching us.

"Looks like your father has sent his manservant to be our chaperone," Dwight laughs as he catches sight of Manson. "You'd think your father doesn't trust me or something."

"I don't think it has anything to do with Father," I offer. "Manson has been in our family ever since we were all born, and I think he worries about us girls more than Father does." I give Manson a small wave. He waves back at me. I can't see his smile, but I know it's there.

The fragrance of the flowers surrounds Dwight and me like a sweet mist. It's quite intoxicating. Rows and rows of red and yellow blooms light up the morning. When Mother was alive, the garden was her realm, her place to come for peace. For the first time, I see what this garden has become for Father. I bet he finds Mother here from time to time.

"A penny for your thoughts," Dwight says as we walk.

"I was thinking how beautiful the flowers are right now and how much my mother loved this place. I feel at peace." A picture of my mother's beautiful face comes into my mind. I feel sad. My eyes fill with tears. I can't cry now – not in front of Dwight. I change the subject.

"Father has done a good job of maintaining the gardens, don't you think? I'm glad. I think it helps him cope with being alone," I confide.

Dwight doesn't say anything for a while. Then I see a sad smile on his face, and he says, "Being alone is the hardest thing there is in this life." We reach the old bench at the far end of the garden and sit down.

"Do you really believe that?" I ask, surprised that he's sharing such personal thoughts.

"Yes, I do. It's not natural for people to live alone." Dwight's eyes rest on me for an instant before he adds, "Of course, I'm talking about your father. He's a man who needs to have a wife, especially with you girls growing up and moving away one day."

"How do you know we'll move away?" I ask, curious. I've never heard Dwight offer any thoughts about Father, nor about us girls. "Lucille will soon be married and they'll live right here near Father. I'm sure Ada will never find a husband."

"Maybe," Dwight responds, "and that would be good for you girls. But what about him? It's not the same as having a wife."

I nod, "I suppose you're right. He might be lonely after a while." I've never thought about Father being alone – as in being without a wife.

"And what about you, Amelia? Will you spend your life in this house with your lonely father?"

I'm at a loss as to how to answer this question. I never liked the idea of marriage, but I suppose, now, with what happened, no one will ever want to marry me anyway.

"I don't know, Dwight. I guess I can't answer your question."

"And I guess it's an unfair question, isn't it? I'm sorry if I've offended you," Dwight says.

"I'm not offended, Dwight." I stop and lay my hand on his arm until he looks at me. "Your question just made me think about my life." I pause. I'm not sure I want to say this to Dwight, but he's been like one of the family. "I wonder what my life will be like in the future." I sigh. "I guess, you're right. The thought of being cooped up with Father for the rest of my life frightens me even more than the thought of getting married."

"Are you afraid of getting married?" Dwight asks.

"I am," I reply. "I see too many of my older friends getting married to men who control their lives. The man goes to work and enjoys his friends. His wife stays home. I guess she does have the management of the house and the children. But that seems boring to me. There must be more to life than that."

"If you could have the perfect life then, what would it look like?" Dwight asks. "What would make a marriage work for you?"

"I'm not sure. I know I need more than children and a house. That's all."

We continue our walk. "You make it seem as if it's boring to be a woman. But if your husband respects you and cares about you, and makes enough money to give you a good life," he pauses and waves his hand as if he held a magic wand that could produce those things, "wouldn't you then find yourself fulfilled – if you had children and a house?" He waves his hand again. "You could visit your friends – and take care of your father."

"I don't think so, Dwight," I tell him. "Besides, I doubt I'll ever find a man to marry me anyway. So what's the point in thinking about it?"

"Your father is right about you. You do speak your mind," Dwight says, smiling. "I like that in a woman. You know how most men view women?" he asks. Without waiting for an answer, he continues. "Most men think of women as fragile, silent creatures who will become hysterical if told most truths about the world. Men keep information about business and politics – and anything that might upset such fragile creatures – to themselves."

"Is that how you feel about women, Dwight?" I stop and turn to face him.

"Sometimes," he replies.

"Well, I'm not like most women," I blurt. "I wasn't cut out for the usual – for the normal things of this life. I want more than marriage and babies. I enjoy politics and I like learning new things." I sigh. "Not that it matters," I finish. "I'm sure I won't get married anyway after...." My voice falters.

"You sell yourself short, Amelia. You'll be married before too long, I'm sure. Sometimes things are right in front of our eyes and until we're ready to recognize them for what they are, we pretend they don't exist." He pauses.

Before he can finish what he was going to say, we are interrupted by Manson, who has found us. "Mr. Dwight," he announces. "The carriage has returned and is waiting for you." He walks back toward the house.

"I see you have Manson's approval, Dwight," I say. "Did you notice how you've moved up from Mr. Deschamps to Mr. Dwight?" I laugh. "Manson only calls family members by their first names."

Dwight smiles and nods. "Your father – and your whole family – has been very good to me. Guess I'd better go," he continues. He turns his hat around and around in his hands. "This has been an interesting conversation, Amelia. I hope we can do this again, soon." With a slight bow, he turns and follows Manson to the house.

"I think that might be nice. Have a nice day." I call after him. I pick a large pink rose and carry it back to the house.

CHAPTER 6

I don't feel much better after three months at home. Sometimes, I vomit in the morning. I feel queasy and tired most of the time. Tonight, I'm not having any luck finding something suitable to wear to Aunt Mary's Christmas party. My dark green velvet dress, one l always felt suited me best, catches my attention. As I reach to take it from its wooden hanger, Ada pokes her head into my closet.

She frowns and scrunches up her nose. "I hope you're not seriously considering that ugly thing," she says, grabbing it and tossing it onto the bed.

"I'm about to give up this whole party thing today. I feel awful," I tell her as I sink into my bed and cover my eyes to stop the tears.

"Let me help," Ada says. "You'll feel better if you get out of this house. You've been cooped up way too long." I see the worry on her face. She grimaces. "Aunt Mary will be upset if you cancel this late."

Aunt Mary is known far and wide for the social events she hosts. She is always planning a tea to honor some birthday, or to introduce a visitor or new arrival to Salt Lake society. I've heard that people actually pray for an invitation to one of her events, but I'm not sure it's true.

She's happiest when she's entertaining. She gets carried away with every event. She plans meals that include foods that she's discovered on one or another of her many trips. She hates it when people agree to attend her events and then cancel. I don't have much choice but to attend as I have no energy to endure her wrath.

"And besides, Amelia, it won't be the same without you," Ada continues.

What a nice thing for her to say. Maybe she has quit being so mean.

But just as I think my sister has magically reformed, she says, "This particular dress has always reminded me of the drapes in the sitting room." She holds it up in front of me. "Anyway, you're way too thin these days to wear this."

She's right. I have lost weight over the past few months. It's hard to eat when I feel awful. I can see my ribs when I undress. I feel tears again. What's wrong with me?

"It's okay, Amelia, I didn't mean to hurt your feelings. Don't cry. We'll find you something to wear and you'll be fine." Ada takes me in her arms. Her body feels warm and comforting and I hold her tight until I stop crying. Her words help me get back together again. This is unlike Ada. This is unlike me. "Let's ask Lucille if she has something you can wear. You're about the same height."

Lucille answers our knock on her bedroom door wearing a light-pink satin, floor-length gown, and Ada explains what I need. "Take whatever you want but I doubt anything I have will fit you," Lucille says. "Most of what I have is pink, and I know how much you love pink." Her sarcasm feels brutal today.

I turn back toward my bedroom. "I'm not going. I don't need a stupid party anyway," I wail.

Lucille reaches out and takes hold of my arm, stopping me. "Wow, I didn't mean to upset you. Yes, you do need this party, stupid or not," Lucille tells me. "Wait here. I'll be right back."

"Lucille will find you something to wear, don't worry." Ada tells me. "Our sister can solve almost any fashion problem."

Lucille returns, handing me a large bag. "There's a dress in there I think will fit you. It's one of Mother's. Before she died, she gave it to me. I tried it on a few weeks ago but it's just too small. Besides, it's more your style than mine."

I stare at my sister and then at the bag. "Mother's dress? How can I wear one of Mother's dresses? Is that even appropriate?"

"I'm sure Mother would be ever so happy if you would wear it," Lucille assures me.

As I pull it out of the bag, I recognize the dress. It's the one Mother always claimed was her favorite. It's dark blue with silver sparkles on the bodice and streams of embroidered birds twirling up and down the skirt. The birds' eyes are made of rhinestones and their beaks are sewn in gold thread. It's the most beautiful dress I've ever seen. I loved this dress when I was a little girl. Mother was beautiful. I rub my hands over the soft fabric and touch the little rhinestones. I think my sister is right. Mother would be pleased if I wore her dress for the evening.

"Hurry up," urges Lucille. "We're already late and you know how Aunt Mary hates late."

As I slip the dress over my head and the soft material falls over my body, I can almost feel Mother in the room. Even the smell of the cloth brings her back to me. I look at myself in the mirror. The dress is a perfect fit. A soft breeze flutters past me. I feel as though Mother's standing right next to me, watching. I wonder what she would say.

"It's beautiful," Lucille says. "You look just like Mother. You're as beautiful as she was." Her voice breaks, and she takes a deep breath. "I miss her."

I look at my sister, surprised. She's never said that she missed Mother, or that I am beautiful. I reach out and hug her.

She hugs me back, and then steps away, laughing, "I think I'm jealous," she says. "If Earl sees you, he might want to marry you instead of me."

"Oh God!" I grin. "Sometimes you say the funniest things, Lucille."

"I know," she laughs. "Sometimes I even make myself laugh. Anyway, it's okay, Amelia. I think you should wear the dress and enjoy it. I think Mother would be very proud. You are beautiful."

Ada stands staring at me, deep in thought. "Wow," she says. "Lucille is right. You look like Mother." She, too, chokes back her tears.

I feel sad for her, for Lucille, for all of us. I still can't understand why Mother had to die. We stare at each other for a moment lost in our own thoughts.

Finally, Ada breaks the silence, "Well, aren't we a bunch of sad sisters. It's supposed to be a night of Christmas celebration. Let's brighten up, shall we?"

Happy to end the sadness my sisters smile at each other. It's not that easy for me. Don't they understand? I sigh and tell them, "I usually look forward to Aunt Mary's Christmas party but this year – I don't know what I feel; humiliated and overwhelmed is all I can come up with."

"You have nothing to feel humiliated about," Ada says. "Overwhelmed, I understand. What you have been through is overwhelming. But, Amelia, nobody but us knows about this anyway, so going to the party shouldn't feel any different than last year."

Maybe she's right. Maybe no one knows. It just feels like everyone knows. I am sure Aunt Mary knows something – maybe not all the details but the way she acts towards me, stiff and strange, tells me she must know something. I worry about how the servants talk to each other. Maybe Dotty will tell Aunt Mary's servants. I put my hands over my face.

Lucille takes my hands away. "Amelia, stop thinking about it. Just come to the party with us. Aunt Mary will be even more curious – and angry – if you don't show up. Then she'll ask questions we can't answer.

I nod. I really don't want to upset Aunt Mary.

Father is waiting for us at the door. He's dressed in his finest suit and ruffled shirt. "We're going to be late and Mary isn't going to be happy with us," he says with impatience.

"Sorry, Father, but it took Amelia awhile to find a dress," Ada tells him.

Father turns to look at me. "Oh my," he stammers. "Looks like you found one, and a beautiful one at that. You look like your mother." He pauses and a look of recognition slowly spreads across his face. "Oh Lord, it's her dress, isn't it?" He lets out a long sigh and whispers, "You look lovely my dear, lovely." Then turning to Lucille and Ada, he adds, "In fact, you all look beautiful tonight. Your mother would have been proud of you all."

We arrive late. The blustery cold pushes us into the house before much can be said. "George, pleased to see you and your girls this evening," Aunt Mary says. "I believe the invitation said seven, if I'm not mistaken, and it is now seven-thirty." She embraces Father before asking, "Is everything all right?"

"Everything is fine," Father answers. "It was my fault we're late, Mary, dear. I was held up at the courthouse and I'm afraid my tardiness then delayed us all. Do accept my apologies."

Aunt Mary motions us toward the dining room. I'm relieved. Father has come to our rescue with his little white lie. We escaped a ten-minute lecture on the virtues of being on time.

Everyone is already seated. Aunt Mary has outdone herself with decorations and elaborate table settings. Baskets of ornaments, holly, and colored candles decorate the entire length of the table. Each setting has the best of silver utensils, crystal glassware and elegant gold-rimmed china. Even the elegant ecru-colored place cards with our names in large black hand-scripted lettering are tipped with gold.

I am startled to see that it's Dwight who stands to pull out a chair for me. "Dwight, I'm happy to see you."

"I'm happy to see you too," he replies, smiling as he slips the chair under me. He is dressed in a shiny black suit and tails, sporting a small black bow tie. I've never seen Dwight look so elegant. He looks like a proper gentleman and I wonder why I'm surprised by that.

He smiles at me again and takes his seat on my right. "Amelia, you look beautiful. The dress you're wearing is regal. I've never seen anything like it." He blushes as he speaks.

I study his face. He's sincere. I've never had a man talk about my clothes before. It's a little strange.

"The dress belonged to my mother," I tell him. "She loved it. I used to love seeing her in it. It's very special to me."

"Yes," he says, still looking embarrassed, "I can see why."

We look at each other. I don't know what else to say. Dwight is familiar to me, yet he seems a stranger tonight. I don't know quite what to make of him. At that moment, though, I'm happy I've come to the party and I'm happy he's here next to me.

I look up and down the long table. Father has been placed between two women: the church organist, old Mrs. Compton and her daughter, Anne, who is a recent widow. I wonder if Father might be one of Aunt Mary's latest match-making experiments. The idea terrifies me and makes me smile at the same time. I wonder if Father is aware of her ploys. I don't think he would like it very much. At least I hope he wouldn't like it.

Aunt Mary likes to bring together people that she thinks would make a good couple. A number of the marriages in our city can be attributed to introductions that she arranged at one of her soirees, dances or teas. We tease her about being a matchmaker, and we point out that all her matchmaking results in more women who need her midwifery skills. She gets quite defensive when we tell her that.

My sisters are seated across from each other. Lucille is next to Earl. He is playing the attentive beau, leaning close to her and laughing at whatever she's saying. I still think there is something not quite right about him. Ada is seated next to Clarence and both are looking a little awkward. Another of Aunt Mary's matchmaking attempts? I try to be subtle in my examination of Clarence. Is it possible that he might be interested in my sister? I find that hard to believe.

The kitchen doors swing open and servants carry out platters of delicious-smelling food. We start with thick, rich barley-tomato soup and follow it with goose stuffed with herbs and wild rice. Everyone is offered wine in sparkling wine glasses or red punch in porcelain mugs.

We call Aunt Mary's husband Uncle Quincy. He's the perfect partner for her. He enjoys the social events she plans and seems to enjoy playing whatever role she assigns him. He's always a gentleman. He smiles all the time and has a loving way about him even when she barks orders at him like he is some kind of servant. I don't think he has an easy time living with her.

We eat and are entertained at our end of the table by Aunt Mary's steady stream of stories about her travels. She laments how every one of the ten different cheeses used in Italian cooking is unavailable here in Salt Lake. It's not the actual subject matter that keeps her audience glued to her every word, but the way she tells her stories. Her hands seem to talk right along with her mouth. Uncle Quincy, seated at the other end of the long table, offers equally entertaining tales.

Dwight seems to enjoy the stories as much as I do. He takes every opportunity to lean over and whisper in my ear. He edges his chair closer to mine. I pretend not to notice. But I do notice after each story he touches me on my shoulder or on my back. I find it comforting. I want the evening to go on.

When Aunt Mary announces that we are all welcome to adjourn to the sitting room, Dwight and I stand with the others. Around us, the house is decorated with seasonal greenery, Christmas ornaments, and candles. I even see sparkling icicles hanging from the ceiling. In the sitting room, servants offer the adults trays full of expensive brandy in Christmas glasses. I choose instead to have a mug of steaming chocolate. Dwight selects hot apple cider. He also takes a brandy.

Uncle Quincy's voice booms out over the crowd. "Attention everyone, let me have your attention," he says. "Those men who would like to smoke, please join me in the library. I have some Cubans I can share." He grins and waves to the men to follow him.

Dwight laughs. "I do fancy a Cuban from time to time," he tells me as he leaves with the men.

I'm disappointed to see Dwight leave, but I join the women in the sitting room. I search out a large comfortable chair in a quiet corner. This room is even more opulent than the others. I peer into a shiny wood cabinet with glass shelves near my chair and see miniature zoo animals: tigers, giraffes, and lions and even a little ceramic insect with painted black wings. It looks so real it makes me shiver.

"Are you cold, my dear?" I hear Aunt Mary's voice. Before I can answer, she has placed a soft wool shawl across my shoulders.

"Thank you," I tell her. She likes us to be polite.

She takes my thank-you as a signal to pull up a chair and sit next to me. "So, my dear," she, begins, "How are you since your trip?"

I stutter. I remember what happened and worry if she knows anything. "I'm better every day," I tell her, hoping I sound convincing.

"I'm glad to hear it," she says. "It's important to be careful when one travels. Other countries can have such awful diseases, isn't that right?"

I stare at her. Is she being sarcastic? I didn't go to another country, just another state. Perhaps she doesn't know the truth. How is it that no one has told her? Aunt Mary always knows everything about everybody.

"Yes, that's true," I tell her. "Other countries do have terrible diseases. So do other states."

She looks at me, and smiles, but I detect in her a hint of disappointment at my answer. She smiles at me again when I offer her nothing more. Then she goes to attend to her other guests.

Ada and Lucille bring their wine and come to sit with me. We spend the next hour or so chatting with each other.

From time to time a friend will walk by and drop in on our conversation. The chatter is pleasant and mundane, and I feel like my sisters were right. It appears no one knows what happened to me. Thank heavens.

I'm surprised at how quickly the time goes by. The men arrive back in the sitting room smelling of cigars and brandy. Half the men stand around sipping their drinks and the other half join the girls they already feel attached to. Dwight comes over to where I'm sitting. I see Father engaged in an intense conversation with Anne. He seems quite animated and she seems quite awed by what he's telling her. I doubt if Father would ever stop loving Mother enough to find someone. I don't think he would do that to us.

It's well past eleven when the party breaks up and my sisters tell me our carriage has arrived to take us home. I say goodbye to Aunt Mary and Uncle Quincy. She urges me to come and visit her now that I am able to get out. I think she feels left out. She tells me again how happy she is to see me recovered from my illness. I feel something odd about her behavior towards me. She seems less friendly than she used to be. But maybe that's just my imagination.

Dwight walks out of the house with me. He takes my hand in an exaggerated gesture. "May I help you into your carriage, pretty lady?" he asks, smiling.

"Yes, you may, kind sir," I tease. "I would be delighted if you would help me." Dwight grins. I feel the warmth of my hand in his. He walks me to the carriage door and helps me in. "I'll talk to you tomorrow," I tell him.

He smiles and moves away. I wave again as the carriage begins its journey home. He waves back. Then I notice that Father is not with us. "Where's Father?" I ask Lucille.

"He left before us," answers Lucille. "Anne's mother left the party early and he offered to take Anne home." Lucille giggles and pokes me in the ribs. I pull away, annoyed at her giggling.

"What?" says Lucille. "You wouldn't be happy if Father found someone to love?"

"Father has us. We are all he needs. He would never betray Mother like that. I just know it." Even the thought of Father with another wife disturbs me.

Lucille gives me one of her looks: the one that says, "You're crazy." Then in her pompous way announces, "Mother is dead, Amelia. She's been dead for three years. We don't have the right to hold Father hostage for the rest of his life. Every man needs a wife."

"I'm not holding him hostage, Miss Know-It-All," I lash back. "I just don't think it's time."

"Father has been alone a long time. He deserves to be happy," Ada adds.

"What's wrong with his being happy with us?" I counter.

I can tell when Lucille is mad. She rolls her hands into tight little fists and her words come out in staccato. "Can you hear yourself? Why are you being so selfish? Can't you ever think about Father? He might need someone else in the house. And besides, we won't be there forever and then he'll be alone."

"Then let him hire another servant," I retort.

Both sisters look at me. I want this conversation to be over. I close my eyes and feign sleep, but Ada continues.

"So much for Father's situation," Ada says. I'm about to breathe a sigh of relief that they've given up. Then, she adds "But, since we're talking about what men need," she giggles and whispers to Lucille.

My eyes fly open. "What?" I demand.

Ada clears her throat and announces, "In case you haven't noticed, Dwight is sweet on you. And I think you shouldn't encourage him so much if you aren't serious."

"What? I don't encourage him. What does that mean?" I respond, surprised she would think that. "He's a friend – a friend of our whole family. He works with Father and I'm nice to him. I think he's a very nice man – and I don't encourage him at all."

"You do, too!" Lucille chimes in. "Like tonight, you two looked just like a couple of lovebirds all snuggled up to each other. I saw how he touched your back and you, all smiles and googly-eyed."

"I was not 'googly-eyed'– as you put it. You want me to be rude to him?" I protest.

I can feel the force of Lucille's stare, even in the darkness of the carriage. But it's Ada who tells me, "Dwight is interested in you, Sister dear. He takes every opportunity he can find to come to our house, eat our meals and stare at you. Don't tell me you haven't noticed. You need to think about how you treat him."

Lucille cuts in. "And he keeps asking us about you. What is Amelia doing? How is Amelia doing? It's becoming a problem. You need to make up your mind. Either tell him you are interested or tell him to go away. It's not fair to the poor man."

"He's never said a thing to me about liking me. He's always around and he's always nice, but he just makes small talk. Maybe he just feels sorry for me. Maybe you've forgotten what happened. I'm pretty certain nobody will be asking me or Father for my hand."

Lucille sighs, "I think you're wrong, Sister." She shakes her head. "Dwight is smitten with you." We fall silent for the rest of the trip.

The carriage draws up to the house and we all pile out.

Dotty opens the door to the house and greets us. "Will the Judge be late this evening?" she asks.

Lucille replies, "Yes, Dotty, if he's not here now and he's not with us, then he'll be late."

"So sorry, Miss Lucille," Dotty says. "I wasn't trying to make trouble."

"It's all right, Dotty," I tell her. "Father had something else to take care of and I'm sure he'll be home before it's too late. You can go to bed now. Tell Manson to wait up for him."

"Thank you," Dotty responds.

As soon as Dotty is out of earshot, Lucille complains, "You are too easy on that woman. She was putting her nose in where it doesn't belong. Father should have let her go along with the other servants."

I'm shocked at Lucille's statement. "We've known Dotty all our lives. She's part of the family. There's no need to be miserable to her. Besides, Mother asked Father before she died to take care of Dotty. Father would never let her go."

"I don't think we should make family out of servants," steams Lucille. "They get lazy."

"Sometimes you're snooty, Lucille," I retort.

Lucille gives me another of her "You're an idiot" looks and says, "Good night, Amelia. I'm sure we can find more worthwhile things to fight over in the future. No?" She gathers up her dress and petticoats and stomps up the staircase.

Ada follows Lucille, but not before giving me a hug. "We're tired, Sister," she tells me. "Ignore her. A fight about the servants is not worth it. See you tomorrow."

"Good night, Ada."

As I gather up my skirts for the climb to my room, I can't help but think about Father and the fact he isn't home yet. I wonder if Anne Compton is responsible for his lateness. I wonder if what Lucille and Ada said about Dwight could have any truth to it. Whether it does or not, I'm not going to think about it anymore tonight. I'm exhausted.

CHAPTER 7

Morning comes too soon for me. The sunlight through the window awakens me and I roll over to shade my eyes. God, it's bright in here. As I lift my head off the bed, the nausea sweeps over me and horrified, I watch last night's supper gush down the side of my bed and onto the floor.

"Darn," I yell, louder than I anticipate.

Lucille rushes in. "Dear God," she keeps saying over and over.

I can't stand it anymore. "Please, stop *dear godding*." I moan. "Just get out of here. I'll be all right. I just need rest."

But Lucille persists, "I'm calling Doc. This has been going on too long. You might think I haven't noticed but I have. You're sick almost every day now. If you have some stupid disease, I don't want it. I'm going to get Manson to fetch Doc."

I feel too terrible to stop her. She's right. I am sick almost every day. I finish retching and lie looking up at the ceiling. I'm tired of feeling this way.

Dotty appears with a large bucket of soapy water and a brush. She uses a large white rag to pick up the chunks of stuff I've hurled and then scrubs away at what is left of the mess on my mattress. She makes me get up so she can roll up my dirty sheets and replace them with clean ones. As she works, she shakes her head and tut-tuts under her breath. Does she think I can't hear her?

"Dotty, what is the matter with you?" I ask, losing my patience. "Doc is on his way. It's just something I ate."

"I know it's not my place to say it, but you've been sick an awful lot lately," Dotty tells me. She is wide-eyed. "Being sick every day doesn't come from something you eat," she mutters as she scurries out.

An hour later, Doc arrives at my bedroom door, smiling, but looking concerned. "Your sisters tell me you aren't well again. Now what seems to be the problem?"

"I feel terrible in the morning. I throw up and am so tired I don't want to do anything, but by the afternoon I feel better."

Doc is quiet for a moment. "Amelia," he says, "have you had your regular bleeding since you returned from California?"

At that moment, it feels like Mother is in the room with us. Her words come back to me. When a woman's bleeding stops, she is going to have a baby. I hadn't understood then, but I do now. The horror of what happened crashes down on me again – I thought it was over, but it's just begun!

Doc has me lie down. He runs his hands over my stomach and pushes on it. "Do you have sore breasts?" he asks.

I nod. Every word he says makes the truth more real.

"You can sit up, now Amelia." he tells me. He writes something on a piece of paper.

I know what he's going to say. "Am I having a baby?" I ask, not wanting the answer I know I'm going to get.

Doc sighs. "It'll take a while to know for sure. There's the possibility your symptoms right now are the result of – mm" he pauses, searching for words. "– of injuries from 'what happened.'" He shakes his head. "But in all honesty, Amelia, I do think you are with child."

"Oh no. Anything but that. What am I going to do?"

"Just take time to think about it, dear," he says, patting my arm. "Your family will help with whatever decisions are needed. I'll check on you in a few weeks."

On his way-out Doc stops to speak to my sisters in the hallway. Their voices are muffled. I stare at the ceiling. My life is over.

Lucille comes and sits on the edge of my bed. Ada stands beside her. "So, what's going on?" asks Lucille. "What did Doc tell you?"

I'm unable to speak. I don't know what to say.

"Are you sick?" asks Ada. "Doc wouldn't tell us. He told us to ask you."

"No, I'm not sick. Please, just leave me alone."

"You're having a baby," Lucille says, her voice firm and clear. She isn't asking. She knows it's the truth.

I nod. Both sisters come towards me, but I shoo them away. "Please, not now. Just leave me alone. I just need to be on my own right now."

"If you need us we're close by," Ada tells me as they leave. But I notice they hesitate before closing the door.

Later I hear Father's footsteps on the stairs. He knocks and enters. He sits next to me on my bed and I see the sadness in his eyes. "Doc told me your situation, Amelia. I don't even know what to say. I'm sorry I took you on that trip and sorry I didn't do more to protect you from something like this." He gathers me up in his arms. He doesn't cry, but I feel his sorrow.

"I'm sorry, Father. I'm sorry about this. I wish I had listened to you. You tried to warn me. I'm sorry," is all I can say.

He pulls away from me. "Oh, Amelia, don't ever say you're sorry. It is I that is sorry for all of this. None of this is your fault. I have only myself to blame. We'll get through this, I promise. Please don't blame yourself."

He holds me for a long time and then, letting me go, says, "Just rest now and I'll come and talk to you again tonight. I have some ideas about this, but you need some time to rest. Remember that I – I love you, Daughter." Almost as an afterthought he mumbles, "It's best if you don't tell anybody about this. At least, until we figure out what to do." Then he's gone and I'm left with my own thoughts.

My father loves me – even after everything that's happened. I hug that thought to me. Maybe everything will be all right. I'm having a baby. The thought travels from my head to my heart and back again. How can this be? Me? Having a baby?

The realization of what having a baby means overwhelms me. That man who broke into my room. He is the father. Bastard. I know the word. I've heard men say it when they're angry and forget or are unaware that women are present. But now that word will apply to me – to my baby. My child will be a bastard. No one will want to be seen with me. And

Father – what will this do to Father? It will ruin him. It'll ruin our whole family.

I throw myself onto my pillow and cry. I will pray to God to let me die. Everyone will be better off.

**

When I wake up in the morning, it's obvious that God has not answered my late-night prayer for an early death. In fact, not only do I not get death, I get worse than death. I get extreme nausea. If I don't move my head, maybe I won't throw up.

The overwhelming desire to vomit subsides and an overwhelming feeling of dread takes its place. What's going to happen to me? Before I can put any energy into the question, Lucille is at the door. I don't want her or one of her preachy lectures this morning, so I roll over and turn my face to the wall. Maybe she'll get the message and just go away.

Lucille sits on my bed and puts her hand on my shoulder. "Amelia, it's okay," she tells me. "We'll get through this, all of us." I feel her breath on my cheek as she gives me a kiss.

I lie still. It's not okay. Can't she see that?

"Amelia," she says. Her voice is sharp, more like her real self. "Turn over and look at me. We have to talk."

"There's nothing to say." I roll over and snap at her. "Nothing. Can I make it any clearer? I'm doomed. It would be better if I were dead."

Lucille rolls her eyes, "You are not doomed, and you won't die. Stop this nonsense and talk to me, sister to sister."

"Nonsense?" I storm, reaching for my handkerchief and wiping my eyes. "What nonsense? How can you call it nonsense? I can't do this. It's easy for you to judge. My life is over and yours is perfect."

"If you keep being so melodramatic, your life will be over." She gets off the bed and stands with her hands on her hips. She reminds me of Mother. "Honestly Amelia, sometimes you can be incredibly unreasonable. Stop this self-pity and get hold of yourself. You're not responsible for any of this. This is not your fault." She pauses to take a breath. "There are some people who might think otherwise. What you need is a plan – and sooner rather than later. A plan for you, for your baby and for the rest of us. We all have to live with this, you know. It's not just about you."

I glare at her and burst into tears. "I just don't know what to do."

Lucille sits back down on the bed next to me and hugs me close, rocking back and forth like Mother used to do when I was upset or tired. She pulls away and says, "We – all of us – need a plan and the first part of that plan is for you to come downstairs and have breakfast. The family is waiting for you. They have something to say."

Lucille brings my slippers and slips them on my feet. "Come on," she says. "I'll help you with your robe. Everything will turn out okay." She takes a deep breath. "I promise."

I follow her down the stairs and into the dining room. Father, Ada, and Dwight all turn and smile at me. Oh God, Dwight is here. I should have known. I should have dressed.

I study Dwight's face. He's smiling, but he looks worried.

"Amelia," Father says, standing up like he would for some honored guest. "Come sit with us. We need to talk."

He clears his throat and then smiles again. "I'm speaking for our whole family, Amelia. We want you to know we love you and will look after you through this." He pauses and looks down at his plate. In a near whisper he adds, "We just want you to know that."

"I don't know what to do." I try to stop the tears, but I can't.

Dwight hands me a handkerchief. "It'll get better, I promise."

I dab at my eyes with his handkerchief. He's kind. I wish I had gotten dressed. I must look like such a mess.

Before anything else can be said, Dotty and Manson arrive with breakfast. Conversation dies away as the aroma of just-baked cinnamon buns, bacon and coffee permeates the room. Dwight and Father load bacon slices onto their plates and pour fresh cream into their coffee. I choke back a wave of nausea and ask for peppermint tea. Dotty hurries to get it for me. I chatter away and try not to look at the food on the table while Dotty is busy fixing my tea. When it arrives, I take a large sip and it settles my stomach enough that I can stay at the table while the others eat.

"Try these cinnamon buns," Dwight tells me, pushing the plate of buns in my direction. "They are tasty."

"I'm sure they're good," I tell him, "but I just don't feel like eating right now. Maybe later."

"Oh," he says. "I'm sorry, I forgot you might not feel well under the circumstances."

I nod and smile but his "under the circumstances" makes me want to punch him in the face.

"I'm going upstairs to dress," I say to no one in particular.

Dwight interjects, "Amelia, I'd like to take a walk in the garden with you when you return. I think we should talk." He's formal and awkward. I wonder if something is going on that I don't know about.

Father nods as Dwight finishes speaking. "You listen to what Dwight has to say, Amelia. He's a good man."

"I'll be back in a little while. I won't be long," I tell him. Why does Father keep telling me Dwight is a good man? I already know that.

I choose a dress and drag a brush through my hair. No use getting too dressed up. Dwight has seen me at my worst.

Dwight and Lucille are talking at the table when I return to the dining room. They fall silent as soon as I enter. Dwight stands and smiles. "Your sister and I need to talk," he says to Lucille.

"I have some things I need to attend to myself," Lucille tells him as she leaves the table and heads for the door. "Nice to talk to you, Dwight."

Dwight takes my hand and leads me out into the garden. We walk to the old bench where we sat the last time we talked. "I'm not good at talking to women at the best of times." He looks at me, takes a deep breath and adds, "And this is certainly not the best of times."

We sit for a few minutes. It feels like this is more than just a walk in the garden. At last Dwight begins. "Look, Amelia, I don't know how to say this or what to say but here goes. I know everything that has happened to you. I know you are with child. I know this a tragedy for you. I want to talk to you about – " he pauses, and his face reddens. He holds his breath until I think he'll explode and then blurts, "m-m-marriage."

"Marriage?" I'm stunned.

He continues before I can say anything more, "I know – you might think it's because I feel sorry for you, but It's not that. I've come to care for you over the months I've been coming to your house. I feel like I'm such a part of your family. I enjoy your company and I think we would make a good match." The words tumble out over one another and he looks away, his face red. He runs his finger inside his collar. "I know this is hard for you, but please consider my offer."

"Is this Father's idea?" I feel anger growing inside. "Has he put you up to this to save his stupid reputation? Because if he has, you can just go away and get out of my life." I can't stop the anger. I feel the tears coming. Oh God, please don't let me cry.

God isn't listening.

"Please don't cry," Dwight pleads. "This has nothing to do with your father and what he wants. It has to do with how I feel. I want to be with you. I can help you and if we must, we can raise this child. If you want – it will be your decision."

I hesitate. "I'm confused about everything," I tell him. "I don't know whether I'm angry or sad or what. I need time to think. Marriage is such a huge step. I don't know what to do."

Dwight nods, looking helpless. "It's a good idea to take some time, Amelia. Marriage is a big step and I know how you feel about it. I want this to be your decision." He pauses. "But we don't have much time."

I take a big breath. I remember I'm going to have a baby.

"You know what I mean, right?" Dwight asks.

"Yes, I know. If I wait too long, people will wonder what's going on. I know, Dwight, the sooner the better."

"I'd appreciate knowing your answer in the next day or two. I hope you understand that I am serious about you."

"I do," I tell him.

He sighs and then stands up, announcing he had better be going to work. He squeezes my hand. "Goodbye," he mumbles. "I'll see you at breakfast tomorrow."

When I return to the house, it feels empty and strange. Lucille and Ada have gone shopping and I'm alone. That's a good thing as I need to think. I need to be sure what I feel. I don't want to get married, but a baby needs a father. What will people say if I have a baby with no father? It'll be shameful for me and for my whole family.

There are too many questions with no answers.

Sam crosses my mind. What would he say? What would he do if he found out I was going to have a baby? Where is he? Why did he disappear without telling me?

***

Early the next morning I hear the family gathering for breakfast. I don't feel like facing any of them and I'm struggling with nausea again. Just as I snuggle farther down under the quilt, Dotty arrives at my bedside. She gently shakes me. "Sorry for waking you up," she whispers next to my ear, "But Mr. Dwight asks that you join him for breakfast."

"What?" I snap at her. "Since when does Mr. Dwight give you orders?"

"He just asked me to let you know he was waiting for you." She frowns and backs away from my bed. "I figured you probably wouldn't be coming down, but I was trying to be polite to that sad man."

"Why do you say he's a sad man?" I ask, sitting up.

"I just feel it. He seems like a man with a big load on his back." She turns away from me as if she's going to leave but turns back to me at the doorway. "And I know he has a soft place in his heart for you." She shakes her finger at me. "If you don't say yes to him, you've lost a good man." She makes a slight bow to me and whips out of my room like I hit her. Damn Dotty.

This whole situation is so sad. I don't think I can ever be happy again – yet I smile thinking about Dotty's little performance. She is right: Dwight is a good man. Would Father make me put the baby up for adoption? What if I raised it and hated it? What would Mother say? What will Aunt Mary say when she finds out? And she will find out.

I get dressed. Can marriage be any worse than the turmoil that's going on right now? When I reach the bottom of the stairs, I see Dwight in the dining room reading the newspaper and drinking his coffee. He looks up, both expectant and awkward, "Oh Amelia, how are you today?" he sputters. "You look well."

I sit next to him. "Where is everybody?" I ask.

"I'm not sure," he answers. "The Judge left for work before I got here today and I'm not sure where your sisters went."

Dotty appears in the doorway, "You want some breakfast, Miss Amelia? You can't live on peppermint tea," she cajoles. "I'll bring you a nice cinnamon bun."

"No Dotty," I tell her, "Just some peppermint tea. It's all I can stomach right now."

She nods and backs out of the room. When she returns, she has my tea – and a cinnamon bun cut into small pieces like I'm a little child or an old woman.

"All right, Dotty," I nod as she sets it down in front of me. "I give up."

Dwight smiles and nods. After Dotty leaves, he comments that she seems to know very well what I like and don't like.

"Well," I confess, "she's been with us for a long time. She's irritating at times though." I indicate the bun she's placed in front of me. "Upstairs, she told me you're a fine man and I should be nice to you," I laugh, and pick up a small piece of bun.

"Well," says Dwight. "I all of a sudden like her a whole lot better than just a minute ago. She's some smart woman." He's smiling again. "Have you thought about what I said? Can you give me any hope at all?"

I smile at him, unsure how to tell him what I feel.

"You're smiling," Dwight says. "I like to see you smile."

"Dwight," I sigh. "I've thought and thought. I'm still not sure what I should do. But I keep being reminded – first by Father and now by Dotty– that you're a good man, and that I should take a chance on that being enough for us to get started on a life together." I meet his eyes. "I hope it's enough for you."

I put my head in my hands as I think of the enormity of what we're going to do, but Dwight gets up from the table and pulls me up, close to him, wrapping his arms around me in a warm hug. "Of course, it's enough. It's all I can ask. It's all going to work out, Amelia," he whispers. "It doesn't have to be all bad."

After a few minutes he tells me "I have thought about all of this ever since your father told me about...." He slows to a complete stop groping desperately for another way to say it. "Your ... situation. What is most important about this baby is what you want. Not what I or your father or your sisters want. If you want to keep the baby, then we'll just pretend it's our baby. I've heard stories about other families, good honest families, who end up with a baby that doesn't look like anyone in the rest of the family. It – he or she – will be our baby. That's all there is to it."

I stare at Dwight, unable to speak. What a beautiful thing to say. He's right. The baby is part of me, no matter what the circumstances. "You're a wise man, Dwight. I think in my heart that we should do what you say. This baby is mine for sure and yours because you want it. That makes it ours for sure."

I hug Dwight close to me and with his arms wrapped around me again, I feel there may be hope for the future after all. Suddenly, I feel a flutter as soft as a butterfly's wings within me – and I know there is hope for the future.

After a few moments I pull away and look at his happy face. "Well," I tell him, "If we are going to get married, then we should hurry up and plan a wedding."

Dwight stops smiling. "Amelia, I don't think we should have a wedding. What I mean is, I don't know if we should have a wedding in the usual sense. I think we should go to some other town or county and just sign the legal papers." He shrugs. "Leave out all the celebration and people."

"Won't people think it odd?" I ask. "Won't that just give people more reason to gossip?"

"Sending out invitations to a wedding that's planned a week before it happens will cause gossip even more, I think," Dwight says.

"I think they'll gossip no matter what we do."

"I need to go to work," Dwight says after kissing me on the forehead. "I'll see you this evening. We can talk to your father about the wedding then."

That evening, Dwight and I tell Father we have decided to get married. His face lights up and he hugs me and shakes Dwight's hand.

"Good decision," he tells Dwight. "Happy to have you officially in the family."

"Thank you, Judge," Dwight responds. "Amelia and I want to get married as soon as possible."

"That's a good idea. There aren't any legal issues," Father tells us. "Waiting will just make everything more obvious. Why don't you go up to Davis County? No one up there will know you. We'll tell people that Dwight is going on a long trip and wants you to accompany him and it's only proper if you're married."

"We could also tell people that because Lucille has already started her wedding plans, we decided it was too much to invite people to two weddings in one year," I add.

"Good idea," laughs Father. "Fact is, that's truer than not."

Dwight smiles at me. "Our next problem now is finding a place to live in a short time period. Any suggestion about that?"

Father immediately interjects, "I insist you stay with us until you can build a house of your own. You'll have everything you need including servants to help with the child for a while."

Dwight considers what Father has said. "That's very generous of you, Judge," he concludes. "We don't have any other option right now."

I say nothing. I hate the idea of being married and living with Father and Lucille and Ada. But I know Dwight is right when he says we really have no other option.

CHAPTER 8

I have a week to prepare for my trip to Davis County. It's not a long trip. Father says it's fifteen miles or so. Dwight says there's a nice inn near the Davis County courthouse and maybe we should spend a few days there. I don't know how I feel about that. It feels funny to think about staying a few days with a man. Maybe it's the nights that bother me. Maybe I'm just afraid. Why can't I just be happy that someone nice wants to marry me?

There's a knock at my bedroom door. I've been so deep in thought I didn't even hear anyone coming up the stairs. I open the door and find Aunt Mary standing there, a look of deep concern on her face.

"Oh, Aunty, how nice of you to visit. Do come in!" I exclaim, trying to look like I'm happy to see her. Why is she here?

"I just heard you are about to be whisked away to be married," she says, entering my room and sitting herself on my dressing table chair. "Your father told me. How can you run off without so much as a word to me? I'm disappointed. I thought we were closer than that."

She really must not know anything about what happened. And worse – Father has told her about the wedding without explaining why the planning has been so hasty and so secretive.

Aunt Mary continues like a runaway train. "And you pick Dwight Deschamps. That's my main concern. Oh, honey, it's not that I don't like him. It's just that he's not of your social standing. Not anywhere close. What can you possibly see in him? I invited him to my Christmas party because your father insisted. He also insisted that Dwight be seated next to you because he wanted Dwight to feel accepted by us and our friends. He explained that Dwight didn't have the best of upbringings and wanted to learn about the nicer things in life. I could hardly refuse such a request, now could I? At the time, I just thought he was trying to be kind to Dwight. Now I'm beginning to think he had other things on his mind. No matter how I look at this situation, I can't understand why you would want to marry someone like Mr. Deschamps."

"You don't understand, Aunty. You just don't understand."

"No, Amelia, no I don't understand."

There is silence between us. How can I tell her? Suddenly, I feel faint. I sink down on the bed.

"Amelia, you're as white as a ghost!" Aunty exclaims as she sits beside me and takes my hand. "Here. Lie back on the pillow. Let me lift your feet up. I'm sorry if I upset you but you upset me. I promised your mother on her deathbed I would look after you."

She feels my forehead and then pulls a quilt over me. "Now, be a good girl and tell me what's going on. Maybe I can help. I know you haven't felt well ever since your trip to Stockton."

"I'm not sure you want to know, Aunty. It's not a pretty story and you'll probably hate me when I'm done telling it." I feel my tears start, but I don't care.

"No need to cry, Honey," she says. "No story can be bad enough for me to hate you. Your mother used to say that crying never solved anything, but it does make us feel better."

At the end of my story, I tell her how Dwight has helped me through the whole ordeal and that he knows about everything. I tell her how kind and caring he is and how he has agreed that we will raise the child as our own.

We sit in silence for what feels like forever. I try to think of something else to say, but more words don't come. Just when I feel like I want to scream, she reaches out and pats my hand. "You poor dear thing, I just knew something had happened. How far along are you?"

"Almost five months," I reply.

"Oh, Amelia," she says, shaking her head and getting up. "I wish you had told me before. I might have been able to help you. I guess if you feel you want to marry Dwight then that's what you should do. I now understand why the haste."

I manage a smile. "Aunty, please don't tell anyone," I plead. "No matter what, don't tell anyone."

"Of course, I would never tell anyone. Whom would I tell and what would I say?" she looks at me with disappointment. Then she perks up. "I want to be at your marriage, and I'll help with the delivery. But of course, you can have

Doc, if you prefer." She stops momentarily to take a breath and then continues before I can say anything. "I hope you have stopped wearing your corsets by now." she says, eyeing me. "You don't look very big. I never would have guessed."

"Why would I have to do that?" I ask, confused by such a statement.

"Silly girl," she replies. "You do need advice. We modern women know that wearing a corset while growing a baby will hurt the child and make it difficult to come out. Besides, before too long you'll be staying in the house. A woman, large with child, is not something society should have to look at."

She pats my hand again, tucks the quilt around me and tells me to rest. Then she leaves, saying, "I'll speak to your father about going to Davis County with you. I agree it's a good idea, but you should have family with you. I'll stand in for your mother. I know she'd approve."

I close my eyes. I'm not sure it was a good idea to tell Aunt Mary any of this. She isn't at all angry with me, and she does know about delivering babies, but I have the feeling she will think it's her duty to take over my life.

Early the next day she's back telling me that it's all arranged. "We'll take our two large sleighs. Quincy will be pleased to give the horses a good winter run. There's room for everyone – you and Dwight, Lucille and Earl – he's almost one of the family – in one sleigh. And your father, Ada, Quincy and I in the other. We'll arrive around one or two in the afternoon, go out for a pleasant meal together. I'm sure they'll have a place to eat at the hotel. Farmington is big enough for that. We'll go to the courthouse the following morning. Now don't you worry about a thing. I have it all worked out." She pats my hand once more. "We will all help you work this out, dear. It's all very unfortunate, but we will get through it."

The next few days drag, but that lets me rest in between bouts of packing. I feel better these days. I start to look forward to our trip to Davis County. Dwight comes for breakfast every morning and often for dinner as well. I look forward to his company.

On the morning we leave, breakfast is quiet. No one seems to have much to say. It's my last breakfast as an unmarried woman in my father's house. The baby kicks me as if to say, "Be grateful. At least, you'll have a husband and I'll have a father."

Dwight helps Manson carry our suitcases out to the sleighs. It's cold. One of those days where you see your breath every time you speak. The sky seems to be clearing, so maybe we won't get any additional snow.

The weather holds and we approach the town of Farmington just as the sun goes down. The nine-hour trip in the open sleigh feels like it goes on forever. Part of that is my fault as I had to ask Father to stop after ten miles in North Salt Lake so I can visit the commode at the rest station there. I hear a huge sigh of relief from Aunty when she hears my request. I think she needs the stop as much as I do. While it's been a cold day, the down comforters and wool blankets keep us warm. It also helps that we are all packed in together and share our warmth. I can't help but wonder if I'm doing the right thing.

Father points out the courthouse, an imposing brick building. We pass the train station where a long black steamer is idling. Sam comes to mind. I think it's odd that Sam disappeared like he did. In my heart, I hope that nothing bad has happened to him. For an instant, I wonder what my life would be like if it were Sam here with me instead of Dwight.

From the outside the Farmington Inn looks like all the other stone complexes in the town, but once inside it is warm and inviting. Large chesterfields and chairs line the sides of the lobby and a large fireplace greets us. From a shiny wooden desk at the far end of the room, the clerk nods and smiles as we approach.

"I'll stay with Amelia and the girls," Aunt Mary announces. "Quincy can stay with you men."

I'm happy that she and my sisters are with me tonight. I doubt that I can ever stay alone in a hotel room again in my life. Our room has two large beds covered by large handmade quilts, with a chamber pot next to each one. The beds look inviting. Even after sleeping half the trip, I'm overwhelmed by the need to sleep. I'm ready for this day to be over.

But Aunt Mary isn't. "What are you going to wear tomorrow, Amelia?" she asks.

"I've let the sides out of one of my party dresses. It should do nicely, and I only have to wear it for a day. Here I'll show you."

She shakes her head when I show it to her. "Amelia," she says, "just because you're getting married in –" she waves her hand in the air, "in a bit of a hurry doesn't mean it can't be special." She picks up her coat. "This dress won't do. We need to find a seamstress who can make this over into a proper wedding gown."

"By tomorrow?" I ask. "We can't get it done by tomorrow."

"Yes, we can," she responds like an army sergeant giving orders. "I'm taking you somewhere to get this dress fixed right now."

Downstairs, Aunt Mary approaches the innkeeper's wife and explains our need for a seamstress. "My own seamstress is just the woman you need," she replies. "I'll send one of my sons down the street to bring her. I'm sure she'll be happy to be of service."

I can't help but notice that Aunt Mary slips a handful of coins to the wife. Within the hour she brings a red-haired, middle-aged woman to our room. "This is Mrs. Timpkins," she tells us. "I'm sure she will be able to help you."

Aunt Mary is quite polite to the woman, even though she doesn't like "immigrant" women especially Irish ones. She's always gone out of her way to ignore poor Dotty. She explains our situation, even the part about my shape. The woman smiles and nods.

I try on the dress and she takes out a large etui of silver dress pins and sticks them through the material in various spots, putting in some darts and taking out others. The fitting takes only a few minutes. I remove the dress, trying not to get jabbed by all the pins she has used. She folds it and wraps it in a large piece of brown paper for its return to her shop where she will make the final alterations.

"I should have this for you early tomorrow morning," she informs us as she leaves.

As I climb into bed, I can't help but think about tomorrow when I'll be a married woman and it will be Dwight next to me. It feels weird even thinking about it. I don't even know what to do with him in my room, let alone in my bed. Suddenly, the horror of Stockton flashes through my mind as if it happened yesterday. The thought of anyone touching me brings back the pain, the violation.

A wave of nausea comes over me and I try to push it away. Will I ever forget what happened? My heart pounds and I struggle to sit up. Then, I feel a sudden flutter in my belly. The flutter comforts me, and I lie back down. The images subside, and I try to relax. I roll over.

My movement has disturbed Aunt Mary in the bed next to me. "What is it, Amelia?" she asks. When I tell her I'm a little afraid about my first night with Dwight, she says, "Marriage takes work."

I sigh. "Mother used to say that." I tell her. "She always said that any good thing comes with hard work."

"That sounds like your mother. I know if she were here just now, she would talk with you about what you need to know about marriage."

"I think I'm terrified by the whole thought of it." Surprised at the intimacy of our conversation, I wonder if my sisters are awake and listening.

"Don't be," she confides. "Just lie there and let him do whatever he needs to do. Remind him to be careful and not push on your stomach too much. You don't want to disturb the baby. If he's any kind of man, he'll be gentle with you." She turns to face me in the darkness. "It takes a while to learn how to enjoy a man and – being pregnant, and with all you've been through – it might take longer than expected." She pats my hand. "Once you get used to it, it can be rather a nice thing once in a while. For a long time, Quincy seemed to have a constant need, but as we get older, it becomes less important. Men are strange creatures but then, you'll find that out soon enough." She laughs and pats my face.

The next thing I hear is Father knocking on our door. He tells us the men are ready for breakfast. Aunt Mary tells him to go ahead without us. We have things to do.

"Okay," Father responds, sounding displeased with our response. "If you say so."

We all tumble out of bed and bump into each other as we dress.

"I'm hungry, Aunty," I protest. "I feel rather faint." Images of Stockton are floating in and out of my head. I shake my head to stop those memories and other memories come in their place. Sam. Would I be happier if I were going to marry Sam? Why does he keep popping into my head?

"You are far away, sister and why are you looking so sad?" Ada asks, interrupting my thoughts. "You shouldn't look sad on the day you get married. We're your sisters. We are trying to cheer you. What's wrong?"

Ada is right. I shouldn't be sad on my wedding day. "I can't stop thinking about Stockton," I admit. "I guess it still makes me sad."

Lucille gives me a quick hug. "It'll turn out okay, Amelia. I just know it. Dwight is a good man. He'll take care of you."

"I had such high hopes for more in life and now I'm going to turn out like everybody else." I shake my head. "I know Dwight's a good man, Lucille, but I don't want just to be taken care of."

While we talk, the seamstress arrives with my dress. Aunt Mary takes the dress from her and lays it out on the bed. Mrs. Timkins has attached delicate white tulle, a gauzy organza and ecru lace to various places on the skirt and sewn sparkling rhinestones across the bodice. She has provided a veil of white tulle for my head with a band of combs protruding from it to keep it from slipping off. It looks like a different dress. Aunt Mary helps me slip out of my everyday dress and into the new one. It glides over my head and she fastens the buttons. It fits perfectly. Lucille and Ada gasp and exclaim how beautiful I am. I feel better already.

In the middle of our celebration over the dress, there's a knock at the door. Lucille opens it and Father enters. He looks at me wide-eyed. "Oh, Amelia, what a beautiful dress. You look lovely. I don't know what else to say," he stammers. He leans towards me and kisses my cheek, whispering, "We will get through this, my dear. I promise."

I whisper back, "Thank you, Father. I'm sorry for all the trouble I've caused you."

***

It's midafternoon when we leave the inn and even though it's a short walk to the courthouse, I'm glad for my warm coat, wool scarf and hat. There's a chill in the air, like we might soon get more snow.

We find Quincy and Dwight waiting just inside the door of the old building. Dwight's face lights up when he sees me as Aunt Mary takes my coat. "You're beautiful," he tells me. He takes my hand. "I'm a happy man."

The legal paperwork for the marriage takes only a few minutes. A clerk reads what the papers say and then we sign our names. The clerk looks at my signature and then turns to me. "Well, Mrs.," he says, "it's my job to inform you that you now have a new name. Today you go from Miss Amelia Lange to Mrs. Dwight Deschamps. Next time you sign, you remember that." He smiles again and stamps the documents. Dwight pays him a small fee and the clerk hands him some papers to keep.

I now have a different name from my father's. Does that mean that Miss Lange has disappeared? Why do I think such thoughts? I should feel privileged that someone, anyone wants to marry me. But I don't feel privileged.

After the signing is complete, Aunt Mary announces she has already made arrangements with the little cafe next to the inn to accommodate us for dinner. "They have assured me they will make it special," she smiles at me. "Amelia and Dwight should have some celebration even under these circumstances. Besides, she needs to get some wear out of her special dress."

We walk back to the inn. Dwight holds my hand, and it feels warm and small inside of his. I keep thinking I should feel happier than I do.

The wind has picked up as we approach the inn and it's starting to snow. I hope it isn't one of those huge storms that come at this time of year. It could keep us confined in one spot for days.

After a delicious dinner of venison stew and thick brown bread, there is much chatter about the day and the coming snow. It's just nice to sit and enjoy everyone's company. The waiter suggests some decadent French dessert whose name I can't pronounce, and everyone is overjoyed to accept. It turns out to be a cream filled pastry dripping in chocolate. I could have eaten two but I'm certain if I asked, Aunt Mary would tell me I'm not being lady like. Whatever that means.

It's late when we finally make our exit towards our room. Father comes up behind Dwight and whispers in his ear. I see him put something in Dwight's hand. Turning towards me he says, "Good night, Daughter," as he walks towards his room, "I wish you both much happiness."

I turn to Dwight. "What did he give you?" I ask.

"A room key," Dwight responds. "He said it's a special gift to us from him. Our clothes have been transferred to the room already."

"Why on earth would he do that?" I add, surprised.

"No idea," answers Dwight, shaking his head. "Maybe he wants to be sure his daughter has a nice place to sleep tonight or he thinks I can't afford to pay for a room." Dwight grins and adds, "Or maybe he just didn't think it right that I should bunk with the men tonight."

Our "gift" turns out to be a large suite, far more lavish than the room I slept in the night before. There are subtle shades of soft green and gold with touches of red here and there, dark cherry wood furniture. Stuffed chairs upholstered in striking gold and bright green Chinese brocade sit in a corner of the room. The bed is covered by a magnificent multi-coloured quilt. The drapes have cherub faces embroidered in perfect lines, up and down the length of the material, which is hung from brass curtain rods at the ceiling.

In the middle of our exploring the room, Dwight takes my hand in his and pulls me close to him. He puts his arms around me and stands, rocking us back and forth like he might do to comfort a child. I feel like a child tonight. I have no idea what to do. I tremble.

Dwight draws back and looks at me. "Are you cold?" he asks.

"No, Dwight, I'm not cold. I'm just...."

"I think you're afraid and it's okay," he tells me. "Frankly, I'm a little afraid myself. And with all you've been through, you have the right to be afraid. We'll just go slow. Come and sit on the bed and I'll get us a drink. It might help us relax."

He brings me a glass of brownish liquid in a small glass. I smell it. "What is this?" I ask. "It smells of alcohol."

"Of course, it does," Dwight says, laughing at my ignorance. "It's cognac. Cognac is for special occasions. Occasions like this one."

Dwight takes a large sip of his drink. I tip my glass to him and then take a large swallow. The liquid hits my mouth and it feels like someone has grabbed me by the throat. I start to choke, and Dwight pats my back. "No! no! no!" he laughs. "You don't gulp cognac. You sip it to enjoy it in all its glory."

"I don't think I got much glory from that sip," I gasp, still trying to recover.

"Try it again," he urges, taking the glass from my hand and holding it up to my lips. "It'll help you relax. I promise."

I put my hand on his as he guides the glass up to my lips and allows a small amount to run into my mouth. This time it tickles my nose. I swallow and I feel its warmth run all the way to my stomach. I take another sip of the drink and then another until the drink is gone. He takes the glass from my hand and sets it on a side table. He kisses me and begins to undo the buttons on my dress. My mind snaps back to the violence of that other night, the sound of ripping cloth and the searing pain. I try to push the vision from my mind, but too late there is loud moan and Dwight stops. "Am I hurting you?" he asks.

"No," I respond. "I just had a bad memory."

"Do you want to stop?" he whispers.

"No," I tell him. "I'll be all right."

He takes his time with me. One by one I feel the buttons come undone. He takes my dress off and begins to caress my face and neck with his fingers. I hear Aunty's words, "Just let him do what he needs to do."

There is a pause in his caresses, and he gets up off the bed. I watch as he removes his clothing, piece by piece. There is something seductive in the rhythm of his movements. I can't help but watch, caught up in everything he's doing.

I feel a stirring, somewhere inside. I remember the same feeling with Sam. I've never seen a man naked before. It's a curious thing.

Dwight comes to me. Our naked bodies lie together, side by side at first and his hands touch every part of me. My heart beats faster, and I feel an ache that takes control. Afterwards, we fall asleep wrapped up in each other. I don't know what has happened to me, but I feel warm and wanted.

The snow comes and it swirls for three days, keeping all of us confined to the inn. Dwight and I spend as much time as we can in our beautiful room. We get up for lunch and dinner and play cards with my sisters when they ask. My sisters make little teasing comments to us from time to time and I sense they would like to tease us more, but Father frowns at them when they try.

By the fourth day, the snow stops. I'm glad we came by sleigh. It makes getting home a lot easier than if the horses had to pull our heavy carriage through the mounds of new snow. There isn't much conversation on the way back to Salt Lake. I watch the slow passing of scenery and wish we could go faster. After the second rest stop, I fall asleep cuddled in a warm blanket with Dwight next to me.

I'm awakened by Dwight telling me to climb down from the sleigh. "Hey sleepy girl," he says, "we're home and you need to wake up and come in the house." I nod, too tired to do anything else. With Dwight's help I make my way out of the sleigh.

It is good to be in my own bed again. Having Dwight here will be even better. As I lie back on my pillows, I think about the last three days. I've learned a lot about Dwight. Maybe I can be happy and married. Maybe everything will turn out. I put my hands on my belly and feel the baby moving. Bringing a new life into the world might make my life even better. I pray that Dwight and I will be able to love this baby.

CHAPTER 9

1907

Halfway through the eighth month of my pregnancy, I am awakened in the middle of the night by a pain that starts at my backbone and travels around my belly. I cry out. I can't help it. I need the pain to stop.

"What's wrong, Amelia?" Dwight asks, sitting straight up out of sleep. He leaps out of bed and turns on the light. "What's happening?" he asks again, looking terrified.

I grab my belly as another pain shoots through me.

Someone is knocking on the door. Lucille and Ada both enter before Dwight can tell them to come in. "Is everything all right?" Lucille asks. "We heard noises."

I can't answer. The pain is steady but lessens a bit. I need to sit up. I reach out my arms to Dwight, "Help me up. Please," I sputter.

Dwight takes my arms and eases me into a sitting position. The pain catches me deep between my legs and I catch my breath as it overwhelms me. I suck in my breath and try not to make a noise, but a loud groan escapes me. "Oh, god, just let me die."

"Ada," Lucille shouts. "Go get Manson to run for Doc right now and then send Dotty to get Aunt Mary. I'll stay with Amelia."

I feel Dwight stand up and move away. I hear the door close behind him.

I cry out again in agony. "You'll be fine." Lucille tells me. "You're not going to die. The doctor is coming." She's holding my hand and watching my face.

Another pain passes. It hurts. "I can't do this," I croak.

"Yes, you can," Lucille says. "You have no choice."

"Maybe if I stand up, I'll feel better. Help me walk a bit," I demand.

"I don't think that's a good idea, Amelia. You don't want to do anything that might hurt your baby."

"Oh, God," I yell at her as another pain shoots up my back. "I can't do this, Lucille; it just hurts too much. I need to stand up."

"You'll be all right," she insists. This time she grabs my arms and yanks me to a standing position. The pain subsides for just a moment and then I feel something gush from my body; something warm and wet. Pink-tinged liquid flows across the floor. "I'll get Dotty to clean this up," she mutters as she turns to leave.

"God, please don't leave me," I wail.

She shakes her head impatiently and pats my cheek, "Oh for heaven's sake, Amelia. I'll be right back."

I lie back on the bed and cover myself with the quilt. Why is Lucille mad at me? I close my eyes. When I open them again, Lucille is sitting beside me holding my hand

and Dotty is on her hands and knees wiping up the mess I made.

"Don't worry, Amelia. Aunt Mary will be here soon." Lucille's voice is softer now. Perhaps she wasn't as impatient with me as she sounded but just disgusted with the mess I made.

After what feels like hours, I hear Aunty's voice before I see her. "What's happening?" she says as she rushes into the room. "Lucille, move so I can have a look. Did someone call Doc?" Aunty runs her hands over my swollen belly.

"I sent Manson to get Doc," Lucille tells her.

I gasp as another agonizing pain sweeps across me. "It hurts, Aunty. A lot."

Aunty says nothing but nods and rubs my hand.

Manson arrives with the news that Doc has gone into the country to deliver another baby and won't be back for some hours.

"Aunty, it hurts too bad," I wail. "Do something!"

"I am doing something," she responds. "I am going to sit here and wait for God. That's what I'm doing. He comes around during these events and determines what the outcome will be. In the meantime, Amelia, if you feel like you need to push, just follow your body."

Time after time, the pain rises up and my belly gets hard. I'm tired. I want it to stop. Aunty stands up. "Amelia, just concentrate on what you are doing. At the end of this you will have a baby. A sweet baby. That's all you have to think about."

"No. Aunty, it hurts too much." I tremble in pain.

Aunty comes close to my bed and I feel her hands rest on my belly. "I want you to tell me the next time you feel like pushing and I'll help you push the baby out," she says. As another pain crawls from by back to the front of my belly I let out a moan and she pushes with all her might. I push with all my might. Aunty stops pushing and finds her way to the bottom of the bed. "One more push," she tells me. "I can see the baby's head. You need one more push."

Another pain comes swiftly, and I push as hard as I can. This time I feel the child slip from me in a great gush. "I've got it." Aunty says, catching the baby in her outstretched hands. "Thank God that's over." I hear her mumble.

There is silence. Shouldn't a newborn baby cry? I try to sit up to see but pain pushes me back on the bed. I can't tell what Aunty is doing with the baby, but shouldn't there be a sound from the baby by now?

"Why doesn't my baby cry?" I ask, fear rising.

"Sometimes babies don't cry," Aunty tells me. "They just gurgle." Making no effort to let me see the baby, she picks up a roll of what appears to be a blanket and places it in a large basket. She comes back to me and leans in with both her hands and again pushes hard on my belly. "We have to get it all out," she tells me when I cry out. I feel something else exit my body and Aunty catches it in a pail. Aunty takes time to clean me up and then pulls a quilt over me and says, "It's okay, Amelia. I'll attend to it. I'll send Lucille in to look after you. She leaves the room carrying the basket and the pail.

"Where's my baby?" I call after her. She doesn't answer. What did she mean by "I'll attend to it."?

Lucille appears looking sad and concerned. "Oh Amelia, Aunty said I should sit with you. What can I do for you?"

"The baby. I didn't hear it cry. What's wrong?"

Lucille covers her face with her hands. "I don't know. I didn't hear any crying either but I'm sure Aunty will take care of it."

Now that the pain is over, I need to sleep. Lucille promises not to leave me and sits stroking my hand.

Hours must have passed because when I open my eyes, Doc is next to me. He asks Lucille to leave while he examines me. "There is nothing more to do," he informs me. "Your Aunt Mary seems to have taken care of everything. I'm going to examine the baby."

"Doc, my baby. Why didn't it cry? Is it a girl or boy? Why won't anybody let me see my baby?"

Doc won't answer my questions either. He looks at me, pats my shoulder, and turns towards the door, adding, "Your aunt will talk to you."

When Aunty returns, she sits by me on the bed. "The baby is dead," she tells me in a low monotone voice. "The doctor examined him and verified that he is dead. He was very small, Amelia. He really didn't stand a chance."

Dead. My baby is dead. What a terrible thing for Aunty to say. At least she said it was a him. At least I know it was a baby boy, a son. I feel like the world is coming to an end. Poor baby and I never got to see him. I wonder if anyone will be sad. Aunty says nothing more but sits for a few minutes before handing me a glass of water and a pill and telling me to sleep.

I awaken some hours later to find Dwight dozing in a chair next to our bed. His head is tilted to one side and his eyes are closed. His arms are folded across his chest as though he is enclosing himself in a giant bear hug. His legs are crossed, and he's removed his shoes. How can anyone sleep like that?

I watch him sleep as the questions run through my mind. What will he say about this? What do I feel about this? All the worries about the baby and the embarrassment and gossip are gone. To anyone who didn't know about the baby, everything looks normal. There is no baby. No need to keep a secret. No need to lie. I feel the tears. I don't care about any of that. My baby is dead. How can I be happy about that? A baby died today, my baby. My face is wet with tears.

Dwight wakens. He reaches over with a large handkerchief and pats my eyes. "It's okay, Amelia. You have your cry. No matter what anyone says, you're allowed to be sad."

"Are you sad about the baby, too?" I ask.

He hesitates and then tells me, "No, I'm sad about you. I'm sad because I see you cry for this child. God had his hand in this. I think justice has been done. There is no place in this world for a child like this. I understand you need to be sad, but it's better if you consider this an act of God and give thanks."

I look at him and then I roll over and put my back to him. He's a man. What can he know? This baby was part of me.

"Amelia, please don't be angry. I know you don't like my words, but I have to tell you what I feel. I promise one thing to you: I will always be honest with you. This is how I feel. I can't be sad about the baby if I'm not sad. But I am sad for you."

"I'm not angry," I mutter to him. "I just can't talk anymore. I need to think."

"Doc says we don't have to register the baby's birth and death. Your father says illegitimate and stillborn children don't have to be registered."

I roll over and try to sit up. Dwight puts a pillow behind my back. "I think we should register him. It is a him, you know." I tell him.

Dwight nods. "I know," he says, "I saw him. He was the tiniest human being I have ever seen. I think he wanted to live. I watched him take what must have been his next-to-final breaths."

"You saw him?" I ask. "You saw him die? He never cried. I thought he was dead when he was born."

"No," says Dwight. "He was moving, and his eyes were open, and he was making noises, but Aunty said he wasn't breathing well and would die soon."

"Oh Dwight," I moan. "What did he look like? Do you think he was normal?"

"I'm not sure I should tell you this, but you need to know. He was dark, dark like chocolate. When I talked to your father about this he wasn't as distraught about this fact as Aunty. He said when Aunty told him about it, she went into a rage like she was crazy. I think he was quite concerned about her sanity at the time."

"Aunty can be very odd at times," I tell him. I sigh and pause, adding, "So, you didn't see him die?"

"No, I didn't see him die," Dwight says, twitching in his chair. "I left after I saw him, and Aunty says he died an hour later."

"Why didn't you bring him to me so I could see him? I needed to see him. Don't you understand that?"

I see the pain in Dwight's face as he recalls, "Aunty said no. She said it would be too disturbing for you to see him and then have him die. I couldn't stand it when she said that, so I left. I'm not very good at things like that."

"So where is he now?" I ask.

"Your father took him to the undertaker. I think they were going to bury him this afternoon."

"What? They are going to bury him without me?"

"He's going to be buried without any of us. Your father's instructions were to bury him and not mark his grave. He says that's best for everyone. He says it's best that no one knows he existed."

I bury my head in my quilt and cry. What does Father know about what's best? Dwight rubs my back and sits with me until I fall asleep.

When I awaken I find Dwight gone. Hours later when he returns, he informs me that we have named the baby George even though it was against my father's wishes.

Dwight intercepted Father and Aunt Mary at the undertaker and was able to make our desire for a proper burial and registration known before it was too late. I was surprised that Father didn't play his judge role and overrule Dwight, but Dwight says he just shook his head, sighed and agreed. Maybe in his heart Father knew it was the right thing to do.

CHAPTER 10

I find myself alone this morning, sitting at the kitchen table eating breakfast. Everyone must be off to work or on a shopping trip somewhere. I am relishing this aloneness.

I hear the kitchen door behind me swing open. "Are you feeling better today?" Dotty asks as she fills my coffee cup. "Your eyes are smiling more," she adds.

I nod. She's right. I am feeling better. It seems like the sadness is taking forever to lift but it is lifting. It's been three months to the day since we lost George.

I still cry from time to time. When Dwight is around, he can sense my dark moods and he holds me close and pats my back and whispers how everything will be all right.

Dwight has helped me to heal more than anyone else. He always knows the right thing to say. He distracts me from my dark thoughts by finding something uplifting to talk about. He takes me for rides out into the countryside or for walks in the park nearby. It hasn't been easy for him over the past three months either. He has turned down work opportunities out of the city, just to be certain I am looked after. He comes and asks me how I am before he leaves the house for any length of time.

Ada has been a big help to me as well. When Dwight isn't around, she sits with me and we talk. In the past three months, I've learned to appreciate my sister. She can be kind and helpful when she wants to be. I've also learned she and Clarence Logan have been seeing each other – with Father's approval. She has confided in me that they are going to be married within the year. When I'm feeling strong, she insists on taking me shopping and we wind our way through the little shops in the downtown looking at clothes and shoes and picking out things she might like for her wedding. I ask her when they will be announcing the date, but she isn't very forthcoming. She keeps saying it depends on Clarence's work schedule, but I think it's something else.

Aunt Mary, however, hasn't come to visit me since George died. Ada tells me to be happy about that because Aunty has gone kind of strange since then. She's been very sad and gloomy. I'm not sure why Aunty should be so sad. It wasn't her baby.

I'm becoming more and more determined to move on. Dwight talks more and more about us having our own house. He has been planning what it will look like. He says that one day he will bring the blueprints home for me to see.

I haven't been excited about the house like he is. I am in my childhood house and have familiar things around me, but it's not that comfortable for Dwight. Last night he told me that if we continue to live here much longer, people will think he can't provide for his wife.

This morning, he and Father come in while I'm finishing my breakfast. "Why aren't you at work?" I ask them.

"You tell her," Father says to Dwight, his voice high with enthusiasm.

"You won't believe what just happened," Dwight tells me. "We have struck it lucky." He sits down next to me. "Your Father has just wrangled a plot of land for us in the nicest part of the city. A Mormon friend of his owns it and said he would sell it to us for a good price, but it has to be a secret until the deal is done or we could lose it."

I look at him, confused. "Why?"

Father explains, "Mormons don't like selling their land to anybody but another Mormon. They see most of Utah as their promised land, so I understand their reluctance to sell any of it off. But I once helped this fellow with a legal issue, and we've been friends ever since. I guess he feels he owes me a favour."

"Here, I made you a rough drawing of the street where the house is going to be," says Dwight, his eyes sparkling with excitement. He unfolds a large piece of paper and points to a small open spot between two large buildings. "That's the place, 66 South 13th East."

"Wow, that's a fancy area. Is that by the reservoir where all the mansions and big houses are?" I ask.

"Well, our house won't qualify as a mansion," he tells me, "but it will be nice. It will be around the corner from the big houses, but you're right, it is in a fancy area. He searches through a stack of papers on the table and unfolds a large blue sheet with dark markings and lots of numbers.

"Here's a blueprint of our house," he explains. "It's a rough picture of what it will look like when it's built."

I like the tall columns that line the front porch. "Oh," I exclaim, "there's another porch at the back. We could screen it in and use it for sleeping when it's too hot inside."

Dwight smiles. "Good idea," he says. "I'm glad to see you take some interest in the house. I was beginning to think you wanted to stay in your father's house forever."

"You haven't given me any opportunity to make decisions about the house," I tell him. "This is the first time I've seen a picture--sorry, I mean blueprint of it. I was beginning to think you were going to build the thing without any input from me at all." I feel my voice rise and my face feels flushed.

Dwight turns to me and stares for a moment before he comments, "You're right, Amelia. I apologize. You seemed so preoccupied that I just didn't want to trouble you with the mundane details. Also, I wasn't sure we were going to be able to buy the land. But now that I know we can and that you are interested, I will bother you every chance I get. Would you like to drive over in the carriage and see the land tomorrow?"

Dwight's eyes crinkle up at the corners. He's teasing me. It's his way of avoiding a tiff. I don't think he liked my comment about not informing me about the house. I smile back at him. He means well, but I get the feeling he thinks the details of the house belong to him. I imagine he will be happy to leave the decorating to me but not anything to do with the building.

"There are black walnut trees on the property." Dwight adds. "I'm going to instruct the builder to save a few for us. They'll make good shade for the north side of the house."

"Show her the drawings of the inside of the house," Father suggests to Dwight. "This is the part she will be more interested in."

Dwight reaches underneath the stack of papers again and pulls out another drawing. "Here's a rough picture of the inside of the house," he says, handing me another large piece of stiff paper. "There are two levels and a deep basement. It even has a tub for bathing and a commode on the upper floor." He points out the various rooms and announces, "I count ten bedrooms, a pantry, a kitchen, a salon, a parlor and a full bathroom."

"Oh my," I sigh. "That's a lot of rooms, Dwight."

Before Dwight can reply, Father says, "Yes, you'll have to fill them all with children."

The room goes silent for a moment and Father's face turns red. "I guess I shouldn't have said that, Amelia." He takes my hand and gives it a squeeze.

I squeeze his hand in return. "It's okay, Father. I know what you mean."

He smiles at me, relieved, "I guess Dwight and I should get back to the business of completing the house transaction before the day is over. See you for dinner."

On the day the builders break ground for our house, Lucille and Earl set their wedding date for Saturday, October 10th. Lucille asks me to help her with the planning and preparation. Now I have something to think about other than just waiting for the house to be built.

Aunt Mary reappears when she finds out about the wedding a few days later. She and Lucille get into a tug-of-war about the details.

"I want pink roses for my bouquets," Lucille frets, "But no. Aunty says pink is not appropriate for an older bride. She says it would be fine if I was seventeen. She also whispered that people might think I'm damaged goods if I use pink. And I can't have blue napkins for the dinner. She thinks they are too masculine. What does that mean? Blue is pretty, especially for napkins. Mother had a whole box of blue linen napkins embroidered with little gold flowers. How can Aunty say no to that? I honestly think the woman is losing her mind."

All I can do is give Lucille a hug and tell her it'll be all right, even though I'm not sure it will.

A few days later, Aunt Mary tells Lucille that more than two hundred guests is in poor taste. As soon as Aunty announces that, Lucille makes a list of guests that totals four hundred. That very same evening Father brings up the subject at supper.

"Lucille my dear, have you produced a guest list for your wedding yet? I have a few of my colleagues that need to be invited."

"Aunty says that four hundred is far too many people. What do you think?" Lucille asks.

Father pauses for a moment and then replies, "Mary did mention to me that she thinks you don't understand the etiquette that must be followed when it comes to wedding planning."

"Father," says Lucille, as her face turns a slight shade of pink and her eyebrows furrow into a frown. "I do understand the etiquette for weddings. But she is unreasonable. She won't let me have pink roses or blue napkins."

I expect Father to roll his eyes and sigh, but instead he gets up and walks around the table and leans over and hugs her. "I'll talk to Mary, but I doubt if it will do any good. While what you want seems reasonable to me, she will still have her own opinion. I am still going to insist on the four hundred guests. I'll tell her I need some of my colleagues to be invited."

He smiles at her and they hug again. "Thank you, Father. Thank you."

Aunty comes the next day and behaves as if everything is just fine. She takes Lucille, Ada and me to meet with her dressmaker so he can design the dresses for Lucille's wedding.

The sign over the doorway reads "The House of Maurice." Maurice is a short, plumpish little man with a long nose. He is wearing a green tunic and black slippers. A picture of a garden gnome pops into my head and while I know that isn't the most flattering description, somehow it fits.

"Mary, Mary, Mary," he chants after the introductions. "So, you have brought me these delightful creatures with which I may weave my magic. Which one is the bride?"

Aunty smiles and points to Lucille. "Weave your magic like you always do, Maurice."

Maurice motions to Aunt Mary, Ada, and me that we should be seated. He takes Lucille by the hand and twirls her around several times.

"What sort of dress were you thinking of?" he asks, studying Lucille's figure.

Aunty breaks in with a description of what she thinks. Maurice cuts her off. "Now Mary," he says, "I didn't ask you. I am asking this lovely young woman who is getting married and for whom the dress is going to be created, what she wants. It is her event you know."

Aunty's mouth opens as if to reply but shuts it again. She turns to Lucille and nods as if giving Lucille the right to speak. Aunty knows if she doesn't listen to Maurice, he will simply refuse to work with her, and Aunty knows he is the best dressmaker that Salt Lake has to offer. It makes me smile to see Aunty put in her place. I wish I had that much courage.

Lucille looks at Maurice with wide eyes. She looks at Aunty and opens her mouth, but nothing comes out at first. Then she says, "Gibson Girl. I want to look like the Gibson Girl."

Maurice bursts out laughing. "I like you," he says straight away. "Yes, you and I are going to get along just fine. The Gibson Girl image makes my life very simple. Of course, you will have to wear a very confining corset to give you a tiny waist and you will have to pad your bosom quite a bit." He walks around her, studying her from every angle. "Your hair, we will pile on the very top of your head," he says while his arms fashion the items in the air as he speaks. A bustle and a long satin skirt, that's easy. I think though, that you and I will make this Gibson Girl just a little different – and very special."

Lucille smiles and bobs her head up and down. I see a sparkle in her eyes.

Maurice calls his assistant to come and take Lucille's measurements. In a few moments, that part is done, and Maurice announces, "Next we choose the material. Come with me." In the storeroom, Maurice pulls down large bolts of fabric, and within an hour all major decisions are made, and they have been made by Lucille and Maurice. Aunty hasn't said a word.

As we pile into a carriage to bring us home, Aunty seems uncomfortably quiet. Lucille asks her what she really thinks about the Gibson Girl look and Aunty says, "It's fine. If you like such things."

Lucille smiles, "Yes, Aunty, I do like such things. Don't you?"

"Well, if you want to know what I really think, the whole thing is ridiculous. Frankly, I think it makes you look like nothing more than a well-groomed hussy."

I gasp and put my hand over my mouth. Part of me is shocked by such a statement but part of me is angry. What an unkind thing to say to Lucille who has worked so hard to have what she wants. I look at Lucille's face thinking she might be upset. Instead, I am surprised to see a wry little smile form at the edges of her mouth slowly turning into a look of pure determination. The rest of the ride home is as silent as the inside of a tomb.

***

Three weeks later the nuptials take place at the Presbyterian Church, down the road from our house.

Maurice has outdone himself. Lucille is the perfect picture of the iconic Gibson Girl, modern but delicate and elegant. Her dress is white satin and has seven layers of twirls in white lace and tulle that cascade around her hips and down to her feet. Little pearls, all hand sewn, flow like a winding river from her bodice to the floor. The pearls are the added little somethings that Maurice included to make the Gibson Girl look a bit different from the usual. Her full-length veil is French silk tulle. Her shoes are silver brocade. She smiles at herself in the mirror before taking the long journey down the aisle. I envy her perfection. I envy her wedding.

I think back to the day I got married. No ceremony. Just signing papers in a courthouse. My dress was special at the time and under the circumstances, but now it seems rather tawdry. I need to stop thinking like this and just be happy for my sister. Just accept that it will always be like this. Sadness drops over me like a blanket.

Just before Lucille leaves her dressing room to head down the aisle, Father enters the room. He barely gets through the door before he stops, mouth open, and stares. After a moment he brings his hand to his mouth as if he wants to touch the words he needs to say. "Dear God, you are a beautiful sight my dear. Your mother would be so proud."

Tears fill his eyes, and he brushes them aside quickly. He walks up to Lucille and kisses her cheek, then places a gold necklace around her neck. "Your mother wanted you to have this, my dear," he tells her. "It was your grand-mother's necklace originally." He bends and kisses her again. "I'm proud of you Lucille," he tells her. "You will always be my special princess."

Lucille thanks Father and hugs him tight. She stares at Ada and me over his shoulder. It feels like we are children again and fighting for his attention. Who will be the winner? I turn to Ada and see her tears. They match mine.

Lucille steps back from her embrace with Father and turns to me. "Don't cry, Amelia," she tells me, as she hugs me, trying not to mess up her hair. "This is a very happy day." I smile as best I can and nod. I do want her to be happy.

We leave her then, standing in the doorway to await the call from the preacher to begin her trip down the aisle. Ada and I make our way to our seats next to Father, Clarence and Dwight who are already seated. The organ music starts and the congregation stands to watch the bride enter. She is indeed beautiful. She looks longingly towards her groom standing at the front of the church. I see the joy on her face. The ceremony is the same ritual that is word for word what all our Christian neighbors have used for five hundred years.

The only flaw in the whole ceremony is the long-windedness of the preacher. He seems to delight in the fact that he has a captive audience and no time limit. In the sermon part of the ceremony, he takes it upon himself to pontificate on the merits of purity and the sanctity of marriage. It feels like he is looking directly at me and talking directly to me. I feel the sadness return. Perhaps if he had talked for a short time, I wouldn't have felt it so deeply but after twenty minutes of this I have visions of running up the aisle to smash his head into tiny little bits. I have the feeling there were others who would want to join me.

The reception is held in the church hall. Good thing it's large and there is enough space to provide meals for four hundred people. There is no dancing or alcohol, as the Presbyterians allow neither in their facilities, but there is much co-mingling, chatter, and laughter.

As I make my way through the crowd to my sister's table to congratulate her, Aunty touches me on the shoulder and whispers quite loudly. "Well, I'm so delighted to see your sister get married in such a respectable way. I'm sure your mother must be very proud." She looks at me without smiling and turns to walk away.

I stop to catch my breath. I think I have stopped breathing all together. Did she really say what I think she said? I turn in her direction and as I step forward with the intention of telling her how horrible I really think she is, I feel a hand on my back. It's Dwight.

"I heard what she said," he tells me. "Just keep walking. You were going to congratulate your sister. I insist that you continue that journey and forget what you heard. We don't need to make a scene. We can deal with this later."

I frown at him. He's right, of course. This is my sister's wedding. I head for her table.

Father has invited a number of guests to the house afterwards to imbibe and to watch the bride and groom open their gifts. I watched as various gifts arrived at our house in the days before the wedding, each bearing a carefully wrapped package and depositing it in the parlor along with all the others. In the end there were so many gifts that I couldn't imagine having room to fit all the guests and the gifts in the parlor.

On the day of the gift opening, Father realizes the problem and insists that we move all the chairs and gifts to the large sitting room on the upper floor as there is ample room there. As the day goes on and as each gift is carefully unwrapped and exclaimed over, I begin to believe this day will never end. I am just grateful when Lucille asks me to take each gift into another room and rewrap it for travel to their new home. At least I don't have to sit hour after hour staring at the extravagance and wondering what she will do with all the items.

Shortly after the gift opening, Lucille and Earl leave for their honeymoon in Europe. They won't be returning for more than a month. When they return, they will be moving into Earl's farmhouse with its thousand acres and the chickens and goats. It makes me chuckle to picture Lucille collecting eggs and milking goats. I know that probably won't happen, but it still makes me smile.

Three days after Lucille leaves, I start to miss her. It feels too quiet. Maybe it was the hullabaloo of the wedding that accentuates the silence, but it does seem strange. I wonder how Father will feel when all of us are out of this big old house and he will have to ramble around in it all by himself. At least Ada is still here to provide us company during the day.

At dinner a few nights later, Ada and Clarence announce that they have decided on a date for their wedding: a week before Christmas. They want to have a small event, at home and with only a few friends and family. "We want nothing lavish. We want it to be a quiet affair," she states. "Nothing like Lucille's spectacle. And I want Aunty to stay out of it."

Father sits back and wipes his mouth with his napkin. "I don't know if there is a way to keep Mary from helping with a wedding," he says.

"Well, I want to do this by myself, with Clarence's help of course. I don't want her telling me what I can and cannot do at my own wedding," responds Ada.

"Then tell her what you want and take the consequences," Father says, shaking his head. "She means well."

"She's too bossy for me." Ada rails. "I want simple and she doesn't know the meaning of simple. I don't intend to tell her about it until the last minute."

"Well, that won't work," I interject. "She'll find out from somebody else."

"I'll figure out a way," Ada insists. "Just give me some time and I'll figure it out." After three weeks of thinking about it, she decides to visit Aunty for afternoon tea. She sends a card by the coachman the day before. Aunty sends a message back that she would be delighted to see her.

Father and I are waiting when Ada comes home. Her eyes are red from crying. "I told her the date and that we want to have a very small gathering at Father's house and that Clarence and I are doing our own planning." She swallows and goes on. "Aunty looked at me like she was in shock." Tears form in Ada's eyes. "She got so angry. I can't believe how angry Aunty got. She made me cry."

Father stands up. He gives Ada a hug. "I think it's time I had a talk with Mary. She seems not to be herself these days." He takes his hat and soon we hear the carriage leave. Ada and I wait up for him. It's past midnight when he returns looking tired and distressed.

"I'm not sure I helped your case any. Mary says if she can't help then she's not having anything to do with your wedding. I take that to mean she also wouldn't be attending. And she made it a point to let me know how disappointed your mother would be. This isn't like Mary. Something else must be bothering her. I'm going to ask Quincy if there is something we should know. Perhaps she is sick or something."

"Well, I don't care," interjects Ada. "Clarence and I are going to have a small family wedding. I don't care anymore whether she comes or not."

Father interrupts, "Well, you should care Ada. She has been a help to you girls for many years. She has done a lot of nice things for all of us. Perhaps we should try to get to the bottom of her behavior before we pass judgment."

"I'm tired of her constant interference," states Ada. "Maybe there is something else going on, but I don't have time for it, whatever it is."

In the end Aunt Mary and Uncle Quincy don't come to Ada's wedding. The little affair that Ada and Clarence want turns out to be a good idea. They are married in Father's living room in front of the fireplace with our family and a group of twenty or so friends. They both look happy. The cook makes a spectacular dinner of roast duck and roasted chestnuts and a white wedding cake with lemon filling and covered with almond paste.

They go to San Francisco for their honeymoon. I envy them that. I've always wanted to go to San Francisco. I think Ada will be happy with Clarence. He's a hard worker and he seems to care about her. She is lucky to catch him. When they return, they announce they are moving to Sacramento. Clarence has better work opportunities there and the climate is more to his liking.

CHAPTER 11

1915

"It's a girl." I'm exhausted and I just want to sleep, but that little phrase dulls the pain and brings joyful tears rolling down my cheeks. From the time we knew I was going to have another child, Dwight has talked about how nice it would be if it was a girl. He will be overjoyed he has his girl at last. Even George and David will be pleased when they get used to having a sister. I try to drift off into sleep, but the memory of the first little George crosses my mind. Dwight insisted that our first son be named George even though there was another little George already buried. I think I was too tired at the time to object.

"Mrs. D. sit up!" Hilda's mannish voice pulls me back from my thoughts. "Sit up now and suckle this babe. In a while you can sleep, but now you need to give this little one a go."

I open my eyes to see Hilda with her gray hair and watery eyes. She looks old, but her hands are like steel, and she has muscles like a man. I presume that's what it takes to do what she does. I hired her on Aunty Mary's recommendation as Aunty spent most of last year traveling

Europe. Aunty was around to help me birth both my sons, but now I'm wishing she was here for my little girl as well. She was never as demanding as Hilda.

"Come on, Mrs. D," Hilda encourages, her foreign accent grating on me. "Give it the old one-two try, and then I'll let you sleep." Father says she's German. When I first met her, I asked where she was born and she said, "Utah." She claims she doesn't talk funny.

I give in and sit up. She plumps a pillow against my back. "Good girl," she says, her voice jaunty now that I've complied. She puts my daughter into my arms. "Now let's have a good look at her," she says, pulling the blanket open. "See how perfect she is, Mrs. D.? How lucky you are."

Hilda has dressed my daughter in the white shirt that Lucille knitted for George when he was born eight years ago. She's also pinned her into a bulky white cloth diaper.

The first thing I see after her outfit, is her belly with the cord sticking out, tied tight with a white string, and dotted with drops of blood. I remember when George and David were born how it annoyed me each time to have that blob of cord sticking to everything and oozing blood every time their diapers got changed. I hope it falls off as quick as it did with the boys. She has a thick head of black hair. I hope it stays that color. Her eyes are closed and still swollen from the birth. Her little rosebud mouth is the sweetest thing about her. She is such a pretty baby. Nevertheless, if the truth be known, I don't like anything about birthing or tiny babies. There's too much work and messiness required to feed them, and I hate the constant need to change dirty diapers. I know I love my children, but I also love giving them to a nanny until they can walk. That reminds me, I should get in touch with the wet nurse before another day goes by.

Hilda interrupts my thoughts again. "I thought you going into labour early would give us a winzig one, but she's definitely not winzig. She's a real fatty." Sometimes Hilda says the strangest things. I ignore her comments.

"You're beautiful," I tell my daughter. Then, she opens her mouth and wails like a banshee – louder than either of the boys ever howled. I look up at Hilda in dismay. I want her to take the baby and make it stop crying.

Hilda laughs at my distress, "She's already a hungry one. Put her to your breast. Now, don't think you won't have milk to feed her. Mothers make as much milk as baby needs." She rearranges the baby, turning her head so she can latch on. I feel the pull of her sucking and I want to throw up. When I look up at Hilda, she's smiling down at us. "Just sit back and let the baby feed," she coos. She puts a small blanket over us. "In case someone comes in."

I nod my compliance. I don't have the energy to discuss this feeding issue with Hilda. She's a good midwife, but a believer in mothers feeding their children. She would never understand.

Hilda watches over me for a few minutes more and then lets out a long sigh. She tells me she has other mothers to visit, including one who is very close to her date. She assures me that my nanny will be able to help me with anything I need. I voice my thanks for her help. As she leaves, she tells me, "You're welcome, Mrs. D. You're lucky to have such a nice baby. Say thanks to God for such a gift."

Hilda's right. I am lucky. I have a healthy baby girl, two healthy sons, and a beautiful house that I love. I am grateful. Dwight makes enough money that we can hire a nanny to help with the children. I list off the things that make me feel grateful. I hope God is listening.

I'd be more grateful if my husband was home more. In the past two years, ever since the house was finished, Dwight has been gone for such long periods that I sometimes feel like I'm not even married. He comes home so tired that he sleeps for days. Then he sits around, bleary-eyed, facing stacks of papers while he decides where he's going next. He seems to be deep in thought all the time and he's difficult to talk to, forgetful, distant. He's different from when we were first married. I shake my head. What's wrong with me? I need to get these negative thoughts out of head and, as Hilda says, just be grateful.

Dwight is happy about the house being completed and so am I. A major part of it was finished in the first few years of our marriage, and the little extras, like sanding the outside steps and building a box for the fireplace wood, are now finished as well. Dwight was thoughtful and con- siderate in those days. He consulted me about all the major building decisions. He even asked me what color I would like for the outside. The big pillars in front are soft yellow and the roof is black – such a nice contrast. Even the black walnut trees at the side of the house have been saved- just like he promised when we first started this project. He was the one to foresee that they would make a shady area where the children can play in the heat of summer. Those were happy times. We talked all the time about everything. The last time he was home he was so irritable we hardly talked at all.

I watch the baby nurse for a few minutes. She fidgets and then disengages from me and lets out a bellow. I'm uncomfortable with this whole feeding business. It's disgusting. Aunty and Hilda would both be upset with me if I said that out loud, but I can't help how I feel.

I hear a rustle at the door and Jane's round and happy face appears. We are fortunate to have Jane as our nanny. She's the daughter of one of my mother's old friends and was recommended to us when George was born. She is good with the children. She tells me David is sleeping and George is playing. "I heard the baby cry. Do you need anything?"

"I'd like to rest a bit more. Please settle the baby and put her in her crib. Then go downstairs and tell Dotty to come up."

Jane nods and takes the baby from my arms. The baby stops fussing. Why is it that some women don't have to do anything, and they can charm a child? I wish I was like that – at least with my own children. Jane puts the baby in her crib at the other end of my room and turns back. "Oh, Mr. Deschamps has arrived home. He was surprised to hear the child is born. He said to tell you he will be up to see you as soon as he gets the horses settled."

"He's home?" I exclaim. I'm never quite sure when to expect him. He's been going into Mexico more and more often in the past five years looking for prospects for Father.

Jane nods and smiles. She spreads a blanket over the baby and says, "I'll tell Dotty you need her. Shall I send her right away?"

As Jane is leaving, Dwight appears. "Surprise," he says. "On the other hand, it's you that has the surprise." His face is smiling but his eyes are distant. He sits down beside me on the bed. "You've been busy," he says, giving me a quick kiss on my cheek.

"I'm glad you're home. You have your girl." I smile back at him, pushing away the worry that comes from noticing his distance. "I wish I could get up and give you a hug."

He smiles again. "A girl is nice." He reaches over and brushes the hair out of my eyes. He kisses me again, my forehead this time. "You're a beautiful woman you know – beautiful and strong. So where is this girl baby of mine?" The words are the right ones, but I sense that he is working hard to stay focused – even on such an important event as a new baby. With the boys, he was excited. What has happened to that excitement?

"She's over there, in her crib. Have a look at her. She's very pretty."

Dwight goes to the crib and gazes down at the baby who is quiet for the moment. "You're right, she is beautiful. Just like you," he says. He comes back and stands by the bed.

"Don't you want to hold her?" I ask. He couldn't wait to hold the boys. Awkward at first with George, but eager, nonetheless. The smile drifts from Dwight's face and he coughs. "Yeah," he says, his voice raspy. "Maybe later. I'm dirty and tired from my trip. I've been sitting in that damn carriage for the past four days. I'll go wash and change clothes before I touch her."

"Dwight, do you want to tell the boys that they have a baby sister? I told Jane that they were to stay in the nursery until someone comes to get them. They'll be excited to see you, too. They may be disappointed it's not a brother. But they'll get used to the idea."

He nods and kisses me on the forehead again. I can smell the road on him and the sweat of a long ride. He will have much to tell me later about his adventures. That is, if he is so inclined.

He nods and walks out of the room and down the hall – in the direction opposite to the nursery. I thought he would be excited to see his boys – and to tell them about their new little sister. Maybe he's just tired.

Dotty arrives, interrupting my thoughts with her profuse congratulations which I accept with impatience. I tell her it's time to let the wet nurse, Mrs. Anderson, know that the baby is here and that I need her services. I want her to come right away – today if she can, but certainly by tomorrow. I finish my instructions by telling her to get a room ready for Mrs. Anderson now.

A look of disapproval comes over Dotty's face. I know that look. I've seen it before. "Don't look at me like that," I tell her. "You don't understand. I can't feed the baby." We have been through this before, Dotty and I. She has given me all the reasons why I should, and I have few answers as to why I can't. "Dotty, I don't want to talk to you about this another minute." I turn my back on her and pull the quilt up over my head.

I hear Dotty walk to the door. "Whatever you say," she says before the door closes. By the tone of her voice, I can tell she's not happy with me. I don't care. It's not her business.

A few minutes later, I hear a soft knock, and the door opens to admit Father, George, and David. George runs in shouting to me and tries to jump on the bed. He's rambunctious. "George, settle down now, you'll disturb your new little sister," Father admonishes him even as he smiles over George's head at me. He's carrying David who is much too old to be carried.

"Where is she, Mama?" he asks. "What's her name? Why is she a girl?"

"She's a girl because God said so," I laugh at George. He's always full of questions. "Sit still for a moment and wait for your grandfather. I bet he'll let you hold her."

"I'm afraid I stopped to visit the boys first," Father confesses, grinning. "I hope you'll forgive me. I really missed them." He stops then, and adds, "And I missed you too." Then he laughs. He's an excellent grandfather and our boys love him. He knows how to play with them – everything from tag to hide and seek. Father built a horseshoe pit in the back garden for them. They've spent hours tossing the shoes even though they haven't any hope of throwing them the full forty feet. The boys seem to turn Father back into a child when he's with them. I never thought I'd see the day when the proper somber judge would let himself be a child. It's quite wonderful.

"Amelia, congratulations," he tells me, setting David on the floor and giving me an awkward little kiss on my cheek. "Hilda says that I have a beautiful, healthy granddaughter."

"Yes, Father, she's over there in her crib. Have a look for yourself."

"She's perfect," Fathers coos as he bends over the crib and lifts her to his chest. "Ah yes, she's as beautiful as her mother." He sways back and forth, rocking the baby as he walks to the big easy chair to sit down with her. I remember Mother telling me how good he was with babies as well as young children. George and David both lean in to see their new sister and Father lets each of them sit next to him and hold her for a few minutes.

"Does she have a name?" George asks, his little-boy voice ringing across the room.

"What do you think we should call her?" I ask. Dwight and I have talked about names, but I can't get Dwight to commit to any name I suggest. He doesn't seem inclined to offer any suggestions of his own. Another of the things that cause me to worry about him. He was so eager when it came to naming the boys.

George chimes in, "I think she should be Babe."

Father and I laugh. It's typical of George. He's a particularly precocious child. I can tell my father loves that.

Father asks, "So, am I to understand that you and Dwight haven't officially decided on a name yet? I don't think Babe would be suitable as a name to be registered."

When I shrug to indicate that I don't have a name for her, Father's face wrinkles into a quizzical frown. "I thought you had that done a long time ago. I remember how for each of the boys you had names picked long before they were born."

I change the subject. The name thing is making me angry at Dwight. On the first day of our daughter's life, I don't want to be anything but grateful and happy.

Father, as if reading my mind, asks, "How are you, Daughter? You look like you could use a bit more rest. God knows you have every reason to be tired. I swear I don't know how you women do this birthing thing. It scares the daylights out of me."

I laugh at this little intimacy. Father was always proper when I was growing up. But, since I got married, he seems to have changed. He talks to me a lot more than he used to.

"I'm all right. It was an easier birth than either of the boys." I smile at him. "But the boys are quite a handful these days, and I have to hire a wet nurse. I hope she can come by tomorrow." I'm babbling now. "I'll be happy to be able to get out of bed in a few days and get on with my life." I haven't seen Father in such a long time and there's so much to say that the words just tumble out.

Father laughs. "Yes, the boys are always a handful. I can tell they missed me." He grins at them playing with each other. "Oh, I received a wire this morning," he smiles. "More good news. Ada has had her baby. A few days ago. A baby girl - just like you." His face becomes serious as he finishes, "It's too bad she's so far away. They named her Sarah."

We talk a bit about Ada and her increasing family. She has four now. Father pretends to be scandalized by how fast the babies have arrived, but I can tell he's proud of every one of Ada's, just like he is about mine. We avoid talking about Lucille today, as if not mentioning her name will prevent her from being hurt by the news that Ada and I have both given birth again. She has become a little like Aunty, planning social events one after the other, as if that could make up for the childlessness she and Earl have had to accept.

Father cradles the baby close to him and dances around the room singing a funny little song he's made up for her. It's his tradition. For each of his grandchildren, he sings a different song, and that song sticks to them. Both my boys could recite the words of their songs by the time they were four.

In the middle of their little dance, Jane returns and offers to change the baby's diaper and take the boys back to their rooms to get ready for dinner. Father gives up the little bundle and hugs each of the boys before they follow Jane to their room. He stands near my bed, and we talk about his latest trip. He explains that he cut it short so he could get Dwight back home to me. "I was worried about you," he says, smiling. But I can tell there is something else on his mind. I know Father much better these days. I always knew when he was angry. These days I can tell when he's worried as well.

Father hesitates like he does when he wants to move the subject to a serious topic. He sits down on the bed next to me and puts his large hand over my small one. "I've been meaning to talk to you, Amelia, but I didn't want to bother you when you were with child. Are you well enough to have a serious discussion about your husband?" The concern on Father's face deepens. "I need you to tell me how he was the last time he was home. Was there anything out of the ordinary?"

"I'm not sure what to say, Father. Dwight was exhausted. I know that for certain. I just chalked it up to his being busier than usual with work. He's more withdrawn than usual, though." I take a deep breath. "I do notice that he's not sleeping very well. I wake in the middle of the night and he's not there. I sometimes find him reading in the sitting room. When I ask him what's wrong, he just smiles and says, 'Nothing. Go back to bed.'"

Father holds my hand and his fingers wind around mine. He appears deep in thought and is silent for a few seconds. "The truth is, I insisted we come back sooner than planned because I want Dwight to see a doctor. I think something is seriously wrong and we need to get to the bottom of it. I've tried to talk to him about it, but he insists that he's just tired."

"What makes you think he isn't well?" I ask, wondering what he's thinking.

The worry creeps further into Father's face. "He has difficulty remembering things that are important, like his work schedule. He forgets words. He doesn't take care of himself. It's like he has forgotten how to do that. I even had to tell him to take a bath a few nights ago. He fought me on that request. He kept saying he already had a bath. Believe me, he stank. I thought that was strange for a man who is always so fastidious."

"What you say doesn't sound at all like Dwight. Are you sure this isn't just the result of being overtired?"

"I'm hoping that's all it is," Father tells me. "I'll leave it for a few days but keep an eye on him and let me know what you think. By the way, isn't it strange that he hasn't come to sit with you? I find that unacceptable."

"Oh Father, he did come to see me. He said he needed to change clothes and wash up first. I'm sure he'll be along any time now."

Father stands up to take his leave. He smiles down at me and shakes his head. "I hope you're right about his just being tired. Promise me you'll let me know if he's acting strangely."

"I promise." I tell him, but I hope I don't have to.

***

I wake to find Jane hovering over me with the baby in her arms. I can tell it's already morning with the sunlight streaming through the window.

"Are you ready to feed?" she asks as soon as I open my eyes.

"No, I'm not," I reply. "I'm never ready to feed. Is there any word from the wet nurse yet?"

"Not that I know about," Jane answers. "But I think Dotty would be a better one to ask than me. I did remind her to make up the room for Mrs. Anderson in the maid's quarters."

"I want you to sleep in the maid's room. Put the baby's crib in the nursery and let Mrs. Anderson sleep there with both the boys and the baby. She'll be nearer to the baby, and you won't be disturbed by the baby at night."

"Won't the baby disturb the boys?" she asks.

"I doubt it." I tell her, trying not to sound too flippant. "They seem to sleep through anything."

Jane frowns. Maybe she wants to disagree, but I'm not in the mood to listen. The sooner Mrs. Anderson arrives the better. I am finished with having my sleep interrupted. I change the subject.

"Do you know if my husband has gone down for breakfast yet? Would you tell him I want to speak to him?"

"I saw him downstairs about an hour ago. I'll check for you." Jane continues to stand beside the bed holding the baby, who is fussing and whimpering.

"I suppose I have to feed one more time," I relent.

"Yes, ma'am," Jane says. "At least until Mrs. Anderson arrives."

I sigh. I can't help it. It's just annoying. I take the baby and put her to my breast. She is a dear little thing. Today her eyes are open, and they are dark, almost black. I imagine they'll change as she gets a few days older. She latches on as if she hasn't eaten for two days, and the milk comes in right away. In my heart, I was hoping there wouldn't be any milk. Then the question of a wet nurse would be much less complicated. I hope Aunty stays in Europe until this is settled. If she returns, she will try to convince me to nurse for a year.

I wonder what Dwight is doing. I hear him talking to the boys, but he doesn't stay long. Maybe Father is right. Maybe something is wrong with him. I wish he would talk to me more, like he used to.

There's a soft knock on the door and Lucille's smiling face appears. "Lucille, how nice to see you. I thought maybe you'd forgotten you had a sister," I tell her.

Lucille laughs. She comes over and gives me a peck on my cheek. "Forget about you, Amelia," she teases. "I've come to see the baby."

I know she's teasing me, but sometimes when she says things like that I wonder if she might really mean what she says– like she did when we were young. She watches the baby nurse for a few minutes.

"You're lucky," she whispers. "I'd give anything to have a baby."

I smile at her. "Don't worry," I tell her. "I'm sure one day you'll have your own. Sometimes it just takes time."

She looks at me and her eyes fill with tears. "I doubt it, Sister dear. I doubt it."

The baby unlatches, and at a nod from me, Lucille takes her in her arms telling me, "She's big and pretty. Just look at those cheeks and that little rosebud mouth. I could just eat her up." She cradles the baby and then holds her up on her shoulder for a burp. She walks towards the far end of the room and finds the large rocking chair to sit in. I feel sad for her. She would make a good mother.

Dwight sticks his head in the door and, seeing that I am awake, walks in. "How are you today?" he asks. He's cheery this morning and my heart leaps with the thought that a good night's sleep has cured all that was wrong with him yesterday.

"I'm better today," I answer. "How are you? Did you sleep well?"

"I slept a bit," he responds. "Always good to be in my own bed."

The baby makes a noise, and he turns, seeing Lucille. "Oh, I didn't realize you have a visitor. I can come back later."

"Dwight, it's just Lucille. She's not a visitor."

"I know it's Lucille," he snaps.

"Good morning, Lucille," he says. That's not like him to switch his moods so abruptly.

"Good morning, Dwight," Lucille says. "I'll take the baby to visit her brothers," she offers. "I'm not a mind reader, but I can tell you two need to talk."

"Thanks, Lucille," I tell her. "I appreciate that."

"That's okay, Sister. Like I said before, I came to see the baby, not you." She laughs and disappears down the hall.

Dwight sits on the bed, kissing me on the lips. "Ah, alone at last," he says, smiling. The anger is gone as suddenly as it came. He smells of pine soap and he's shaved. My father's words about him not bathing come back to me.

"We are indeed alone," I tell him. "I was missing you and wondering why you didn't want to see us."

"It's not that I don't want to see you, Amelia. It's that I am not feeling well these days and I don't want to bother you with my troubles."

I feel a strange sense of relief on hearing this. "Father told me he's noticed you're not yourself, and I've not seen enough of you to figure out how you are. Please tell me what's been happening."

"I'm not sure I know myself," he answers. "I'm sure it's not serious enough to see a doctor. I just haven't felt well for a while. I don't sleep soundly. And my bones ache." He stops and laughs. "Maybe I'm just becoming an old man."

"Perhaps," I smile, "but you're not that old. I think you should go see Doc. He might be able to help you feel better. You seem to have lost some weight."

He pauses as though he has more to say but shakes his head. "I'm going to play with the boys for a while," he tells me. "I should spend more time with them." He kisses me again and heads for the nursery, turning back only to say, "I'll see Doc if it gets worse. I promise."

A few minutes later I hear the baby cry and Lucille returns with her. "Guess it's feeding time again," she says as she lays the baby across my lap.

"Are you going to feed this one?" she asks. Lucille has always been blunt.

"No," I tell her. "No, I'm not. No matter what you or anybody else says, I'm not going to feed her. I find it repulsive."

Lucille says nothing. She just gives me a strange look. After a few awkward moments of silence, she asks, "Why is the world so unfair?"

"What do you mean by that?" I ask.

"Father told me today that Ada had her baby. Amelia, that makes four babies in seven years for her. And three babies in eight years for you. I haven't had even one baby in that length of time. Where's the fairness in that? I ask God why he is punishing me, but I don't get an answer. It makes no sense. You have three children and I get the feeling you'd prefer to have none." She waves away my feeble attempt to protest. "You don't even want to feed them. What's wrong with the world? Those who want children can't have them and those who don't want them have them."

I'm not sure what to say to my sister. I feel sad for her, but angry at the same time. "Lucille, you're wrong about my not wanting children. I love the boys and of course, I love this little girl. I just don't want to feed her. It makes me feel like some sort of animal or something." It's hard to explain my feelings to Lucille who wants to experience everything I find repulsive about babies. "I'm sorry you don't have children. I don't know why. I know the world seems upside down sometimes. But please don't accuse me of not wanting or loving my children."

Lucille's angry demeanor softens. "Amelia, I'm sorry. I didn't mean to suggest you don't love your children. I just feel left out. What is life without children?"

"Is Earl giving you a bad time about not having children?" I ask.

"No. He says it doesn't matter. But I know he wants a son. He says some women just can't have children. He insists that he will love me, regardless of whether we have children or not." Lucille wipes her eyes and reaches out to hug me. "Why is the world so complicated, Amelia?"

I wish I knew. Lucille and I spend the next hour chatting. I know she would rather play with the boys, but Dwight is in the garden with them kicking a ball, and she doesn't want to interrupt them. Before she leaves, I make her promise to come over often and she says she will.

I make my first trip downstairs for dinner the next day. The cook has made a special meal in my honor: roast venison and wild rice with bits of garlic and ginger. Father comes to join us. The boys are excited to have me back, but I think they are more excited to have dinner with their grandfather. Jane takes the baby to the nursery. Dwight arrives and takes his seat next to me. He seems anxious. We hold hands around the table to give a prayer of gratitude for our food and a healthy new family member. As I clasp Dwight's hand in mine, I feel it tremble. What is that? A new symptom? I glance at him, but his eyes are shut in prayer.

When the prayer is over and Dwight picks up the fork to eat, his hand is still shaking. I turn to my food but as I do, I see Father watching Dwight. I say nothing. But boys being boys, George and David don't let the shaking go unnoticed. In between bites of venison, George asks, "Father, are you cold? Your hands are shivering."

Dwight laughs, embarrassed. "Yes, George," he tells him. "It's cold in this room."

"How come I don't shiver?" David asks.

"Don't know, David. I guess I'm just old." We all laugh and continue eating.

Dwight leaves the table before anyone else. He says he wants to take a nap. As soon as the boys are finished eating, Jane arrives and takes them to their rooms.

"You want me to have a talk with Dwight?" Father asks.

"I think so. He said he would see Doc if things got worse." I shake my head. "To me, this shaking means things are getting worse, but he doesn't seem to connect it with his other symptoms. That worries me. I don't know why he hesitates to see Doc. Doc's like a member of the family."

"I agree. I'll talk with him right now. I hope we can get to the bottom of this soon." He gets up from the table, takes a deep breath and then says, "Wish me luck."

I nod. I feel helpless. Dwight has always been so strong. Now he seems weak. What if something is so wrong that he can't get well? What would I do without him? The questions whirl in my mind. How would I live with three children and no husband? I can't imagine what my life would be like without him.

The strangest thought comes into my mind: Sam. I wonder again what happened to him. Sometimes I'm certain he's dead but at other times I know he's not. I wonder if indeed he's alive, does he ever think of me? If something happens to Dwight, maybe Sam would find me and marry me. I give my head a shake. Will the memory of Sam ever fade and leave me alone? Sometimes I think the craziest things.

Jane summons me to feed the baby again. Where is that wet nurse? It's been three days and she still hasn't appeared. I walk up the stairs to the birthing room. I'll feed her there tonight while Jane puts the boys to bed. I need a change of scene and I need to think. I'll be glad when I can go back to sleeping with Dwight in our bedroom. Though right now, with this strange shivering, it's better if he has his own bed.

I settle into my old familiar rocker to feed, and the baby attaches herself to me. The door opens, and Father appears catching a glimpse of my bare breast.

"Oh, I'm sorry to interrupt," Father stammers as he looks away. I note a touch of pink on his cheeks. "I talked with Dwight, and he has agreed to see Doc. He insists on going by himself. Remind him, will you Amelia? I'm worried that he won't follow through."

I assure Father I will remind Dwight to make an appointment. Father nods and says goodnight. I can hear his footsteps as he makes the trip to see the boys. I imagine him hugging each one and singing their special songs to them. The carriage wheels grate on the cobblestones as he heads home. Every time Father goes away, I miss him. I wonder if he's lonely in his big old house across town. He has Manson with him from the old days but that's all. I wonder if he misses Dotty. She came to live with me when George was born.

When the baby has finished nursing, Jane agrees to take her to the nursery to sleep. Her gurgling baby noises in the night have been bothering me and I need to sleep.

I reach over to turn off the light when I hear Dwight's' voice, "Thought I should say good night," he says. His voice sounds like the old Dwight again. "I'll be happy when my wife can sleep with me again," he says with a smile.

"I'll be happy too, Dwight." I tell him. "Come over here and at least give me a hug."

He hugs me. I feel a slight tremor move through his body. Before he lets go, he whispers, "I promise to see Doc as soon as I can. I know you're worried about me."

CHAPTER 12

My first thought the next morning is about Mrs. Anderson. I hope she arrives today. I hear Jane's footsteps in the hallway. "Good morning, ma'am," she says as she enters my room. "Good to see you awake. Your baby needs to eat." I get out of bed and sit in the rocker to feed. Jane hands her to me and I put her to my breast.

"Jane, where's Mrs. Anderson?" I ask.

Jane frowns and looks at the door. I have the feeling she wants to flee my question. I sense she's not telling me everything.

"Well?" I ask again. "I asked you where the wet nurse is."

"Ma'am," Jane says, her voice tentative, "you should talk to Dotty about Mrs. Anderson. I heard her say that Mrs. Anderson has gone to feed another child."

"What? What are you talking about?" I shout, dislodging the baby's mouth. She begins to wail and then latches on again and starts sucking. "Don't be silly. Why should she go to another child when she agreed to come here?"

Jane doesn't answer my question but tells me, "I'll fetch Dotty for you. I think you should speak to her about this."

Oh Lord. Now what will I do if what Jane says is true? As the minutes pass, my heart starts to race, and my face gets hot. What is keeping that woman? Why does she frustrate me so? The baby lets go of my breast and begins to cough. She burps, bringing up some milk. Even the sour smell of that burp nauseates me. Gagging, I put the baby on my shoulder and pat her on her little back. She lets out a loud wail in my ear, then another cough. She spits up all down the side of my neck and down my back. "Jane, damn it! Where are you?" I yell. The baby startles and starts to wail.

"Jane!" I yell again, louder, to be heard over the now-screaming child.

Footsteps come running up the stairs and Dwight appears. He takes the baby and holds her to his chest, his hands gentle as he rubs her back. "Amelia, what in the world is wrong with you? Why are you shouting and scaring the baby like that?" He's half whispering, but his voice is harsh.

I wipe at the smelly milk on my neck and arms. "She coughed up her milk and covered me with it. It stinks. I need Jane to clean her up. She's a mess."

At my words, Dwight holds the baby away from himself and laughs. "You're right, she is a mess and now so am I. Wow, she has quite the voice. I could hear her wail from clear downstairs. Here, you hold her, and I'll go get something to clean her up."

"Just wait a minute, Dwight," I tell him. "I'm in no mood to clean up after the child. Let's just wait for Jane. She should be back in a minute."

"I'm not waiting for anybody. I'm going for rags," he says, as he passes the baby to me and leaves.

A wave of sadness passes over me. I know Dwight is right. I should at least clean up after the baby. The baby. The baby, I repeat. It's time to stop calling her "the baby." I don't understand why we can't agree on a name for this child. This can't go on. She needs a name.

Dwight returns with a few cloths and with Jane who is carrying a half-filled pail of water."I'll take the baby, Ma'am," she tells me. "You use the water in the pail to clean yourselves up and I'll take the baby to the nursery."

Dwight is already dipping the cloths into the water and wiping the sourness from the front of his shirt. He smiles as he hands me a clean cloth. "Isn't this fun?" he asks, his tone sarcastic. I take the rag he offers.

"I think it makes more sense to just change our clothes." I'm angry. Angry at Dwight for accusing me of upsetting the baby. Angry at Dotty for not getting Mrs. Anderson here. Angry at Mrs. Anderson for not being here.

He looks at me and smiles again. Then he asks, "What's wrong with you, Amelia. You seem very unhappy."

"What's going on?" I repeat. Maybe I should tell him. "Do you want to know?" I ask.

He nods.

"Well, to begin the wet nurse hasn't arrived and Jane just told me she heard from Dotty that the wet nurse isn't ever going to arrive. Then, the baby started choking and that frightened me – and – and," I burst into tears, "We can't keep calling her the baby. Dwight, our baby needs a name. I'm starting to hate everything about this – this whole thing." I choke back my tears.

Dwight frowns. "You know there is an answer to this, Amelia," he says, his voice stern. "Just get another wet nurse. Where's the list Hilda gave you?"

Before I can answer, Dotty knocks on the door and comes in. "Jane says you want to see me?"

I dry my eyes with the handkerchief Dwight hands me, and I try to get myself under control. "Yes, Dotty. I do want to see you. I want to know where Mrs. Anderson is."

"Mrs. Anderson?" Dotty repeats, and then hesitates.

"Dotty, what is wrong with you? I asked you a simple question. Where is Mrs. Anderson?"

"I'm sorry but I didn't ask her to come until yesterday," she tells me, backing away with each word that comes out as if I might hit her. "And now Mrs. Anderson says she has another baby to feed, and she doesn't want to feed two babies."

"What? You told me the day before the baby was born that you would go and tell her we wanted her services. You didn't go? You lied to me? Why on earth would you do something like that?" I ask in disbelief.

She hesitates, then plunges ahead. "I, I guess I just thought it would be best if you fed your own baby."

So that's it. Dotty is just like all the other women in this family. They all think they know what's best for me. "Dotty, I have a mind to send you back to Father's house. I won't ever trust you again. You've been with me my whole life, but I don't want to see you around me. Pack your things."

"Whoa. Wait just a minute," Dwight says, before Dotty can take a step towards the door.

"Dotty, just go back to the kitchen," he tells her. "I'll come and talk to you later." Dotty bows her head and mumbles something to Dwight as she backs out of the room.

Dwight turns towards me. "Why are you so miserable? Dotty is a good worker, and she has the baby's well-being at heart. You would see that if you'd stop being so obstinate about not wanting to feed the child. We'll find another wet nurse – and if we can't find another one, it's not the end of the world. According to Jane, you have enough milk to feed two babies."

"What do you know about it?" I ask, sounding as nasty as I feel. "It's easy for you to judge. You're always working and never here. You have the easy life. I'm always forced to do what everybody thinks is best for me. Why don't I get to decide?" Tears overwhelm me, and I cover my face.

Dwight puts his arm around me to hug me close. I feel his warmth, but I'm so angry I push him away. "No! Can't you understand that I don't want to feed the baby? Why can't you understand anything about me?"

"All right," he tells me after a few minutes of silence. "I will try to find you another wet nurse. You seem to be determined not to feed this baby yourself. No matter what any of us say. However, I am not going to let you send Dotty to your father's house. We need her around here a lot more than he needs her. She is a good woman and she works hard."

"Just get me a wet nurse, Dwight and I'll keep Dotty as long as she keeps what she thinks to herself."

Dwight nods. He looks tired. I wonder if I've given him a task he can't do, given the fact he might be sick. I have no idea if what Father says about him is true or not. At least he's rational today.

"Did you make an appointment with Doc yet?" I ask, determined to change the subject.

"No, not yet," he tells me. "I'm not sure I want to."

"Dwight," I state. "Don't be so ridiculous. We need to get to the bottom of this."

Dwight chuckles. "Look at who is calling me ridiculous. You don't want to feed the baby. I don't want to go to the doctor. If you ask me, I'd say we're both a touch ridiculous, wouldn't you?"

I don't answer.

"I'm going downstairs to tell Dotty she can stay."

I nod. Maybe feeding the baby isn't the worst thing in the world. Maybe I should just do it. It's not forever. I'm tired of fighting everyone and everything.

There is a shuffle at the door and the boys appear. "Time for dinner, Mama," David tells me, rushing through the door and hugging my legs. I ruffle his hair and he turns his face to me for a kiss. He is the sweetest of my two boys, always looking for that extra hug. The anger drains out of me as I look at my sons.

George is the serious one. He's loving in his own way, but more standoffish than David. I can imagine George will be the studious one. He might even follow in his grandfather's footsteps and be a judge. David – well, I don't know, maybe a musician. As if Dwight would ever stand for that. I laugh at the idea. Oh well, I can dream, can't I? It feels like such a long time until they grow up.

I do love them. But I don't think I'm the best mother. Perhaps I'll do better when they are older. I enjoy George's company more now that he is eight than I did when he was younger. He often has very interesting things to say and he's full of questions about the world. I think he considers himself the man of the house when Dwight's away. That's when he hovers over me and is bossier with his brother. It makes me smile when he plays protector. I should be more grateful for what I have.

I follow the boys down the stairs to dinner. The table looks warm and inviting. It's set for more than our little family. As I settle the children in their seats, Dotty enters carrying napkins and buns. She sets them on the table. "I'm sorry I upset you," she says softly when she passes my chair. "I shouldn't have done that."

I nod. I wonder how sincere she is. It feels like Dwight must have coached her to apologize.

Dotty announces that Father, Aunty Mary, and Uncle Quincy will arrive soon to join us.

"Who invited them?" I ask amazed that I wasn't informed ahead of time.

"I think the Judge did," she replies.

"Where is Dwight?" I ask.

"Mr. D went to change his clothes."

Dwight returns in time to hear the arrival of our guests and goes to greet them. Aunty makes her entrance in a fur-trimmed dress with shiny gold shoes and bright red lipstick. Red lipstick and fur must be the latest thing in Europe. Typical Aunty.

"Oh Honey," calls Aunty from across the room. "Oh Honey," she says again, breathless. "I heard you had the baby. I can't believe you didn't wait for me. I hear it's a girl. How exciting." She walks around the table and throws her arms around my neck. "Darling, you do look well."

"Yes, Aunty, I am well. It was an easier birth than usual. I am fine," I tell her.

"Well, thank God. We arrived home just this morning and when your father told me about the baby I had to come and see that you're all right. He was very kind and invited us to dinner."

I shake my head. No one ever has a choice when it comes to Aunty.

"I'm going to run upstairs and see that baby before dinner is served," Aunty says as she dashes towards the stairs. "I'll only be a minute," she calls over her shoulder.

While she's gone, George shuffles himself off the chair and runs up to Uncle Quincy. "You should make your wife be still," he shouts. "She is like a noisy whirly wind."

Everyone bursts into laughter. He's right, and even though we know we shouldn't laugh, no one can stop. When I get control of myself again, I tell him, "George, that's not a very nice thing to say about Aunty. She's happy to see us, and she gets excited."

"Are you talking about me?" asks Aunty from the door. "Your babe is sleeping. She looks peaceful. What a beauty she is. What have you decided to call her?" she asks.

I look at Dwight and he opens his mouth to say something, but then shuts it again. Father cuts in. "They haven't decided yet," he explains.

"What do you mean you haven't named her yet? She's five days old. How long do you think she can go without a name? She does have to be registered, you know," Aunty declares.

Dwight holds up his hand. "Registration can wait until we decide. Amelia wants to name her after one of her dead sisters, Edith May. But I told her we should name our first girl after its mother, Amelia May. We can call her May."

"There are enough Amelias in this family," I tell him, trying to be polite. "I don't want anymore."

"See what I mean?" Dwight says. "She's stubborn as a mule sometimes. So, the baby will remain 'Babe' at least until we can decide otherwise."

I nod and sigh. That will probably be forever.

With everyone seated, and Dotty setting the food on the table, Father stands and announces, "I'm glad we are all gathered here tonight as I do have news to share. News that will affect us all in a very good way. I've put the final touches on a deal to buy a business in downtown Salt Lake. Dwight and I will be partners and Dwight will run it. It's time for Dwight to stay home, and this will provide an excellent income for him while the family grows. He's finished going to Mexico. I am not investing any more money there."

I'm shocked. I hadn't heard about this. Again, everyone works behind my back. I turn to Dwight. "How long have you known about this?"

"Isn't it wonderful?" he asks. "I'm relieved. I can stay home. You'll have me much closer, and I'll be able to see the boys every day." He looks at me as if that explains it all.

"But that's not the point," I insist. "Why didn't you tell me this before now? The planning must have been going on for a long time and you never said a word."

"I know. I wanted it to be a surprise. You were so busy with having the baby. I thought you'd be happy with the news." He and Father look back and forth at each other. Dwight looks confused, like a little boy who has brought his mother a present and she doesn't like it.

I'm dumbfounded. How could these men make a decision like this and not at least ask what I think? "What kind of business?" I ask, still feeling left out.

"We'll be manufacturing steel-framed windows used in industrial buildings," Father tells me. "Not very interesting to a woman, I'm afraid."

"Is that lucrative?" I ask, curious.

"It can be," Father answers, "and it has been. We get the client list from the original owner and we're keeping the accountant that they use. Eugene is his name. He seems to be a smart fellow and I trusted him from the minute I met him. Anyway, like I said, I don't think it's that interesting for you. What's important for you to know is that your husband will be home every night."

Dwight seems to be listening to Father but he offers nothing more to the conversation. I can't tell if he's happy about this proposition or not. Perhaps he's pretending for Father's benefit. Maybe he hasn't had much say in the arrangements.

Aunty says little through this whole conversation. It's odd for Aunty to be so quiet, so I ask her if she's tired.

"No, not particularly," she answers, laughing, "I'm just concerned that you haven't named your daughter. You could always name her after me." This statement causes everyone to burst out laughing. Good old Aunty. Some things never change and maybe that's a good thing.

After dinner, when everyone has gone home, I climb the stairs to my temporary bed in the birthing room. I try to sleep, but my mind keeps going back to the dinner conversation. Why wouldn't Dwight talk to me about this before all these plans were made? Why would Father invest in this if he thinks Dwight is so sick? It makes no sense. I won't sleep tonight without figuring this out. I turn on the light and look around. I'm tired of this room and tired of this lumpy bed. It's time to go back to my own room.

Dwight is sitting up at the desk writing in a notebook. "Hello," I say.

Dwight jumps as if poked with a stick. "Oh, you startled me."

"I'm tired of sleeping in the other room, Dwight, and I need to talk to you. I'm sleeping here tonight."

"I'm not sure that's a good idea," he tells me outright.

I stare at him, not believing what I hear. I thought he would be happy to have me back.

He adds, "What I mean is, I'm not sleeping well these days. I may stay up quite late and bother you. You need your rest."

"Oh, it sounds like you'd rather I sleep in the other room."

He lowers his eyes and then nods. "It's not that I don't want you here; it's just that I don't think you'd be comfortable." He closes the notebook. "You said you wanted to talk to me. What about?"

I'm disappointed and confused. "I want to remind you to make that appointment to see Doc right away. Also, I'm curious about this window business."

"What about this window business?" he asks, ignoring the reminder about the doctor.

"You seem irritated with my question, Dwight. I'm your wife and I just want to know what you think about this business deal my father seems to have made on our behalf. Did you have anything to do with it? Or did Father go ahead on his own as he's often been known to do?"

Dwight is silent for a minute. He looks at me, then gets up and brings me a chair. "Here," he says. "You shouldn't be standing in your condition. If you want to talk about this, you better sit down." He waits until I'm seated and then begins. "Amelia, I don't want to bore you with all this business talk. It's just men's business. I think your father has a good idea and I think it's a sound business decision. Your father is banking on the availability of more steel for this enterprise when the war is over." Dwight pauses, but I don't say anything. Now that he's talking, I don't plan to stop him.

"If we are still at war in a couple of years, then I would say he was crazy, but it appears from the books that this company is doing reasonably well, despite the war. I appreciate that he has chosen to partner with me. He could have picked Earl to help him. I guess he sees Earl as already successful and wealthy enough for two lifetimes. Perhaps he feels sorry for me. I know he hates to see you alone so much." Dwight takes a deep breath. He seems exhausted as if he'd been running a race.

"But is it what you really want to do?" I ask, pleased he has shared this much.

"Does it matter?" Dwight looks hard at me. "I've done a lot of things I haven't particularly wanted to do, Amelia." This is the longest conversation we've had in months but somehow, I feel as though I'm talking with a stranger.

"Do you think I wanted to go wandering around Mexico for a large part of my life? Not really. But it brings in the money we need to live well. So, I did it. You need me around more. Are you having reservations about this? I thought it would make you happy. We'll have more security and I'll be home more."

"No, I don't have reservations, Dwight. I only thought you might have told me before the final deal was made. My life is affected, too, you know."

Dwight laughs out loud. "Oh, Amelia. Why do you always want to be involved in everything? Why can't you be content to be looked after? It seems you don't trust me or your father to make the right decisions for you. You have your children and a beautiful house to look after. These are the things that should occupy your mind – not business and money – those things belong in a man's world. How would you feel if I asked to change our daughter's diaper? Wouldn't you feel strange about that?"

No, I think. If you want to change a diaper, go ahead, but I don't say anything.

Dwight continues. "The only point of concern I have is that we could have trouble with the Mormons. They aren't happy to have a Gentile running a lucrative business in the heart of their territory." He grins. "We may have to convert to get this whole thing off the ground. Your father's connections can only get us so far."

"Are you serious, Dwight?" I ask. Even though I'm concerned by his comment about converting, I'm more pleased to see him grin. I can't remember the last time he seemed happy enough to say anything lighthearted.

"Not really," he answers, laughing. "I think it could be a problem in the future, especially if they push the issue with our clients, most of whom are of that persuasion. Anyway, nothing to worry about, my dear. I'll take care of it if and when it becomes a real problem."

So many things to think about. No wonder Dwight is tired. I decide to end the conversation. Tomorrow is another day. With a good night's sleep, maybe Dwight will be more himself again. "I want to sleep in my own bed tonight. That birthing bed is too lumpy, and I need to rest. If you must work, why don't you use the desk in the parlor downstairs? You can sneak into bed when I'm asleep and I won't even hear you."

"It's all right. I'll just go to bed when you do. I am tired." He runs his fingers through his hair and yawns. "Of course, that doesn't mean I'll sleep," he says.

Just as we get into bed, I hear the baby cry. In a minute, there is a light knock on the door. It's Jane. "Ma'am," she calls through the door, "The babe needs to eat."

I follow her down the hallway to the nursery. I'm tired, but, when Jane places the baby in my arms, I feel a sense of surrender. I'll feed her. It's the way it is. I'll take no pleasure from it, but I'll no longer fight it. Perhaps then everyone will leave me alone.

I need to change my thinking about this. The only benefit I can see in nursing is that it provides a break in the daytime from chasing the boys or giving orders to the cook. At night, it's lonely. I find myself thinking back to how things might have been. Maybe if I had never gone to Stockton, my life would have been different.

In the dark, alone with the baby, my mind wanders to thinking what it would be like to be married to Sam. I dream about him sometimes. He comes floating out of the blackness. Sometimes, he's dressed in Mexican garb, wearing a sombrero, an eye patch and waving a spear. Other times he appears in a black shroud waving a white flag. I don't understand the spear, or the flag. Both seem odd accessories to either outfit. He always reaches for me, and I will myself to go to him, but he fades away before we touch, smiling that wicked smile I remember so well. I often wonder what happened to him and why it irritates Father so much when I ask about him.

"Ma'am," Jane's voice says. "Ma'am. I'll take the child now if you like. She's sleeping."

"Oh, yes. Thank you, Jane. I think I nodded off as well."

As she reaches for the baby she asks, "Shall I help you back to the birthing room?"

"No, I'm going to go back to my own room tonight. I'm tired of that lumpy bed." She came to get me in my own room; I don't know why she asked such a question. Jane frowns but says nothing. She knows it's not her business.

Dwight seems to be sleeping when I slip beneath the covers. But when I settle in beside him, his hand creeps over and he begins to rub my back. "You're a good mother, Amelia. Just remember that," he whispers, his voice croaky with sleep. His hand slips down to my hip but stops there. His breath is uneven and raspy.

I lie in the stillness for a few minutes, listening to him breathe. Something doesn't sound right. I turn over to face Dwight, touching his face and then his shoulder. His flesh is hot. The sheets are damp with sweat. "Dwight! You're as hot as an oven. What's wrong?" I ask, sitting up.

A moment passes before he mumbles, "What? Are you talking to me?"

"Yes, I'm talking to you. What's wrong? You're feverish."

"Oh," he answers, groggy, "It happens."

"You mean this has happened before?" I ask, astonished.

"I told you not to sleep with me. Didn't I?" he snaps.

I don't know what to say. "You need to see Doc," I tell him.

There is dead silence from his side of the bed.

I leave him and find a bed in one of the guest rooms near the nursery. I'm sure Jane will wonder what is going on in the morning, but it doesn't matter. I'll check on him later in the night.

By the time I awaken, however, it's morning. I sneak into the room to see if Dwight is awake. I find him shivering under the quilt, his forehead still hot. "You're sick, Dwight. I'm going to call Doc – and Father."

Dwight doesn't answer. He looks at me glassy-eyed and then shuts his eyes.

I decide to find Dotty and get her to call Doc but when I enter the kitchen, Manson is there having his breakfast with Dotty. "Manson, what are you doing here? I ask. He's supposed to be living at Fathers house these days, but this is the second time I've found him having his breakfast in my kitchen. Manson jumps up from the table, looking embarrassed but I don't have time for him to answer my question. "Manson, as long as you are here, I need you to fetch Doc for me. Mr. Deschamps is ill. Once you know Doc is on his way please stop and tell Father. I need him here."

Manson drops his napkin in his plate of half-eaten food. "Yes Ma'am," he mutters and heads for the door.

I take Dwight a cool cloth for his head. His eyes are closed as if he's sleeping, but he's mumbling. Then, he moves, stretching his legs across the bed and raising his arms to the ceiling, shouting, as if he's trying to get someone's attention.

"Dwight," I whisper. "Dwight, wake up. What is it?" I shake him, trying to get him to open his eyes and calm down.

He kicks back the covers and tries to get out of bed. His night clothes are soaked with sweat. He looks around like a trapped animal. "No!" he yells. "No, you can't leave him! He'll die!" he shouts, his voice raspy like his breathing had been the night before.

Jane and Dotty both appear in the doorway. "What's happening?" Jane calls out. "We heard a commotion. Is everything all right?"

"Dwight is having a difficult time, a nightmare I think." I tell them, being as calm as I can.

"Manson has gone for the doctor," Dotty tells Jane over Dwight's shouting.

Dwight goes quiet. He stares at us and then lays back in the bed. He pulls the quilt up around his face and starts to weep with muffled sobs. We stand transfixed, afraid to do or say anything. Where is the doctor? Dwight turns to face me, but his eyes stare straight ahead, uncomprehending. He doesn't recognize me. It's like he isn't there, like something has control of him.

He gets out of bed and stands up. He starts spinning around in small circles, around and around. We watch, helpless. At one point, Dwight shouts, "He's returned. Thanks to God, he's returned." Then he stops spinning. His head must be full of ghosts.

It seems like forever before we hear the carriage arrive. Doc comes up the stairs as fast as his old legs will carry him. "What is going on?" he asks. I explain as quickly as I can what has happened.

"Get out of the way you bastards," Dwight shouts louder than before.

Doc nods and tells Dotty and me to go to the nursery. "You better stay in there with the children," he tells me. "I'll come and get you when things are under control."

Dotty and I join Jane and the children. The children know something is wrong and begin to fuss and ask questions. The three of us pretend that all is well and tell them that we are just playing a game. George, too smart for his own good, looks at us with indignation. "I don't think this is a fun game, Mama. I want it to stop."

"I do too," I tell him. "I do too."

The noise from Dwight's room stops. Jane engages the boys in a clapping game. "Pease Porridge Hot, Pease Porridge Cold, Pease Porridge in the pot nine days old." The rhythm of the clapping and fun of reciting the rhyme distracts them and helps to relax me. I join in. Thank heavens for Jane.

Moments pass, and I hear a sound from outside. Another carriage is arriving. It must be Father.

"You can come out now," Doc's voice comes from the hallway. "I've given him an injection and I think he'll sleep for a while."

I hear Father's footsteps on the stairs as I open the door. He and Doc talk together in low voices. Part of me feels as though I should be demanding they tell me what's going on, but another part doesn't want to know. I stay in the nursery with the boys. A few minutes later, Father appears at the nursery door.

"Amelia," he says, "we need to talk to you. Let's go downstairs to the sitting room. It's more private there."

I look at him, wary. "What's wrong with Dwight?" I ask, close to tears. "How can he be fine one minute and not the next?"

"Get dressed and come downstairs. It's time you had some answers." He asks Dotty to sit with Dwight while we talk. She nods and heads for the bedroom.

Once I've dressed, I find the two men in the sitting room. They look worried, and they both rise when I enter. Father closes the door and tells me to sit.

"What's happening?" I ask again. "I don't understand any of this behavior."

"Doc has something to tell you and it might be difficult to hear." Father says, as he sits down again.

"Amelia, somewhere, Dwight has picked up an insidious disease that's just now showing itself. It's a very unusual kind of malady." Doc pauses, glances at Father, and then goes on. "It can be carried inside a person's body for many years without any symptoms whatever. Then over time, it begins to make itself known in small ways. Fatigue. Sweats. Shivering. Trembling. It shows up in many ways. At times, it can be contagious, and at other times, it hides and isn't transmitted to others."

"How do you know this is what Dwight has?" I ask, confused by all of this. "Dwight hasn't been sick for very long. Has he?"

Doc and Father exchange glances. "We've known for a few months." Father says.

"What? You've known Dwight has a serious condition for several months and no one told me?" I ask. I can't be too surprised that they've kept me in the dark. Again. "Does Dwight know?"

"Yes," Doc answers. "He came to me before his last trip. Given his symptoms I concluded that this insidious disease is the proper diagnosis. But due to the seriousness of such a disease I asked him to take a blood test called the

Wassermann test to confirm my suspicions. Unfortunately, that test was positive."

"Why didn't you tell me before now?" I ask, dumb-founded. "Why didn't Dwight tell me? I kept telling him to go to the doctor and he said he would. Why wouldn't he tell me he already knew and so did the doctor?"

"He asked that I not tell you until you had the baby." Doc says. "I agreed to wait – but I said I would tell you if he got worse. This episode he had today is a definite sign he is getting worse. Dwight told your father a month ago because I felt someone should know to keep track of his behavior."

I don't know what to say. Doc has always been honest with me. I have always trusted him. But I still don't understand why he wouldn't have told me first.

"Dwight will need supervision. He may awaken tomorrow without any symptoms and be symptom-free for quite a while. I am hoping for that. At some point in the future, he will need full-time care, but that could be years from now." Doc hesitates and then adds, "On the other hand, it could be a matter of weeks or even days before he is no longer himself." I shudder when I think of how Dwight was last night.

Father breaks in, "People tend to be afraid and anxious about this diagnosis. We must never tell anyone about this, Amelia. People will think we are all contagious, especially you. Doc and I have made plans."

"I still don't understand. What disease is so terrible? You tell me these things, but you haven't told me what the disease is. Is it consumption?" I pray it's not that.

Both men stare at me. It's hard to read their faces. They look sorrowful – maybe even frightened. What disease is so terrible that they aren't to name it? "Is it consumption?" I ask again feeling my heart begin to race in fear that it might be. No disease that I know of is worse than consumption.

"What? Just say it, for Heaven's sake." I demand. "Say that he has consumption and I will live with it. For God's sake, say something!" I shout at them.

"Dwight has syphilis," Doc says.

My mind races. Syphilis. It makes no sense. I frown at the word. Syphilis. "Isn't that the war disease?" I ask, trying to remember what I know about it. "Isn't that the disease that men get when they go away to war?"

Doc sighs and stands. "Yes, Amelia, it is known as 'the war disease.'" He walks up and down, his hands behind his back. "But," he continues, "men who never go to war can contract it as well. Sometimes it even affects women. I have a book that explains it in more detail. When I have a moment, I'll bring the book for you to read. You can find out what it is, and what the future may bring."

We are interrupted by knocking. It's Jane. "It's the babe, Ma'am," she says. "I've been trying to soothe her, but it's you she needs."

I get up and follow Jane up the stairs. For once, going to feed my baby is a relief.

CHAPTER 13

It takes a week before Doc brings me the book. I'm playing in the garden with the children when he walks up and hands me a green cloth bag tied with hemp twine. I stow it in my closet for later as I'm afraid of what I'll find in it. If Doc is afraid to tell me about the disease that has infected my husband, it must be truly terrible. Worse, Father and Doc seem terrified to call this disease by its name. How could just the name of a disease upset these grown men? Maybe I'm imagining their fear and reluctance. But I don't think so.

I can't go back to sleeping with Dwight - not since his episode. He hasn't encouraged me to return to our bed either. He appears to be back to normal in some ways since that outburst but I'm afraid the delirium might recur. He has barely talked to me since that day and I haven't bothered to approach him. He goes to work and checks in with the children for short periods of time but mostly he keeps to himself when he's home. It's like living with a stranger. I need to figure out how to talk to Dwight about this, but I don't know how.

It's evening when I cut the string on the green bag and pull out the book. It's old, with a stained, brown leather cover and a thick binding. The pages are edged in shiny gold making it look like some official guide to something. The title is etched in the leather in beautiful script: *Venereal Diseases and Their Causes; A Medical Text.*

Doc has left a note in the inside cover of this tome. It reads, "Start at page 135 and read about syphilis."

The vocabulary of the book is complicated. It's meant for doctors. But, after I've read for a half hour, I get the picture. I put the book down. The illustrations show the private places on a man's and on a woman's body. The disease is shown in such detail that I can almost see the pus running out of the sores. There's no reason to read further.

I bury my head in my pillow and cry. How can I make sense of this? The book says the disease comes from being intimate with an infected person. It says if a person becomes infected with syphilis, the disease can hide inside that person for many years.

I've never seen any sores on Dwight's body. Is that what happened to Dwight? Did he love somebody else before me? He never told me. How could he do this? How can it be that I am well? Could I also be infected with this – this horrible disease? It says right in the book that a man can infect his wife, or a wife can infect her husband – or a child can be born with syphilis. No wonder Doc and Father don't want anyone to know.

Dwight's voice pierces my pain. "What's wrong?" he asks. "I heard you crying. Is there something I can do?"

At the sound of his voice, I am blinded by rage. Anger crashes out of me like some horrifying monster. I throw the book at him. "Yes!" I scream. "There's something you can do. You can tell me how this happened!" Dwight catches the book and looks at the cover. The concern on his face turns to shock as he reads the title. He bows his head, "Doc told you."

"Yes, but not all of it. Not the awful parts. Those he made me read about in that book," I rail.

Dwight walks towards the door, placing the book on my dresser. "When you're more rational, we'll talk." He closes the door behind him.

More rational? How in God's name can anyone be rational about this?

I toss and turn in the night and dream strange dreams: I'm walking in a park and it's night. I come to a gate with a sign that reads, "Syphilis Only." I try to open the gate but when I tug on it, the lock remains firm. There's a desperation in my tugging. The harder I try to open it, the more desperate I become. Finally, I try to kick my way in. I hear a noise behind me, and a dark spirit descends. "You cannot enter. This is holy ground," it says and when I look over my shoulder at it, it has Sam's eyes.

I wake with a jolt. I lie in my bed wondering why does Sam haunt me? Why do I dream of Sam at a time like this?

The door rattles and Jane appears, tiptoeing in with the baby. "Ma'am, are you awake? Are you able to feed the baby?"

I roll over and sit up. "Yes, Jane, I'll feed her."

"I heard you call out," she says, her voice gentle in the darkness. "Are you alright?"

"I must have been dreaming," I tell her. "I didn't realize I called out."

She puts the baby in my arms. I wait a few minutes before I let her feed. I need to relax. I need to be a better mother. I need to talk to Dwight. I need, I need, I need. I need to stop the needing. I take a deep breath and begin to feed the baby. A calm comes over me as I examine her sweet little hands and fingers. It's funny how what used to be such a terrible ritual has turned into something peaceful. I feel some of the worry drain out of me. What I really need is to find out from Dwight how he got so sick. I'll focus on that one need.

Father has never said a bad word about Dwight – even with this disease. He would have spoken up if he thought Dwight was immoral. I hold onto that thought for reassurance.

I finish feeding the baby and Jane takes her back to the nursery. I change out of my night clothes and go looking for Dwight. He's not in his bed. I find him in the library reading and drinking brandy. He looks dishevelled. He's startled when he looks up from his papers and sees me standing in the doorway.

"Amelia," he says and then pauses. "You look calm. Should I be watching for a weapon?" he asks. A small smile crosses his face.

"Perhaps," I answer, not in a mood for teasing. "I might need some kind of weapon, if only to use it to pry some answers out of you."

He's silent. Finally, when I think he isn't going to respond, he tells me, "Amelia, ask me anything you like, and I will answer you truthfully."

The anger starts to build up again. "I don't know if that's possible," I spew, "since we've been living a lie throughout our whole marriage." I pause and take a deep breath. "I don't understand why you didn't tell me about – this terrible disease long ago. I'm angry that you kept this horrible secret from me, as much as I'm angry about the disease itself. You knew about this even before we were married."

Dwight moves to comfort me, but I step back. "Dwight. I want to know how you got this – this – and when. It matters to our lives and the lives of our children."

"You're right, Amelia, I owe you some answers as difficult as they may be for you to hear." He moves to sit down, and I do the same. "Honestly," he says, "I don't know when I got this disease. In my twenties I traveled to Mexico often with friends and with your father, to explore the country and the investment possibilities. Doc says I should have had a sore on my body – or some other symptoms – but I don't remember ever seeing anything like that. Whenever my friends and I went to Mexico, we visited taverns in small towns, and sometimes – when we were," he pauses, grimacing, "lonely, we found girls to spend the night with. The girls were poor. We paid them for their services. We were young back then. We never considered what we did could be dangerous or wrong. It was what we did on our travels."

He takes me by the shoulders and looks into my eyes. "I didn't know. Honestly, If I had known, I never would have married you. It's only been in the last few years that I have started to have strange symptoms. Doc just attributed my lack of energy to long hours at work and gave me a tonic. It's just lately that he realized there was something else. He really had no reason to suspect syphilis until I started to have a problem with these episodes of delirium. I had them a couple of times on the road with your father. Doc recommended that I take the Wassermann test to get a final diagnosis. That's when I knew."

I see the pain in his eyes.

"I think God has protected us, "he adds. "He hasn't let you or the children become infected. I think that was God's will."

How can God be involved in something like this? It's unbelievable to me, but I don't say that. I ask instead, "How do you know that I'm not infected? How do you know that the children aren't either? I read in that book that all of us could be carrying this around and never know until years from now."

Dwight looks at me for a moment and then blurts, "No, you are clear. I know that for a fact."

"Dwight, how can you be so sure?" I ask, curious as to why he is so confident.

"I'm not supposed to tell you, but Doc had you all tested. I know you are probably mad about that, that we didn't tell you, but I needed to know. A month or so ago when the children had that cold and Doc came to the house, he did it then. You he tested weeks ago. You thought you were getting a test for something else."

"You had us tested without our knowing. How is that even possible that you could be so secretive? How can I ever trust you about anything ever again?" I can't even yell at him I'm so angry. It never ends. Everybody is always doing what they think is in my best interest. This just must end.

Sadness comes into Dwight's eyes. "I knew you would be mad, but we needed to know and I'm sorry for that. I know how you feel about going behind your back. The truth is, Amelia, you won't have to trust me for long. According to Doc I probably will be dead before too long anyway."

The reality hits me. "It doesn't make for a very nice future. Does it?" I say, more to myself then to Dwight.

"The other thing Doc told me, Amelia, is that we shouldn't sleep together – anymore. The disease can become contagious again at any time. Doc said I should be the one to tell you." Dwight runs his fingers through his hair. "Doc was very firm about that." He looks at me and says, "I'm not sure we can live with this, but we must try, for all our sakes."

I'm unable to speak. How do I talk about this? It's like he's dead already.

"Your father says we must continue to live together – as if nothing has happened – as if nothing is wrong. It's important to your family, to my work and to your father's work, that no one ever knows about this. Doc hasn't written anything down. We sit, looking at each other for what seems like a lifetime.

I break the silence by asking, "What will happen to me and the children if – when – you go away?"

"Oh, Amelia, don't worry about that. Your father will look after you. You'll have this house and the business is doing well. I'm sure you could find someone to run it for you. Your father has many business contacts. He could find someone who would be happy to buy the business at a good price."

He pauses, and nods, "As for you and the children, I'm sure you could go live with one of your sisters if you get too lonely. They both have big houses. I'm certain Lucille would love to have the children around her."

Dwight's words crash in on me. How can he think that I would want my father to take care of me? How can he think that I would be happy to live with my sisters? Anger boils up again. He really doesn't know me at all. He probably never did. I know I'm being unfair, but I can't help it. I need to get out of here.

"I can't talk any more tonight. I have a lot to think about," I tell him, keeping my voice even. "I'm going to bed in the guest room. We can talk more tomorrow."

When I wake the next day, Dotty tells me that Dwight has already gone to work. I don't know whether to be relieved he's gone or angry that he didn't wait to talk with me. Once I finish nursing the baby, I fill my morning with a shopping trip with Lucille. She talks at length about her latest house project. She has talked Earl into expanding the sitting room and adding some bedrooms. Earl never seems to deny her anything. Maybe he feels sorry they don't have any children.

Chapter 14

1918

Father and I have kept the secret of Dwight's illness for more than three years. Since March of this year the newspapers have been printing nothing but news about the influenza epidemic. The government has told everybody to wear masks made of gauze. They are so ugly, like putting a rag over your mouth, but we do it. We've also been warned to stay inside and not go out unless it's necessary. I'm not sure what necessary means, but I do know that Dwight and Father both continue to go to work; at least Dwight goes when he feels well enough. They wear their masks and shrug off the danger of the disease as if it's nothing to be worried about. Father says he's too old to get it and Dwight doesn't seem to care if he gets it.

I can't help but wonder what is happening to the world these days. Our soldiers fight a terrible war and then in victory come home to contaminate us all with either this terrible sickness or some other. Syphilis crosses my mind.

Father did make one major change since the epidemic started. He sent Manson to work at my house and he hired himself a new man for his horses. I think he's worried I might have an emergency and not be able to go anywhere. It does make me feel safer and I think Manson likes being around Dotty and Jane rather than just being with Father.

The schools are closed for the year which is unfortunate but probably for the best. I worry about the children. More children seem to die than old people which is, I suppose, where Father gets his nonchalant attitude. The children are full of questions about the quarantine signs on the doors of houses where people are sick. I just tell them those people are sick and we must stay away from them. I don't see much difference between the sick and the well as we are all ordered to stay in our houses these days. I imagine if Dwight were to get sicker at least we could tell everybody he has influenza, and they'd believe us.

One good thing about this epidemic is that Aunty Mary can't throw her elaborate Christmas party this year. I'm sure she would be asking too many questions if she could see how thin Dwight is.

It's also been easy to keep Dwight's secret from Ada. She lives in Sacramento, and we communicate by letter. But every time I'm alone with Lucille, I wonder how she would react if she knew the truth about Dwight's condition. I do wonder why she hasn't asked any questions about his obviously deteriorating condition but I'm happy she hasn't.

Dwight promised to let the children celebrate the New Year by setting off firecrackers. He and the boys are already outside, and Babe is anxious to join them. I watch from the window as Dwight helps George light them, one after another. As I do many times, I find myself wondering how many more years they will have together – we will have together.

In the past few months there have been times when Dwight hasn't been able to get out of bed to go to work. I can tell it bothers him when he can't meet his business obligations. Last month, in the middle of the night, he got up, dressed, and went to Doc's clinic to sleep. He didn't tell me why, but I think he was afraid of his own actions. Sometimes he has trouble walking, and sometimes he isn't quite right in his head. That frightens me the most.

Just before Christmas, Doc came to the house. He was checking up on how I was doing. I told him I am afraid for us all. He said he had a new drug for Dwight to try and he wanted me to monitor how it was working. He said it might give us some extra time. Dwight seems a bit better since he started this new injection. I can only watch and hope for the best.

Babe pulls on my arm. "Want to see crackers." I laugh at the funny sweet way she talks. I can't believe she is already three. I keep telling Dwight we must come to some agreement on a name for the child, but he keeps insisting on Amelia and I keep insisting I don't want the child named after me. So, we keep calling our beautiful curly-headed daughter Babe. I know it sounds like the name of a horse, but Dwight won't give in, and neither will I, so Babe it is, until next year, when we will be required by law to register her birth at the courthouse.

Babe insists she wants to get herself into her winter garb until I explain that Papa and the boys might finish with the firecrackers if we take too long. She flutters her long black lashes at me and puts her hand on her hip as she tells me, "Okay, Mama, you do. But hurry."

I button her coat, put on her hat, and help her step into her heavy wool leggings and boots before she dashes out the door. I fasten my own coat and hurry along behind her, hoping that Dwight sees she's there before he lobs the next firecracker into the air. She runs straight to Dwight. He shouts something at her, his voice harsh and rough. Before I can intervene, he shoves her to the ground. George and David rush to help their sister, scrambling to get her out of the way as Dwight turns his anger on them, shouting a long line of disgraceful profanities.

Babe runs to me sobbing. "Papa says mean words," she wails. "Papa's mean to me," she says, stamping her little foot and grabbing me tighter. "He push me," she sobs louder.

"Dwight!" I shout. "These are your children. Stop yourself. They don't need to hear this."

My shouting catches his attention. He stops shouting but I can see his eyes are vacant. The next instant they are filled with fear. "Enemy soldiers. Find some cover," he yells and breaks into a run for the house.

In a minute, he's inside, frantic to lock the door. With Babe clinging to my leg, I walk towards the boys whose eyes are following their father into the house.

"What's wrong with Papa?" David asks.

"Papa's having one of his spells." I keep my voice as calm as I can. "We're going to the carriage house. I want you to walk as fast as you can. We're going to go see Grampa."

David frowns at me. "What about Papa?" he asks.

"Someone will look after him," I tell him as I hurry them along.

Manson is busy grooming the horses when we arrive. "Manson, please prepare the carriage. I want you to take us to Father's. Then get Doc Parker and bring him here. My husband needs his help."

Manson looks at me and nods. Thank heavens for his steady help at times like these. The children are quiet. It's as if they know the situation is serious. Dwight's behavior has been up and down, but he has never pushed or touched any of us before. He could have really hurt Babe.

The carriage is soon ready, and Manson lifts the children into their seats. They've seen Dwight's strange behavior before, but the violence of this tirade has upset them. All three sit still in the carriage, close together. They don't argue with each other like they usually do. George is more protective of his brother and sister than I've seen him in a long time. I don't have any way to comfort them and although it's not a long journey, a matter of ten minutes or so, it feels like it's taking forever.

Father heard us approach because, by the time we stop, he is at the carriage door. I can tell by the expression on his face that he understands something is wrong. He takes Babe from my lap and helps me step down. The boys jump down by themselves. We shepherd them into the house and Father sends them off to the kitchen to see if the cook has any sweets.

"Is it Dwight?" Father asks as they disappear, some of their exuberance coming back as they each try to be the first one there.

"Yes. He's seeing things again. Manson is on his way to get Doc." I hesitate. I know that every word I say will bring us closer to the time when Dwight will have to leave, but I tell Father every detail of what happened. "Now I'm afraid for the children." I meet Father's eyes, which hold the same concern as mine. "Maybe, I shouldn't have let the boys play in the yard with him – but I thought he was okay." I shake my head. "Jane is away, and I didn't have a chance to get Dotty away from the house before I left."

As he reaches for his coat, Father says, "I'll go see what I can do. Someone should be with Dwight especially if he's alone with Dotty." He takes my hands in his. "Have faith Amelia. We'll do something about this situation soon. I'll be back as soon as I can."

I have nothing to say. He is right. We need to do something to help Dwight and soon.

When Father hasn't returned by dinnertime, the cook offers to make us supper. As the hours pass, I put the boys to bed in one of Father's guest rooms, and across the hall I curl up with Babe in the old oak bed that I slept in when I was a child. It feels like the haven it's always been for me. The darkness closes around me, and I feel Babe relax. The sound of her regular soft breathing tells me she's asleep. I move her farther across the bed and tuck her under the quilt that Mother made for me when I was little. How different things would be if Mother were still alive. Babe looks like her. Maybe that's what makes me feel that Mother is close to us right now.

I hear the carriage arrive near midnight and I decide it doesn't matter that it's late. I need to talk to Father. I find him in the kitchen. The cook has left him a plate of food warming in the oven. As he starts to eat, I ask, "How is Dwight?"

"It's not good," he tells me. "Come sit while I eat." I pull up a chair on the opposite side of the table. Father offers me a cup of tea and pours it for me.

"Now, about Dwight," he begins. "Dwight was argumentative and unmanageable. It took the three of us to subdue him enough to give him an injection. And it took twice as much of the drug as it should have to calm him down."

A sense of foreboding settles over me.

"We need to send Dwight to a place where he will be looked after," Father says, watching me. "If we don't do it soon, somebody is going to get hurt. And if he continues to be so ... erratic – if he gets violent – then, people will ask questions. I don't want to have to answer them. Next time...." His thoughts trail off into a moment of silence.

"Doc says we should send him to Stockton." The words fall into the quiet room as if they have actual physical weight. "I'm sorry," he says.

"Stockton?" I ask.

"There's a hospital in Stockton that has agreed to take him. Ada and Clarence are in Sacramento. That's twenty miles away. They can be sure he's well looked after." He pats my hand. "And because it's so far away from Salt Lake, no one will know he's ...." Father waves his fork in the air. He still can't bear to name the disease. "No one will know he's sick."

"You've found a hospital that will take him? What does that mean?" I guess I shouldn't be shocked. Again, Father has it all planned out. He's found a place for Dwight. He's been planning to send him away and he hasn't mentioned any of this to me before. "It's hopeless, isn't it?" I ask, not really wanting an answer. I stand up, wanting to run away from it all.

Father stands, too. He puts his arms around me, and I hug him close. He's as heartbroken as I am. He feels warm against me, and I can hear his heartbeat.

Father lets me go and points to my chair. "Amelia," he says, as I sit down again, "it's not easy to find a place that will take – these kinds of patients." He stumbles over the words, and I try not to think that he's talking about my husband. "If they're unreasonable, erratic, violent, not every hospital is equipped to handle that." He sits down. "For the safety of the children, I'm afraid we have no other choice."

He's right. I'll try to think of it as just another decision that must be made. I can't think of it as sending my husband away – maybe for good. "You say that Ada and Clarence have agreed to make sure he's taken care of. That means you told them about Dwight."

He pauses. "Just Clarence knows the whole truth," he says. "There's no need to burden your sister with the details. We just told her Dwight is very ill. Doc Parker and I have been looking for places that might take him in and look after him for some time now."

He pauses. "We didn't want you to have to worry about it when the time came. Stockton has an institution that specializes in this kind of disease. I've talked with several lawyers who have placed people there. They say it's reputable. Clarence took time to visit the place and was impressed with the reception he got. He says he hasn't heard anything bad about it."

"I hate this," I interject. "It just seems unfair."

Father reaches over and takes my hand. "I know this is difficult, but I don't know any other way."

I know Father is right. There is no other way unless God intervenes, but I don't have much hope of that happening.

"When are you going to take him?" I ask, my heart pounding as I give in to what must come.

"I'll send Clarence a wire in the morning. That way he'll know we'll be arriving in the next few days. I'll ask him to alert the hospital to expect us." With this epidemic going on we will have to get special documents to travel. Doc says he'll fill them out for us stating we are influenza-free."

Thank heavens for Doc. He always comes through in times like these.

Father takes a deep breath. "I saw this coming a number of days ago, so I made some arrangements ahead of time. I know you hate it when I do that without your input, but I felt it necessary, and I didn't want to upset you before we had to implement the plan. I hope you can understand that."

Father looks at me. I suppose he's looking for some sort of affirmation, but I just nod for him to continue.

"I've decided that Earl and I will travel with Dwight to Sacramento by train. Clarence will meet us with a carriage for the final twenty miles to the hospital. I've already reserved a secured compartment with an upper berth for Dwight. Doc suggests we keep him asleep for most of the trip. He will give him some medicine to sedate him. I hope he'll sleep the whole way. If not, Doc is giving me another syringe that I can use if I need to. I've been assured that my signature will suffice for the admission papers. Doc is sending his medical records along with a letter explaining the situation. I think we have everything we need."

"Yes, it appears you have everything in order and yes, I hate it when you don't consult me but at this point, I am rather glad you did what you did to get Dwight to the hospital. It's all so awful, isn't it?

Father pats my hand again and nods as he rises from his chair.

"I do have one question. If Earl is going with you, that means you also told him. This is supposed to be a secret."

Father sits down again. "Yes, I told Earl. Lucille, like Ada, only knows Dwight is sick, not what's wrong with him." He looks at me. "It's not something that women need to know about."

I flinch. Why not? There it is again. I'm a woman and I am forced to know about these things because they're happening to me. What do they think will happen if my sisters know these secrets? It would be nice to talk to my own sisters about this, but I guess I'm as afraid to tell them as the men are. What if they couldn't stand the shame and they turned their backs on me?

"What do I tell the children?" I ask, afraid of the answer.

"Tell them the same thing we told your sisters. Tell them their father is sick and he's going to the hospital. That's enough." Father's answers clump my grown sisters in with my children. I understand not telling the children when they're this young, but my sisters are a different story.

I stare straight ahead. I think Father is wrong on this. I will let it ride for now but once Dwight is in the hospital I intend to go to my sisters for support. If they disappoint me, then so be it.

"You should take the children to stay with Lucille for a while," Father continues. "In case there's more trouble. We may not be able to leave for a day or two."

"While we're gone, if you need money, go see Eugene. He does the books at the office. He'll see to it you have all the provisions you need. But, if you stay with Lucille, you shouldn't require anything."

I should feel grateful for everything Father is doing – but I don't feel grateful. I feel insignificant, like a child. I'm being sent to stay with my sister, just like my children are. We're all being gotten out of the way so the men can handle the problem. Dwight's my husband. Shouldn't I have some say in what happens to him?

I stand up and stare at him. "Father, in case you haven't noticed, I am no longer a child. There are some decisions I should be making about this and my life. You act as though I am incapable of doing anything for myself."

"Look, Amelia, I'm just trying to make your life easier right now. You've been through a lot of difficult things. I would think you would be a mite grateful for what we are all doing for you. I know you are troubled about all of this, and I just don't want you to worry about anything. I'm just trying to look out for you. Anyway, I must get going now. When I return from Stockton, we will have a family meeting. We'll figure out how you are going to be taken care of in the future."

He has just decided the rest of my life for me – without even giving me a chance to say anything about it.

"You should go back to bed, Amelia," Father says. He kisses me on the forehead and I turn away. I want to tell him what I really think but he keeps talking.

"Tomorrow will be a different day. I'm going back to your house to be certain that Dwight is looked after before his journey tomorrow or whenever we can make it happen. I'm sure Doc has taken care of him, but I don't want to leave the help with the responsibility of subduing him again should he wake up. I'll sleep there and tomorrow we'll prepare for the journey."

He continues talking as if I'm no longer there. "I also need to go to the courthouse to check on things there. I've been so busy with Dwight that I'm afraid I have neglected my duties. Good thing I have some clout with my colleagues, or they would find some way to fire me." He chuckles to himself.

"What have you told them about Dwight?" I ask.

"I told them my son-in-law is terribly ill and that you need me to help you find the proper medical help for him. They are very sympathetic. My court clerk even told me he knows it's serious or I wouldn't be missing work. I guess a perfect work ethic gives me some credibility in this situation."

He hugs me. I feel resentful and guilty at the same time. I hear a voice that keeps telling me I need to be more grateful.

Father continues, "We'll get through this, my dear. Somehow, we will get through this." He reaches for his coat and then says, "Remember, we've been through worse." Before I can say anything more, he's gone. I want to believe him.

I check on the boys. They sleep like little angels. How sad that they will grow up without a father. How did the world get to be such a heartless place? I whisper, "I love you" and I promise them they will never be without their mother. I go back to my old room and snuggle in with Babe. It's close to three o'clock. and I try to lie still so I don't wake her. It's not a night to sleep.

By the time Babe wakes up, the boys have already gone looking for breakfast. Babe insists on going to join them and I watch her make her way down the steep stairs. Just as she reaches the bottom of the stairs, Lucille appears, dressed in a bright yellow sweater and wool skirt. She smiles at Babe.

"What are you doing here?" I ask. I'm not dressed yet, and my sister is here, in bright yellow and all smiles. I don't think I can face the day if it starts like this.

Lucille runs up the stairs and grabs me in a tight hug. "Oh, God," she moans. "Father told me about Dwight. I'm shocked, and sorry, Amelia. What a terrible thing to deal with. I'm here to take you to my house. Father said it would be best for everyone. What a terrible thing to happen to anybody, let alone my poor sister."

She moves in to give me another hug, but I step back. "Look, Lucille," I tell her, "If you really want to help me, then stop moaning. Stop telling me how terrible it all is. Do you think I don't know that? I have known about this for the past three years, so it isn't anything I didn't know was going to happen. Just don't make it worse than it is with all your *oh gods*, and *oh mys*. If you want to be helpful, play with the boys or help me pack. Do something useful."

Lucille looks blank. "I'm sorry," she says. "I'm just sad for you. I can't help it. I don't mean to make it worse."

"I know you don't, but it does," I tell her.

"Father told me Dwight's sick, and he might not get better. What's wrong with him anyway?"

What do I say to her? Damn Father's ideas. "Father doesn't want you to know."

"Oh," she pauses. "What? Why?"

I look at her. It feels like the words are stuck in my mouth.

"Is it that bad?" she asks.

"Lucille, Father said I shouldn't tell you or anyone for that matter, but I can't keep it inside any longer. It's a horrible thing Dwight has. It's more than horrible."

Lucille comes close to me and puts her arm around my shoulder. "Oh Amelia," she says, "you always were the queen of drama. It can't be that bad."

"It's that bad. Not only is it bad, it's shameful. Do you know what syphilis is?" I finally ask.

Lucille looks at me and cocks her head to the side as if she can't understand what I've said. "Isn't that some sort of war disease? I heard the soldiers bring it back from the war or used to."

I nod. "That's what I always thought but it's not just from the war. Doc gave me a book to read about it. I don't want to explain it to you, but I'll let you read it when I can go home again."

"That's a bit odd, don't you think?" she says. It's hard to tell what Lucille is thinking.

When I say nothing more, she changes the subject. "Come and join us for breakfast when you're ready. The boys are quite hungry this morning and we should go rescue Cook." Lucille heads towards the kitchen.

I head for my old room to get dressed. I must find a way to get through all this. Maybe after Lucille reads the book, she won't be so cheerful. Maybe she'll abandon me forever. I hope I'm wrong. I would be sad to lose her too.

I used to think that God would protect me from all this, but now I wonder if there is a God. Mother would be angry if she heard me say that, but I can't help it.

CHAPTER 15

I'm searching for someone. I walk through burned-out buildings, plowing through the belongings of unknown people, until I reach an old house that stands unscathed in the destruction around me. I make my way towards the door, but before I can open it, a mist appears and through the mist, a man materializes. It's a familiar face. It's Sam. I call out. He turns, but as he does, his face contorts like a strange puzzle until it settles into being Dwight's face. I shout again, but the image is gone.

I am awakened by my own cries. It felt real. I sit up. Sam is gone and now Dwight is gone – even in my dreams they are gone. I lie back down and pull the covers over my head. I feel an unbearable weariness. Can one feel weary from a dream? I want to go home. It's only been one day and one night. I never sleep well at Lucille's.

I should get up and see what the children are doing. The light under the door tells me it must be morning. If Dotty were here, she'd be knocking on my door and lifting the curtains. She annoys me when she does that. Funny, I'd welcome her intrusion today. Anything that feels like normal would be a relief.

As soon as I open my door, I hear the children's voices coming from the kitchen. The sound of them laughing and talking makes me happy. If I keep that sound in my head, it will help me heal. I'm sure of that.

"Hello, Mama," David shouts as I enter the kitchen. "Come sit with us and watch. Aunty Lucille is teaching us to cook porridge."

Babe is standing on a chair with a spoon in her hand attempting, with Lucille's help, to stir a large pot of porridge on the stove. George is standing by watching and David is running his small wagon around the kitchen making sounds like a horse. Duncan, Lucille's cook is sitting at the table leafing through a newspaper. He keeps looking up, frowning at the goings-on. I think he's not happy we have invaded his territory.

"Do you want some of this slop?" Lucille asks, smiling.

"Slop?" I ask.

"Oh, yes," she answers. "George and I have decided it looks more like pig food than people food." She laughs as she says this, and George is delighted.

"Aunty Lucille, you are so funny," he tells her. Turning to me, he says, "It's good slop, Mama. We made it people food because we put raisins in it and David put in lots of sugar."

"I think we should stop stirring for now, children, and get to eating or we will be here all day," Lucille instructs. George holds Babe's hands while she jumps off the chair.

The slop porridge is quite good. There is little conversation until we finish our food. "So, what would you like to do today? Any ideas?" asks Lucille.

George announces, "I want to go to Liberty Park. They have a new elephant there and I didn't see it yet."

"Oh my!" Lucille exclaims. "A real elephant? I haven't heard about that. Have you, Amelia?"

"No. Who told you that, George?"

"Papa did. He said he would take me there sometime." George puts his hand over his mouth the minute the words pop out. He bows his head and lowers his voice, "Sorry, Mother, I guess Papa can't do that, can he? I hope I didn't make you sad."

"It's okay, George. You can talk about your Papa anytime you want. If visiting the elephant today is what you want to do then that sounds like a good adventure. Run off now and get ready," I say.

Lucille protests as soon as they leave the kitchen. "You're not going to take them to Liberty Park, are you? There's no elephant and you know it. Dwight must have been delusional when he told them that. I for one don't want to make a trip to the park for nothing."

"Lucille, don't you know that with children, there is never a nothing trip? They always find something interesting and even if it turns out there's no elephant, does it matter? Don't be such a spoil sport. The children enjoy the park. It's a nice day and we can find a place to eat, and they can play. Can you ask Duncan to prepare a nice picnic lunch for us?"

Lucille frowns. "Why can't the children play outside here? We have chickens and horses and acres of land to run around on. This is a farm, you know."

"But you don't have an elephant. I think the children would like to see such a creature. In fact, I would like to see such a creature myself. It's not every day they can see an elephant."

It's lunchtime before we reach the park. Lucille's driver drops us off at the picnic area and agrees to return to pick us up in a few hours. The day is hot, and the picnic basket is heavy. Lucille and I carry it between us. Even though it's only a five-minute walk to the wooden picnic tables, it's a relief when we can finally put the heavy basket down and sit on the bench. The children are so excited to look for the elephant that I'm convinced they won't be interested in food. However, Lucille insists they should eat before we set out in search of the beast.

The food basket contains scones with marmalade, cheese, cucumbers, pickles, apples, and lemonade, and some small pink cakes in the shape of hearts. These little pink delights catch the children's attention, and they reach out to grab them.

"Whoa," frets Lucille. "What little piggies we have today." She pushes cheese, some cucumber, and a scone towards each child. "You have to eat your proper food first before cakes."

I eat in silence. It's better than admonishing my sister. I agree with her about eating the proper food first, but the tone of her voice and her overbearing ways trouble me. I don't want a fight. I'm here to have fun with my children.

The boys finish what's in front of them and Lucille gives each a little pink cake. Babe has half her scone left on the plate and refuses to eat any more.

"That's enough for her," I tell Lucille. "She's only four."

"Well, if that's enough for her, then she doesn't need a cake."

Ignoring Lucille, I take a cake from the container and give it to Babe.

Babe smiles, a wide smile, and chews with her mouth open and full of pink frosting. Before she swallows, she says, "It's good cake Aunty. I like it."

"You give in far too easily," Lucille tells me, reaching across the table to wipe Babe's mouth. Babe turns away and shakes her head.

Aggravated, Lucille snaps, "You must like behaving like a dirty little pig."

Babe stares at Lucille with eyes wide open and blows the food remaining in her mouth down the front of Lucille's blouse.

Lucille's eyes widen in horror. "Oh, look at me," she bellows. "You've ruined my blouse, you wretched little thing! If you were my child, I'd spank your bottom! How could you?"

Lucille turns to me. "You should teach your children better manners and more respect!"

"I'm sorry, Lucille, but she's just a child." I am shocked by Babe's behavior, but more upset by Lucille's anger. "Spitting food is not proper behavior, but you calling her a dirty little pig isn't proper either," I add.

If looks could kill, Lucille would have had me dead at this exact moment. "You have no idea how to raise children," she snaps. "Your cavalier ways will not do them any good later in life."

I stare at her and she turns away, using a napkin to rub at the spots on her blouse.

George interjects, "Can we go find the elephant now?" he asks.

"Yes, George, I think it's time." I turn my back on Lucille and get up from the table. "I'll pack up the rest of the food and we'll be off."

"Never mind," Lucille announces, "I have no desire to go wandering around the park with this mess down the front of me. You go on with the children and I'll stay here."

I frown at Lucille. If that's how she wants it, then so be it. I leave with the children.

George falls in step with me and Babe and asks in his most serious voice, "Why is Aunty so grouchy? I know Babe shouldn't spit on people, but she wasn't happy that Aunty called her a pig."

"I think Aunty isn't used to having children around. She gets impatient. We will have to try hard to be quiet and on our best behavior when we are in her house, so we don't annoy her so much."

"When can we go to our house?" George asks.

"I'm not sure. I was thinking we would stay with Aunty Lucille until Grampa gets back."

"Why?" George whines. George never whines.

"What's wrong, George?" I ask. "Are you unhappy?"

"I don't want to live with Aunty Lucille," he blurts.

"Well, don't worry, dear. We're just staying with her for a short time. It's temporary. Just until Grampa comes back."

"That's not what Aunty said."

"What do you mean? What did Aunty say?"

"She told me last night that we're going to live at her house from now on."

"She told you that?"

"Yes, she told me and David last night when she came to say goodnight. She said we have to stay here because our Daddy is sick." George flings himself against me and spreads his arms around my waist in a sudden and desperate hug. "Please don't make me stay, Mama. I don't like Aunty Lucille's house.

David turns and watches George's dramatic performance. Then he runs to hug me as well. "Me too," he says, tears filing his eyes.

Babe isn't interested in all the theatrics. "Elepant," she says, pointing straight ahead. "I see an elepant."

She's right. In front of us is a gate with a sign that shows a picture of a large elephant. "Elepant," she says again. How does she know what an elephant looks like?

I turn back to the boys. "Don't worry about living at Aunty's. We'll go back home soon. Don't you worry. Right now, let's go see the elepant."

The children's unhappiness dissolves into laughter at my use of Babe's word. They run ahead to the elephant enclosure. They squeal with delight when they see the strange creature. This elephant is indeed real. I'm glad I didn't let my sister's negativity talk me out of coming here. It's the biggest animal I've ever seen, and I'm as intrigued with it as they are. As we stand gazing at it a man appears inside the enclosure. He walks around the elephant and approaches the outer gate. He releases the gate latch, letting himself out, and stops in front of George.

"Well, little fellow," he says, "I have the feeling that you like my elephant. Bet you have some questions you'd like to ask."

"Yes, sir," George answers. "Is he yours, Sir?"

"Sure is. But you know what, lad?"

"What?"

"He's not a he. This here elephant is a she and she's soon going to be a mother. How do you like them apples?" he says, a wide grin covering most of his round face.

Looking around, George says, "I didn't see any apples." His gaze goes back to the elephant. "How come her nose is so long?"

"That's her trunk," the man answers.

George continues to ask questions and a crowd starts to form around us. The boys keep asking questions and the man keeps answering them. After a few more minutes of talk, the man says he must go, and the crowd moves aside for him.

We return to the table where Lucille is sitting reading a newspaper. She doesn't react to us until George calls her by name. "Oh, she exclaims frowning. "You're back. You certainly took your time."

George immediately starts to tell her how we did find the elephant and how interesting it was and just as David is about to cut in, Lucille turns to me and says, "Is he making this up? You know I hate that sort of game."

"Oh Lucille, what's wrong with you anyway? Why do you have to be negative about everything? Yes, we found an elephant. We also found a man that told us all about it. You missed something special. The elephant was real."

Lucille says nothing more. She stands up, picks up the basket and begins to walk towards the carriage stand. We follow her like a brood of baby ducks in a line behind their mother. I'm not sure how much longer I can take this.

Later that evening, after the children are in bed, I knock on Lucille's bedroom door. "Can we talk, Lucille?" I ask when she opens it.

"About what?" she asks as she steps aside for me to enter. She sighs heavily and I sense she is still in a pout about this afternoon.

"Well, I'm anxious to go home. My children are asking for their own toys. I think they're lonesome for their own things around them. I do appreciate –"

Lucille cuts me off. "Father said you must stay here. There isn't any food at your house. For your own good, you need to stay with me."

I stare at her. "Is there something I don't know?" I ask her.

"What do you mean by that?" she asks. I feel her anger.

"I mean, you sound angry about me wanting to take my children home, back to the house they know. Is there a reason why I shouldn't do that?"

"Father told me that you must stay here until he comes home," she answers. "He feels you need me to look after you. After all, you've had a difficult time these past days. He doesn't want me to leave you alone."

"I'm not alone, Lucille," I tell her, disturbed by her statement. "I have my children, which means I will never be alone."

"Yes, Sister, but that's not like having someone older looking out for you."

"And just why should I need someone older to look after me? I'm thirty-two. I'm not an infant."

Lucille looks down at her feet and then up at me but says nothing.

"Well?" I snap.

"I know you're not an infant but, I can't imagine how crazy I'd be if Earl were to get sick and leave me."

"Do you think that now that Dwight is gone away, I'll go crazy or something? That's the stupidest thing I've ever heard, Lucille. Why don't you just come out and say that Dwight is as good as dead. You don't understand that my husband has been dead to me for the past three years. I have come to terms with being alone. I assure you I am not going to go crazy now."

"Well," she hesitates, before spitting out what she wants to say. "You need to consider your children."

"What about my children? Are you afraid I might neglect them because Dwight is dying?"

"Sometimes widows do things they don't mean to do." Lucille's voice is calm, as if she has all the answers. "Earl and I are happy to take you in."

"Take us in?" I rage. "You know what, Lucille? I don't think you are happy to take us in. I think you're doing it because Father told you to, and I'm not staying here another day."

Lucille looks at me. She starts to speak and then stops. We stare at each other. I calm myself down and say, "Look, Lucille. I'm sorry about this, but frankly, if we're talking about what's best for the children, I don't think you even like children. You like travel, and reading, and politics and all those kinds of things that don't include children. When my children raise their voices in play, you shush them. You shout at them when they run up and down the stairs. You even criticize the way they eat. Those actions don't endear you to them. They think you're grumpy all the time. Why would you want to have us stay here?"

Lucille's eyes fill with tears, so I stop.

"Why don't you have better control over your children?" she babbles, as if I hadn't spoken. "You're not raising them the way we were raised. You let them do anything, and I find that unacceptable."

"And, Sister dear, just what do you know about raising children?" I counter. "It's not like you have a lot of experience."

The blood drains from Lucille's face. "You are mean. I take you in and you mock me. How dare you say that to me? I'm trying to be helpful."

Lucille storms out of the room and heads down the stairs. I follow her, but I get only to the hallway. The children are poking their heads out of their bedroom. They must have heard our whole conversation.

"Aunty Lucille acts mad. Is she?" David asks in a whisper.

George doesn't wait for me to answer, "Of course, she is. She's loony like Papa. Right Mama?"

"Of course, she's not loony. Neither is Papa. Where did you get that idea?"

George looks at me wide-eyed with wisdom and self-confidence. "Grampa said so. I heard him tell Doc that Papa is crazy as a loony bird."

My heart skips a beat. I'm aghast. I can't help it. "I'm sure Grampa was just joking, George. It's not very nice to call someone crazy or a loony bird for that matter. Promise me you won't repeat that to anyone." I take a breath.

George looks at me, his eyes sad. "I'm sorry Mama," he says. "It's what I heard Grampa say. I couldn't help it. They were talking outside my door. I was trying to sleep."

Poor George. He's growing up fast. And overhearing grownup talk makes it even faster. Maybe I owe him the truth about how things are. He knows anyway.

I send David and Babe back to bed, telling David he can show her the new book Grampa gave them. Babe is happy to go with her brother. She likes books.

"Let's go find some comfy chairs in the sitting room," I tell George. I need time to figure out what I'm going to say.

He sits straight up in a leather wingback chair, his feet a few inches above the floor and I sit opposite him. He looks almost grown up.

"Do you think Papa is gone forever?" George asks, his voice soft and sad.

I smile at him. What can I tell an eight-year-old that won't make him afraid?

George fidgets as he waits for me to speak. Expressions of curiosity and sadness take turns on his face. "Mother, do you think Papa will come back to us?" he asks again.

"I'm sorry George, but I don't know," I tell him. "Papa is very sick. Grampa and Doc are very worried about him."

George cocks his head. "Aren't you worried about him?"

I take a deep breath. "Of course, I'm worried," I say. "Why would you think otherwise?"

"You don't seem worried. You seem mad – not loony, but angry. Are you angry?"

I bow my head. I don't want him to see me cry. I don't want him to be afraid like I am. "Maybe I'm mad – angry – a little," I tell him. "Angry that I can't help Papa get better. Angry that he's far away and we can't see him." I take another deep breath. "Part of me is relieved he's in a special place that can take care of him. At the same time, I'm sad that it has to be like this." I put my hands out to George. "Do you understand, George? It'll be hard for all of us and we'll miss him. But, we have each other and that will get us through, no matter how difficult the times get. We just have to remember to love each other."

George slides out of his chair and comes over to me. I scooch over and make room for him. He climbs up beside me, takes my arm and puts it around his shoulder. Then he looks up and smiles.

"Don't be sad, Mama," he tells me. "Grampa told me before he left that I should be the man in the house now."

"Grampa said what?"

"He told me to be your man in the house." George repeats.

Then it hits me. "Oh, you mean, man of the house," I tell him.

"That's right," he responds, eyes bright with pride. "Man of the house. I will be your man of the house."

His words melt my heart. It is just like serious George to be in cahoots with Father to watch out for me. Maybe they are right. Maybe I do need a man of the house, especially one as dear to me as George.

"Do you think Papa will die?" George asks.

"I think it's possible," I tell him.

"Do you think we should pray?" he asks.

"If you think it will help, George, we can pray."

I get down on my knees. George follows what I do, and we hold hands for a moment of silent prayer for his Papa. George tells me, "I prayed that God will make Papa always be in a good mood and make him not sick anymore."

"That's a very good prayer, Son," I tell him. "A very good prayer indeed."

The next morning, Jane appears at my door with David and Babe in tow. I'm surprised to see her as she asked for time away to visit her sick mother. She hasn't been gone more than a week.

"When did you get back? It's good to see you! How did you know where to find us?" I ask, excited and relieved to see her. I put out my arms to hug her. This isn't like me at all, I think even as I do it.

Jane returns my hug, but I sense a reluctance as she pulls back, telling me, "I'm happy to be back. I missed you all. Dotty said you were all here, so I thought I'd come by so you know I've returned."

"What about your mother? Is she better?"

"My mother passed on," she says, her eyes filling with tears.

"I'm so sorry, Jane. It's difficult to lose anyone, especially a mother."

"Dotty told me that you have had your own heartbreak," she replies. "I'm sorry to hear your dear husband is also sick. I hope he gets better soon. I heard they took him to a hospital in California."

"Yes, I'm afraid so. We pray for a recovery but I'm afraid there isn't much hope."

"The world is in a terrible state, isn't it?" Jane blurts out. "The war is over, but all those poor men dead and gone. For what? Nothing. Now this Spanish flu is killing people. I don't know what God is thinking. People must be full of sin for God to punish us so harshly."

Jane's sudden religious rant startles me. I've never seen this side of her before. I shouldn't be surprised, though. Most people think like she does. "I don't think God had anything to do with it, Jane." That kind of thinking has never made sense to me. "It's just the way the world is. Besides, I want a loving God in my life, not one full of spite for his own creation." It annoys me when people believe that God punishes people.

Jane looks at me. I sense she would like to argue but after a moment of silence, she says nothing.

"I'm happy to have you back, Jane," I tell her, glad to change the subject. "It's time for me and the children to go home."

"I can help with that," Jane offers. "The boys can gather up their things themselves, and Babe can help us all." She sighs and takes the children to start packing.

I watch her shepherd the children into their room, telling them they are going home. I'm surprised by the sense of relief Jane's words bring. I will manage. It is indeed time to get on with my life.

It's good to be home again. It doesn't take long for Jane, Dotty, Manson, and I to have the house in good order and centered on the children's schedule. Being at Lucille's felt like an eternity but being home makes it all right again. I play games with the children and plan meals with Dotty. Dotty has taken over the cooking duties along with my help and she does the cleaning and the laundry with Jane's help.

Dwight always told me to let the help shop for me, but now I'm beginning to enjoy getting out. I'm grateful he set up a household bank account when we first married. He was always generous and seemed to understand our needs. Of course, he was the one who put the money in the bank in the first place and paid all the bills. Now I need to change those arrangements.

My first visit is to the bank. I explain that Mr. Deschamps is very ill and has been taken away to a hospital for treatment. The manager is sympathetic and agrees that I should draw from the account to pay for what the children and I need. I don't correct their assumption that these arrangements are temporary – until Mr. Deschamps is well again, the manager explains to the teller. The teller informs me that there's enough in the account to keep things running for a few months if I'm frugal.

I think of Dwight, and I feel the tears. They sneak up on me these days. I brush them away before the teller can see.

CHAPTER 16

Father and Earl are gone for fourteen days. Dotty knocks on my bedroom door, awakening me late in the evening, to inform me that Father has returned. I throw on my dressing gown and run down the stairs into his arms.

"It's good to be back," he tells me in the middle of our hug. "I just got off the train. I went to Lucille's, but she said you were here. This whole trip has taken much longer than I anticipated. Good to see you." He hugs me tighter. Then he holds me away from him, his eyes studying mine. "You look good to me. How are you doing? Why are you here and not at Lucille's?"

I ignore the question about Lucille's and tell him I'm managing well. "Tell me about Dwight, tell me what happened. Tell me everything." I sound pathetic, like I'm begging him. But I have spent every day wondering what was happening with Dwight.

Father looks thinner and there's a weariness about him that is troubling. "I don't think you want to hear everything, Amelia. It was a difficult trip. Knowing I might never see Dwight again made it worse. It was a difficult job to get him into the hospital. They required a lot of paperwork and a lot of money. It was exhausting to say the least." He shrugs off his gloomy tone and the look of weariness goes with it. "You'll be glad to know that Clarence and Earl were both most helpful. They both validated my belief that this is the best thing for all concerned. That, however, didn't make it any easier."

"Tell me everything anyway, Father. No matter how difficult. I need to know. He's still my husband and I want to know it all."

Father puts his arm around me and squeezes me close to him but says nothing. He was always close to Dwight, even before we were married. This whole situation pains him more than he lets on. I feel his age and his sorrow.

"Father, you look like you could use something to eat. Let's go see what we can find in the kitchen. Perhaps Dotty can fix you something before you go home."

"Good idea," he says, a small weak smile on his lips. "I think I could use a bit of something."

As we enter the kitchen, we find Dotty sitting on a stool glancing through the newspaper. She smiles and Father smiles back at her.

"I'd like eggs, cheese and some toasted bread, if you can manage it at this hour." Father laughs and Dotty nods her compliance. "Oh, and some jam would be nice if you have it.

While Dotty prepares the food, Father and I chat for a few moments about weather and other insignificant things. Without thinking, I complain about the amount of work there is to do around the house.

"I was afraid of that," Father answers. "That's why I told you to stay with Lucille. Earl and I planned that you would all stay there until we returned."

I don't respond. I think it's better to let him eat first before we have an argument. I drink tea and we spend the next few minutes in silence while he finishes eating.

"Let's go to the sitting room," he suggests when he finishes his meal. "It's more comfortable and we can talk in private. I don't want the help to overhear our conversation."

I settle into a big chair in front of the fireplace and Father pours himself a small glass of brandy. Dwight always kept a bottle of it on the mantle. I'm surprised. I seldom see my father drink anything stronger than tea. He stands looking at the glass for a few seconds and then settles onto the chesterfield. He sighs.

"Father, it's late," I tell him. "I know I'm impatient, but I need to know about Dwight, and I want you to get home so you can rest. So, tell me about Dwight. How is he?"

"Sorry, Daughter. I know you're anxious to know. In all honesty, the trip went better than I had anticipated." He pauses to take another sip of his brandy. "Between Earl and me we were able to keep Dwight quiet and content on the train. One of us was always awake and with him just to be sure he didn't cause a ruckus. He was quite placid, and we didn't have to use as much sedative as we had anticipated. Dwight even talked about going to a safe place. He seemed to understand what the trip was about. I think he was just as afraid he might hurt someone as we were."

"That's good to hear," I interject when Father pauses for another sip of brandy. "I'm glad he didn't make it difficult for you."

"Once we got to Sacramento, we transferred him from the train to Clarence's carriage and took him straight to the hospital in Stockton. The hospital was expecting us, thanks to Clarence's efforts ahead of time." Father sips his brandy, his eyes troubled again. He glances at me.

"We were met by Dr. B. J. Smythe-James. He's a leading expert in this disease. I felt he knows what he's doing. I had the opportunity to have a long talk with him. I gave him all the details on Dwight's behavior over the past few months. He assured me that we were right in bringing him to the hospital. I think Dwight will be well taken care of."

"I hate that you had to leave him alone there. I wish he were closer, so we could visit."

"Even if we were closer," Father states, "we couldn't visit. The doctor told me that it's better for these patients to have no visitors. It just upsets them."

"That's terrible!" I exclaim. "I thought at least Clarence could visit him from time to time. Then we would at least know he is getting the best possible care."

Father shakes his head. "Clarence will get reports about his condition, and he's promised to forward those to us by letter. I'm sorry this is so difficult for you."

"I'm sorry too, Father. I just wish there was more we could do."

"Yes, well," Father says, shaking off the sadness I hear in his voice. "Not much else we can do except pay the bill – and it could be a large one. The care he's receiving doesn't come cheap." He drains his brandy. "I know that Dwight talked to you about your financial situation before he was too sick." He takes a deep breath. "But I wonder if he gave you any idea of your present financial circumstances."

I stare at Father. He's switched to his "judge" voice.

"I've been to the bank," I tell him. "I told the manager Dwight has taken ill and is away for treatment." Father looks startled. "I have enough funds in my account to last a few months depending on how much the house will cost to run. Can you tell me what the business is making and what it is worth?"

Father goes silent for a few moments. "Let's discuss this in a few days. I have some options for you – but" he says as he gets up, "I think I should give your situation some more thought. Right now, I'm tired and I need to go home. Don't worry. We'll find a way to look after you – no matter what happens." He picks up his hat and gloves. "We'll get you some answers soon." We hear the carriage, and he hugs me before he goes out. "It'll turn out just fine. I know it will."

I nod and wave goodbye. I'm a fool for not asking Dwight more questions about our finances before – before all this. At least I have the house: With that, I can stand on my own.

***

A couple of mornings later, I awake to all three children jumping into bed with me. I'm not sure where Jane is. They each hug me and want a cuddle. We snuggle under the covers. There's something satisfying about having my little ones around me like this. I'm glad they want to be with me. I like hearing them giggle when I tickle them. Life's going to be different without Dwight, but at least I have our children. "Don't worry," I coo to them. "I'll look after you."

"Will you do what's appropriate?" George says. He's been listening more closely than I thought.

I laugh. "That's a big word, George. Where did you hear that word?"

"Jane told it to me," he answers. "When I was little, I asked to sleep with her, but she told me it wasn't appropriate. She said I can only sleep with you, or my brother or Papa. She said appropriate means doing what's the right thing to do. Jane always uses big words. She says she gets them from reading books. She says I should learn one new word every day so I can get smart like her. Jane is really, really smart. I bet she could be a banker or somebody famous, she's that smart."

"I think you're right George. Jane is a very smart lady. You must like her very much."

"Yes, Mama, I do," he says. "She's nice to us."

A sense of loss comes over me. This woman has found her way into my children's hearts. They love her. That must be a good thing. I should be grateful for Jane. If my children love her, the least I can do is appreciate her for helping me. Why does that make me feel so inadequate?

The children go off to find Jane and I get myself dressed for the day. I want Father to return so we can have our talk about what to do next. I will need money to run the house.

Later in the morning, when I enter the kitchen to talk about what to have for dinner, I find Dotty and Manson. Manson, for some reason, spends a lot more time than is necessary in my kitchen visiting with either Jane or Dotty. Sometimes I wonder if Father has put him up to spying on us, or perhaps he and Dotty...

They look up from their conversation, surprised, I suppose to find me there. Manson greets me, explaining that he has just returned from Father's with provisions. I peer into the baskets and see root vegetables, bread, cheese, eggs, smoked pork, and all sorts of other items wrapped in brown butcher paper. "There's enough for at least a week," I say.

Dotty smiles at me when I finish picking through the baskets. "Your father's coming for dinner tonight," she says.

"Did he send word to me about that?" I wonder out loud.

Dotty is embarrassed by my question. "Why yes, ma'am," she answers. "He sent word through me."

Why am I hearing about my social events from the help? I'm starting to feel out of place in my own kitchen. Manson and Dotty share a camaraderie. I am the outsider. I shake my head to get rid of that idea. It's my house and it's my kitchen.

I spend a portion of the late afternoon in the yard with Jane and the children. Jane throws the ball to the boys, while I sit on a bench watching Babe play with her dolls on a thick wool blanket on the ground. Jane thinks the ground is too damp, but it doesn't seem like that to me. Babe likes the outdoors. I can't see her being forced to play inside when it's a nice enough day for the boys to be outside.

We are hustling the children back into the house when Father's carriage pulls up. The children run to him. He bends down and picks them up one by one except for George, who's too big to be swung around. George gets a quick hug and then Father turns back to the carriage which is still open. Aunty Mary steps out followed closely by Uncle Quincy. They have been in Europe for so long this year that I had almost forgotten they existed. Why has Father invited them to dinner – at my home?

Aunty is dressed in a fur coat, a fur hat, and even fur boots. She looks like a giant rodent. I hope she thinks my smiling face means I am happy to see her. I'm glad she can't read my mind. She hugs me in a prolonged clasp, and I almost choke on the smell of her perfume. Lavender. Now I remember why that smell always irritates me. Uncle Quincy gives me his usual quick hug and hurries towards the house.

"Oh, my poor dear Amelia. Your father has been filling me in on your situation. How terrible for you and your babies," she wails. "I can't believe this could be happening to you. But don't worry, dear. We're your family. We'll help you."

I smile at her. To say anything would be a mistake. I let her go through her litany of poor girl and poor babies. Maybe then she'll let it rest. I hate it when people tell me how terrible it is. Do they think I don't already know how terrible it is?

As we head back to the house, another carriage makes its way down our lane. Lucille waves at us through the carriage window. I wave back. I haven't talked to her since I left her house. I wonder why she has chosen to visit on this particular evening.

Father interrupts my thoughts, "Ah good," he says. "Our little gathering is now complete. I asked Lucille and Earl to come for dinner," he says to me. "I hope you don't mind."

"I wish you would ask me," I tell him, "Before inviting guests to my home."

"Oh Amelia, for heaven's sakes! She's your sister," Father says, sighing. "I would think you'd be delighted to see her. You two aren't fighting again, I hope."

"I find her difficult these days. She's been telling me how to raise the children."

"Maybe you should learn to ignore her when she does that. It's not worth a fight and I'm sure she means well," Father says in a voice less stern than I would have expected.

At dinner, Aunty is her usual impossible self. She talks a mile a minute, but I don't interrupt as I ordinarily might. I have no heart for a confrontation right now. Besides, I need to talk to Father. I'm not sure how I'll do that with everyone here.

After dinner, Jane whisks the children off to their playroom to tire them out before bed. Manson builds a fire in the sitting room fireplace and Dotty brings cups of tea for me and Lucille. Father pours brandy for Earl, Aunty, Quincy, and himself. Aunty takes the chair next to mine and sits down. After several minutes, the room warms from the fire. Father's demeanor appears to be warming as well, but I attribute that to the fact that his brandy glass is nearly empty. Aunty chatters on about Europe and her new clothes.

"Well," Father interrupts Aunty, "I think we all know why I called this little meeting."

Everyone falls silent. We all turn towards Father. What meeting?

"We're here to discuss the plight of Amelia and her children. I want her to know that she is looked after and that none of us will let anything happen to her in this terrible time."

I look around. Everyone is nodding and smiling. Aunty reaches out and takes my hand in hers. "Dear, dear child," she whispers to me. It's all I can do to keep from snatching my hand back. I force myself to sit still and listen.

Father begins, "As you are aware, Dwight and I own a business together. When he passes on, the business will come to me." He pauses, as if to be sure we all understand. "While my name is on the documents as half co-owner, he always ran the business as he wanted. I was on there, more or less for my name, to make it easy for him to borrow money and to entice clients. I don't know much about how he ran the operation or what his financial situation was. He always assured me that things were solvent, and the business was going well."

He pauses again and looks around at all of us. "When Dwight was removed from the day-to-day workings of the plant, I had to become more involved. I've been spending a good deal of my time learning the ins and outs of the place. Thank heavens, we have an exceptional group of workers who are interested in keeping the place up and running.

The accountant is competent and has been helpful by filling me in on the actual state of the company.

"The long and short of it is this: There is room to pull a small stipend out of the company every month for the foreseeable future. I think that stipend should go to Amelia to care for herself and the children. I'll check in each week to be sure that things are going well and there are no problems."

"But Father," interrupts Lucille. "We've already decided that Amelia and the children would live with Earl and me."

"Lucille, I haven't got to that part yet. Have patience. I'm trying to explain all of this so Amelia understands."

"What?" I mutter, standing up, astounded by Lucille's words. "Who decided that?"

"Now just a minute, Amelia." Father throws a look of disdain at Lucille, and she bows her head in compliance. "Don't get upset. Let me finish what I wanted to say in the first place before you get defensive."

I stay standing. "Go on," I snap.

"I'm trying to explain to you that we are all concerned for your well-being and that of the children. It's hard for women without husbands to survive." He pauses again and sips from his brandy glass. Then he refills it, though it isn't yet empty. When he's sitting down again, he continues, "I think you should put your children into the care of your sister." He holds up his hand to stop my protest, "Yes, I know, you will never stand for that."

Lucille attempts to speak, but he stops her with a look. "But, Amelia, you must keep in mind that our family has resources. We will share them. We will do our best to help you keep your head above water." Again, Lucille starts to speak, and again, Father silences her with a look. "Amelia, we don't want to make this any harder on you than is necessary. As I said, a woman alone is very vulnerable."

"Dwight's business is also very vulnerable. Selling steel-framed windows to new developers is a tough business. It's been even more difficult because of the war and the epidemic– and the fact that we live in a Mormon community. As you know, being non-Mormon has its drawbacks here. I have great hope for development now that the war has ended. Dwight has run up some debt in the last few years. That has to be paid off." He puts his glass down on the small table next to him. "If you sell the house, you can pay the debt."

I break in. "What are you trying to say, Father? Am I destitute?"

Father turns away. I hear him draw in his breath and sigh. His shoulders droop. He uses his most solemn voice. "You're not destitute, my dear, but with a debt of that size, you have no choice but to sell the house." He holds up his hand as I try to interrupt. "Let me finish," he says. "You have the possibility of a small income from the business." Again, I start to speak. Just as he did with Lucille, he silences me with a look. "Lucille and Earl have offered to take the financial burden of the children off your hands and give you all a place to stay. When we sell the house, you will be able to contribute somewhat to your upkeep." He falls silent and looks around at all of us.

I take a deep breath. I promise myself I'll stay calm. I tell myself I can handle this. "So, it's been decided," I start off. "I shall be relegated to the life of a pauper, living off my sister and her husband, and I'll have no say over my own children. Is that what you're proposing?" I look at each of them, so they know they are all included.

"Amelia don't be so dramatic," Father tells me. "You will not have the life of a pauper. We'll make you and the children as comfortable as possible. It just makes more sense to sell your house. Look at it this way, dear. You can keep some money from the sale of the house to put towards the education of your children."

Lucille nods through all of Father's speech. She interrupts to tell me, "Yes, Sister, Earl and I will be delighted to have you and the children under our roof. It will be best for all of us, and most important, best for the children."

Anger and fear well up from every pore of my body. I take a breath. No damn way this is going to happen. I make my voice firm. "I can't accept any of this." I take another deep breath and remind myself that I'm going to stay calm. "I think you mean well. But, let me make it clear," I continue, "I will look after myself and my children. I don't need any of you. If you want to help me, I'll accept that. But you must help me find a way to look after myself. Don't take over!"

I stare straight at Lucille. "I would rather live on the street than live with you. You are always criticizing me and my children. My children weren't happy at your house even for the short time we were there."

"I don't doubt that they were unhappy, but it's you that makes them unhappy," Lucille spits back. "You need some criticism. I watched you. You need help. Your children run wild and they say terrible things and you never correct them and – ."

"STOP!" I hear. "Stop it. Both of you." Father's voice is loud and clear. "Stop it!" he says again.

"No, Father. You stop it," I yell before I can stop myself. "I'm not doing any of this. No matter what you say. I intend to fend for myself, with or without your help. I'm going to do it myself and my way."

I run up to my bedroom. I have no tears. I see that as a good thing. The clock chimes midnight before I hear horses leaving the carriage house. I wonder what they've talked about for all the hours I've been sitting here. I wonder if I even want to know.

I sit upright on my bed most of the night, staring through the window at the stars. I need a plan. I can't do what they propose. I will not give up this house. When I can't find any answers anywhere inside myself, I turn to God. It seems that prayer is all I have. All I ask for is a plan.

CHAPTER 17

When I wake up the next morning, the sun is shining through the open curtains. I hear the children chattering in the hallway as Jane urges them downstairs for breakfast.

And I have a plan. God must have been working in my dreams. I whisper, "Thank you," to the unknown for answering me.

I wash, dress, and join the laughter in the dining room. The children are full of energy this morning. They all run from the table to meet me with demands for hugs and kisses. George is dressed for school. He seems grown up in his uniform. I watch from the door as he sets off on his half-mile walk to school.

After breakfast, I talk with Jane about what she plans for the children today. She says, "The library is opening a whole section of books just for children and I thought David, in particular, would like that." She smiles. "Manson will take us in the carriage. It's too far for the children to walk."

"I also am in need of Manson's services today," I tell her. The first step in my plan requires that I talk with Father. Jane's face falls with disappointment.

"We can share Manson," I tell her. "He can take us all to the library, and then deliver me to my destination. I'm not sure where I'm going. I need to talk to Father and I'm not sure where he is today. I'm sure Manson must know."

Hesitating for a moment, Jane says, "Manson is in the carriage house. I made arrangements with him last night to pick us up this morning. I should have asked you first, but the evening just rolled by and I didn't want to disturb your family meeting."

I nod in reply to Jane and put on my coat and head for the carriage house to find Manson. As I walk, I rehearse what I'm going to say to Father.

I find Manson attaching the horses' reins to the hitching post. "Hello, Manson," I say hoping not to startle him. "There's been a change in your plans today."

He looks up, surprised to see me. "Is something wrong?"

"No, Manson, nothing's wrong. I just want to let you know that Jane and I need to share the carriage today. She wants to go to the library, and I need to find my father."

At that moment, our conversation is interrupted by the arrival of Jane and the children. Manson lifts David and Babe into the carriage. Then, he helps Jane up as well. He holds her arm to steady her as she climbs up into the carriage and she turns to look at him. "Thank you, Manson," she says, beaming.

Manson turns to me and as he helps me up into the carriage, he says, "When I worked at your father's house, I used to drop him off at Mr. Dwight's place of business each morning. He might be there. Otherwise, he will be at the courthouse."

"Well, in that case, Manson, drop the children off first and then we'll stop by the office.

After dropping Jane and the children at the library, Manson pulls up in front of the two-story, brown brick building. It's quite a magnificent structure that houses the offices and design departments for the business. The sign extends across the entire front of the building: "Manufacturers Specialties Company Building Supplies, 418 Boston Blvd." There are several adjoining buildings behind which are the actual manufacturing plants. I've only seen this place once with Dwight and only from the outside, but in the days when he would talk to me, he always said the place gave him comfort. Just looking at it today I feel a strange excitement about the possibility that I might own this place one day-- that is if Father would ever let that happen.

Manson comes around to the carriage door to help me out, but I ask him to go in and see if my father is there. Moments later he returns and opens my door. "Yes, your father is in," he says with a smile as he helps me climb down from the carriage.

"Thank you, Manson. Can you return and pick me up in a few hours?"

"Yes, ma'am. I have to pick up Jane and the children at three o'clock. I will check with you then to see if you're ready to go home."

I pause before opening the office door. It was me who suggested to Dwight that the sign, "Owner and Manager Dwight M. Deschamps," be hung across the front door. I see he took my advice. It looks very elegant there.

I step inside, but it appears no one is here. The doors to the three offices are all closed but I notice Father's coat hanging on a coat stand in the corner. That must be why Manson assumed father is here.

I notice a large space next to the offices with a desk and five large comfortable-looking upholstered chairs set up in a row along the wall. They appear like they are waiting for well-dressed clients to appear and lounge in them. I decide to try one out. I'll gather my thoughts further before I attempt to find Father. Just as I make myself comfortable, one of the office doors opens.

A small wiry man appears, smiling broadly. "Ah, Ma'am," he says, as I stand to greet him. His voice is pleasant as he reaches to shake my hand. "Good day! I thought I heard someone enter our premises, but I was unsure. Our receptionist is away for a short period of time this week. How might I be of service?"

"I'm looking for Judge Lange. I was told he would be here."

"Yes, indeed, he is here, somewhere. I believe he is roaming about the premises checking on the workers. I'll see if I can find him for you."

This must be the accountant that Dwight and Father both have talked about from time to time, each time telling some story about how competent and honest he is despite his odd behavior. Before he can go in search of Father, I venture, "You must be Eugene Preston."

The strange little man looks at me, tilting his head, as if trying to figure something out. "Yes, in fact, that is who

I am. And who shall I tell the judge is looking for him, ma'am?"

"Tell him it's his daughter, Amelia."

"I presume then that you are the wife of our benefactor and owner, Mr. Deschamps. Would I be correct in that?" The man is prim, amusing in his demeanor. What a gentle soul.

"Yes, you are correct in that, sir," I tell him, wondering why I feel drawn to copy his manner of speaking.

He searches my face for a moment. "I am at your service ma'am. I assume, since you know my name, that you also know I am your husband's accountant and, if it's not too forward, his greatest admirer. I pray every day for him."

"Thank you for those kind words," I tell him. Dwight used to talk about how much he thought of Mr. Preston. He told me his accountant was the wisest man he'd ever met, and that he once saved him from making a bad investment. Dwight said Mr. Preston was a genius with money and numbers as well as being able to judge if people were honest and ethical. Dwight said he never knew Mr. Preston to be wrong, and he trusted him more than he trusted some in his own family. From all that Dwight once told me, I feel like I already know this man.

Mr. Preston's voice breaks into my thoughts. "I'll go now and fetch Judge Lange."

While I wait, I try to practice in my head what I'll say to Father. It's times like this I need courage. Above all, I can't let him dismiss me.

Father appears after what feels like forever and by the look on his face, he's not happy to see me. "Why are you here?" he snaps.

"I need to talk to you. Better now than later," I tell him, my tone matching his mood.

"If this is a continuation of your personal issues, Amelia, then this is neither the time nor the place for us to talk. Go home and I'll stop by after I'm through here."

"Father, I'm not going home. If you won't talk to me now, then I will wait right here until you do." I return to the chair I had been sitting in when Mr. Preston found me.

Father doesn't reply to me. He turns to Mr. Preston and says, "See, Eugene, I told you she was difficult. Now, you see it for yourself." He waves his hand at me in dismissal.

Mr. Preston looks uncomfortable. He pauses before he says, "I have some things to do in my office, sir. I'll leave you two alone."

Father looks back at me as Mr. Preston walks away. "Well, Daughter, I guess you win. We can sit in Dwight's office. Say what you want to say and get it over with." He opens the door and ushers me in.

Father seats himself behind the desk and indicates I should sit in the chair across from him. The one set out for visitors. I'm not a visitor. I pick up the chair, carry it around to his side of the desk, and sit down.

"What are you doing?" he asks.

"I want to talk to you like you're my father, not some clerk in your business," I tell him.

Father's frustration shows in his clenched jaw and rolled-up fists. I don't care. I need to say what I've come to say. Be damned what he thinks about it.

Before he can say another word, I start. "Don't you understand that you're not helping me? Try to see it from my point of view. You and Lucille are trying to take my children and my house away from me." My voice rises and I take a deep breath to restore my sense of calm. "You make plans without consulting me and you expect me to be happy with what you decide. It's just wrong. You take Dwight away and give me the barest details about his health – even the location of the hospital. You treat me as if I am a child."

Father opens his mouth to speak, but nothing comes out. I don't know if he's too shocked to say anything or if he thinks better of what he wants to say.

"I will not give up my children to my sister. She thinks she knows everything about raising children, but she's not even kind to them. I will never let her have a say in raising them. Not now, not ever."

I stand up. Then I sit down again. I take a deep breath to calm myself. "And as far as the house is concerned, it's my house – and I'm not selling it."

I look around the office. "Furthermore, this is Dwight's business. If you won't help me support myself, then I shall go to work here. You don't need this work as much as I do." This whole argument makes me tired.

"Now, just a minute," Father interrupts. "I don't work here Amelia. I stop in from time to time and check with Eugene to see how things are progressing. I am a partner after all, even if I'm only a silent one. The workers know their jobs. Right now, the business needs someone to oversee it, to contact prospective customers, but that's all." He puts his hand on the desk as he speaks. "That's the only function I perform now that Dwight is not here. It's still Dwight's business and will be until he dies. Then it will be partly yours." He shakes his head. "Amelia, it's no business for a woman." His voice is quiet, but the tone is firm. "If you tried to work here, you would be blackballed immediately. You are not a man. And to add further, if our Mormon clients knew they were dealing with a woman they would probably shun us as well."

"But what about Dwight? He got on well with them. You said yourself the business is doing well. They must trust him."

"They trust him because they trust me – and they probably think that I will convert one day," he chuckles as if he is in on a private joke. "As long as they think that, they'll do business with us. Otherwise, they won't. And for certain, they won't do business with us if a woman is in charge." He stops as if he has just rested his case. "Just go home and we'll talk more later."

I pause. Frustration pours out of me. "No, Father, I'm not going home until I get this settled. You don't seem to understand that I not only want to learn the business I need to learn the business. I don't want to be dependent on your monthly stipend and I don't want to stay home with three children and spend my life telling the maids what to do. I may be a woman, but I am not the woman you want me to be. I don't see me ever getting married again so I need something inspiring to occupy my mind. Jane can look after the children during the day when they return from school, just as well if not better than I can. They love her. If you won't give me a chance with this business, then I will find another way to earn my living and you might not like what I have in mind."

"Is that a threat?" Father asks frowning.

"Perhaps," I answer, trying to sound as serious as possible. "It's more like a promise."

Father startles me with his sudden loud gasp. "You're as stubborn as your mother ever was. When she wanted something, she never gave up," he says, his voice fading at the end. "I wonder what she would say about all of this."

"I think she would say to give me a chance."

Father looks at me and shrugs his shoulders. I sense the fight is ebbing out of him as his voice is softer and less aggressive. "The only thing wrong with you working here is you know nothing – absolutely nothing – about running a business. You would run the place into the ground in a month or less. I guarantee it." He leans back in his chair shaking his head.

"Thank you for your confidence, Father." I tell him, trying my best to keep the sarcasm to a minimum. "Do you really think I can't learn? I'm not stupid. No, I don't know anything about this business but why can't someone teach me?"

"Look, Amelia, I never said you were stupid. It's just – that – a woman running a manufacturing business is absurd."

"Why does anyone have to know a woman is in charge? What if people think Eugene is in charge? He could seek customers on my behalf, and no one would ever need to know any different." I pause. I rest my case.

Father scrunches his eyebrows together as if deep in thought and when I think he might argue some more, he proposes a solution. "Why don't we ask Eugene what he thinks? Dwight always said he is a genius. Perhaps he can talk some sense into you."

"Ask whomever you like," I tell him, making my voice confident even if I'm not. I may have lost this fight. Eugene will probably agree with Father.

Father disappears down the hall and into Eugene's office and shuts the door. I wait. After some time, they reappear absorbed in conversation. They look very different next to each other. Father, tall and solid. Eugene, small and thin as a pencil. My father's size has always been intimidating.

"You'd do that?" I hear Father ask Eugene as they come towards me.

"I would, sir," Eugene answers. "It might prove interesting, and it would certainly brighten my days."

Father's mouth is agape with disbelief. "You're a better man than I am, that's for sure." They laugh together but stop when they realize they are within earshot of me.

"What's so funny?" I ask.

Eugene pulls up a chair and places it adjacent to mine.

"Eugene has taken your side, my dear." Father tells me. "Why, I can't imagine, but it's his decision. He has agreed to train you in what you need to know about this business. That way, you will be here to make decisions when major issues arise – once you show you're capable of that, of course. The three of us can meet next week to determine exactly what it is you will be doing."

I nod. I feel like leaping from my chair and throwing my arms around Eugene, but of course that would not be proper. I dreamed that it would come to this – that I would get a chance to try, but I never believed it would ever happen. "Thank you, Mr. Preston. Thank you," is all I can think of to say.

"Just so you know up front," Father interjects, "the stipend I offered you to stay home is the same one you will now have to work for. The business is doing well enough to support you and pay the workers, but you will not receive more than you were originally offered, at least until you prove yourself. To start with, you will also have to come to work every day. We will see how that goes," he says, his sarcasm obvious.

I turn to Eugene. "You're going to do this?" I ask, puzzled.

Eugene nods "I'm very fond of Dwight. I'm doing it for him as I believe it's what he would have wanted."

That revelation startles me at first. But when I think back to how Dwight once was, Eugene is probably right. Dwight would want me to do what I must do to take care of myself and the children. I think he might even support my need to work outside the house.

"Thank you, Mr. Preston. That is very kind of you. I look forward to working with you." I smile at this funny little man. Thank you, Dwight.

Eugene breaks in with a smile and says, "You may not say that after a few days. I've been told I am a bit of a perfectionist. I believe the word some of the workers have for me is 'fussy.' Your father has indicated we will have a meeting next week to determine what your tasks will be so I will leave it at that and get back to my work."

I watch as Eugene turns towards his office. He turns suddenly and smiling at me says, "Welcome to the company, I'm certain we shall get along splendidly, and I would appreciate it if you would call me Eugene."

Father interjects with raised eyebrows, "Ha, you may think differently after a week or so with her."

"I think she will be more than acceptable," Eugene says with confidence. He is obviously not afraid to tell my father what he thinks. I can see why Dwight was so fond of him.

I hope I can live up to his expectations.

CHAPTER 18

1920

It's been a year since I started work here. I arrive at nine o'clock and go home at three – or whenever the work that Eugene has set out for me gets done. I've learned much about the business. I started out doing bookkeeping and general secretarial tasks. Our original stenographer left the business shortly after I began working. She said she was ready to retire and could see that I would be a worthy replacement.

I smiled at that comment because I was struggling at that time. I took a typing course back when I was in school, but it was such a long time ago that I had to relearn it from scratch. I also had to learn the books. That task helped me learn the most about the inner workings of the business. I have developed an inner desire to learn about finances and what keeps us afloat through all these up and down days of the war and the issues with the epidemic. I think I have a good grasp of this business now. Thanks to Eugene.

There were times when he was "fussy" as he calls it. Once when I was just learning the books, he made me stay at work until long after the supper hour to find a missing penny. He said if the books are off by a penny and you don't know why, then it could be off by much more than that. As frustrated as I was with him over that episode, I now understand how important that lesson was. I eventually found that penny and when I did, I was proud of myself. Proud that I didn't go off in a huff. He made me mad, but he was right.

I am growing to appreciate Eugene, even with his strange ways. He's been a patient understanding teacher and Dwight was right when he once commented to me that Eugene is the wisest man he'd ever met. He has a way with our clients. He seems to know after one or two encounters whether they are true to their word. I think he's saved the business a lot of heartbreak in the past.

I remember six months ago how uncomfortable I was around Eugene. At least I was until the day that changed our relationship. I arrived at work to find the giant ledger open on my desk. That happened only when I had made some mistake. But that day was different. I hadn't made any error for Eugene to call to my attention. He had simply forgotten to close it the night before.

That was not like Eugene. It didn't take long before I realized that something was wrong. He got up from his desk several times during the morning and paced the floor, all the time looking grim and worried. Usually, I found it best to remain silent and let him work his own way out of whatever quandary he was in. His quandary usually involved the books and talking to him just made him even more withdrawn.

Not being able to stand this odd behavior another moment, I broke the silence and asked, "What's the matter, Eugene? For heaven's sake, you are fidgety today. Is there something I can do for you?"

Eugene stopped pacing and stared at the floor. "I apologize. You are correct. I am too fidgety for work, too fidgety for eating, too fidgety for anything. I don't know what to do. It's all too ridiculous for words." He went back to pacing the floor.

"Eugene, if you're going to continue to pace the floor like a caged animal, I shall have to go somewhere else in the building to work. What is the problem?"

That's when he blurted it out. "I have to take some days away. I shall need at least a week."

"What? Are you ill?"

"No, no, I'm not ill."

"Has someone died then?"

"No, no. No one has died."

"For goodness' sake, Eugene, I'm not going to play guessing games with you. What is going on?" I put my pencil down. "On second thought, whatever it is, you don't need anyone's permission if that is what you're looking for. I can manage fine without you if it's just for a week."

He stared at me. "You mean I should just go?"

"Well, it would be good manners to tell me or Father, so we know you haven't vanished in the night. I'm certain Father wouldn't mind if you went somewhere for a week. He knows you will make sure that all the accounts are up to date before you leave."

"Oh," Eugene blinked several times behind his glasses. "Thank you, Amelia, for pointing this out to me. I should have been able to figure that out for myself. But the idea of not working for a week so overwhelmed me that I couldn't think beyond it." He took off his glasses to clean them, which he did when he had a tough bit of totting up to do, or when the totals didn't match on his first try.

"I can't think straight," he muttered to himself as he went back to his desk. "Yes, I will take the week," he murmured. He put his glasses back on and picked up his pencil, but it was only a minute before he put it down again, muttering to himself.

At that point, I'd walked over to Eugene's desk. "What in the name of all that is holy is going on, Eugene? Can't you tell me? You have made me so curious that I can't work."

He looked at me and then smiled. The smile continued to widen until it covered his whole strange little face, and a touch of pink colored his cheeks. "I am getting married on Saturday." His voice was almost a whisper.

"But that's wonderful, Eugene! Why didn't you tell us? I didn't know you were courting anyone. Is she someone I know?"

"No, she's not anyone you know, I'm sure. She's from away. Her name is Catherine." He looked down, as though anxious to get back to his books, but suddenly he pulled out a picture of his bride-to-be and I nearly fainted. She was beautiful.

"Are you having a large wedding?" I asked.

"No, Amelia, we are getting married at her parent's house. We've been advised by the Salt Lake City Board of

Health Commissioners not to have gatherings of more than ten persons until this epidemic is over. I thought the worst of this was over, but they are still forbidding large group gatherings."

I thought it was unfortunate: I would have liked to be there. Eugene said he would bring Catherine to meet me one day. I wanted to meet a woman that would marry Eugene. I thought she would be interesting or on second thought I realized I actually wanted to meet a woman Eugene would marry. She would have to be special.

He put his glasses back on and bent over his work again. The fidgeting finished.

I looked at him, sitting at his desk, quiet and focused on whatever was in front of him. I had never seen Eugene as marriageable. He's too odd. I'd always thought of him as a person too engaged in his work to be a husband. To me, he seemed old to be getting married, though I had to admit that he would be a good provider. He worked hard, and he had been very kind to me. I remember thinking I should rethink my judgment of him.

***

Eugene arrives back at work after his wedding relaxed and happy. Standing in the doorway to his office to welcome him back, I can't help but notice the first thing he does is place a picture of Catherine on his desk. It's a lovely gesture. It makes me a little jealous.

I return to my office and sit back in my chair. I sigh and wonder what it would be like to have someone in my life who wanted to put my picture on their desk. I shake my head to rid it of such thoughts and turn to the project at hand but stop again. I like this job. I'm learning new things all the time. The job fills the days, and it doesn't leave me any time to think about Dwight and his situation.

I've had three letters so far from Ada. In the last one she wrote about how she and Clarence insisted on seeing Dwight. He didn't know them. I cried after reading that. I hate thinking of him suffering in some hospital far away. Maybe he isn't suffering. Ada said he seems happy. "He's living in his own little world," she wrote. Perhaps that's how I should look at it: pretend he is happier there than here.

Eugene startles me out of my reverie. "I noticed your father's carriage has pulled up at the side door. It's odd he wouldn't come to the front."

The side door swings open and Father steps inside pulling the door closed to keep the snow from swooshing in behind him. He removes his coat and fur hat and stamps his feet to get the snow off his boots. His eyes dart around the room and then he sighs, his shoulders sag as he comes towards me. He doesn't say a word, even when I call a welcome to him. He walks like he's in a trance.

"What is it, Father?" I ask, afraid to know.

"Oh, my poor girl," he says as he draws near. "It is over at last. Our Dwight has gone to meet the angels. At last, he is free. Thank the Lord."

He reminds me of a southern preacher giving a sermon and it strikes me funny. I would laugh except for the content of his announcement.

Father takes me by the shoulders and pulls me close to him. I'm not sure if he's afraid I'll run away or fall apart like a broken doll. Dwight is gone. Dwight is free. I cling to Father for a moment. I pull back as I smell brandy. That's odd; Father seldom drinks during the day. He must have made an exception today. His eyes are red and sad. I suspect he's had this news for a while but has been trying to get himself together to tell me.

"I'm sorry to bring you the news, Amelia." He leans forward to add, "I wish this all could have been different. Dwight was a good man. Regardless of that insidious disease, he was a good man." Father's voice breaks. "I was proud to have him as my son-in-law. Even now, I'm proud to have him as my son-in-law."

"It's okay," I tell him. "It really is okay. I've known this was coming for a long time."

After a moment of quiet Father whispers, "I thought you'd be more upset."

"I am upset. Upset for my children. Upset by the shame of it. Upset that I have three children to look after without a husband. But then, I have been surviving for the past year on my own. It's not the best, but it's not the worst. Somehow, I feel that God is with me through all of this." I wonder what Father would say if he knew I feel more anger than sadness. What is wrong with me? Can someone use up all their tears?

"Indeed," Father answers. "I am happy to see you have a semblance of faith left. But I am sorry for you, Daughter. In fact, I'm sorry for the family. I will always be grateful to Dwight for all he was to my family. He helped me out in my own time of need. It'll be a while before I get over his death."

I wonder what Father would think if I told him I'm already over Dwight's death. It's the anger around the reason for his death that haunts me.

"There are a few unpleasant logistical details we need to discuss now that Dwight is gone," Father continues, his voice shifting into business mode.

I look at my father, stunned. His ability to change moods makes me feel off balance. "I'd rather wait for any of those discussions until I tell the boys. They need to know as soon as possible."

"I'll take you home," Father says, as he helps me into my coat.

Eugene offers his condolences and tells me to rest. What a nice thing for him to say. I have the feeling I won't get a lot of it in the coming days.

Father and I ride home in silence. As difficult as it all is, at least now it will be possible to make real plans for the future. I think about how I'll tell the children their father is gone. Maybe Father should do that. I'll let him tell Earl and Lucille, and Aunty Mary and Uncle Quincy as well. I don't know what I'll tell other people. I still can't tell the truth. We wouldn't be able to continue living here if I did.

"I'm not going to tell Babe," I say to Father as we pull up to the house. "The boys are old enough to understand, but I'd rather leave Babe out of it. I'm sure her brothers will tell her in their own time, anyway. When we get inside, I'll have Jane take Babe into the nursery. You and I should be prepared to comfort the children if they are upset."

We enter the house, and the boys and Babe come running to us, excited to have me home, but more excited to see their grandfather. Father lets Babe jump up on him and the boys get hugs. It's a scene I've seen played repeatedly on each of his visits. This time is different, though.

After all the hugs have been given, he reaches into his coat pocket and brings out a small package for each child. He must have thought they'd need something extra for this event. Someone has decorated each little box with a brightly colored bow. "Here's a special little gift from your Grampa to keep you sweet and happy," he says with special pride.

The children tear the boxes open and discover each one contains a large piece of peppermint candy and a chocolate bon-bon, treats only seen at Christmas. David shoves the entire bon-bon into his mouth in one bite. He chokes on the sweetness. Babe giggles with delight and takes dainty bites out of hers. George holds his box in one hand and extends the other to Grampa. "Thank you, Grampa," he says. Then he pops a peppermint candy into his mouth.

I leave Father to deal with the children. I take Jane's arm and lead her to the hall, out of earshot of the children and tell her that Dwight has passed. "

"Oh, I am sorry for your loss, ma'am." Jane says. "Oh, my goodness. Of course, ma'am," she says again. "I don't know what to say. That is terrible." Her eyes tear up and I'm afraid she's going to cry.

"Just take Babe, Jane. She doesn't need to hear our conversation with the boys."

"Yes, ma'am, of course." She goes to Babe, leading her by the hand to each of us for a kiss before leaving the room. Babe is content. She has her candy to pacify her.

We take the boys into the sitting room and close the door. "George, you and David sit in the big chairs. Grampa and I want to talk to you about something important," I tell them.

"Okay, Mother," George says, "Is something wrong?"

Children are so perceptive. "Something has happened," I reply, "And Grampa and I want to tell you about it."

George and David climb into their chairs and scooch around to get comfortable. They both hang on to their candy. The candy was a good idea. Maybe things won't seem so terrible if they have a sweet.

Father looks at me and I nod when I think the children are settled. "I have to tell you some sad news, boys," Father says. "You know that Papa has been sick for a long time." He waits for both boys to nod.

"Well, he was really, really sick. We took him to a hospital where Aunty Ada and Uncle Clarence live. It's far away because the doctors were the best doctors for his sickness. I'm sorry to tell you, but Papa isn't coming back. Yesterday he died. The doctors worked hard to help him, but they couldn't."

Neither George nor David say anything. They just stare.

George listens with earnest attention. His eyes begin to mist. "Why do people die, Grampa?" he asks, in a sad voice.

"I don't know, son. They just do. When it's their time, they just go on."

"Where do you think they go?" George asks.

"Well, if they are very good, they go to heaven, but if they are bad, they go to hell," Father responds.

"Oh, for God's sake, don't tell him that!" The words pop out of my mouth before I can stop them. "That's just scary nonsense."

"It's what we believe," Father says, puffing himself up like a determined peacock. I hate it when Father talks religion. I hate it most when he is so adamant in his beliefs – and insists that I believe as he does.

Knowing I should remain silent, I snap anyway. "Well, it's not what I believe. Heaven and hell exist right here on earth. No one goes to a place when they die. They become spirits!"

Father frowns. "We will have this discussion some other time," he grouches back at me. Then, turning back to the children, he adds, "Papa is in a better place, boys. God is looking out for him now."

Both boys look at him and then back at me. I can't tell by their faces what they are thinking. George lets a few seconds pass before he states, "I'm sorry that Papa died. I think we will miss him very much. Thank you for the candy, Grampa. It's very good."

"You're welcome, son. Now take your brother and go find your sister. I think you've had enough grown-up talk for one day. Perhaps Jane will find you something fun to do."

Both boys jump down from their chairs and dash across the room to the door, calling for Jane as they go. I thought they might be sadder than they are, but maybe they knew in their hearts long ago that he wasn't ever coming back. Maybe that's a good thing. They will have plenty of time to learn what it means for their lives. A profound sadness covers me. Is it sadness or loneliness? Sometimes it's hard to tell the difference.

Once the boys leave and the door closes behind them, Father sighs. "I think it's time we talk about several matters around Dwight's passing. I don't think we should put this off any longer," he tells me in a quiet voice. I am surprised by his gentle tone. Where is my "let's get down to business" Father?

I sit waiting as he fumbles with the lock on an old briefcase. He must have brought it with him when he arrived, but I was too concerned about the boys to have seen it.

"Let's see," he begins, as he sifts through the papers. "Over the last few months, I have taken the liberty to examine some of Dwight's business and personal papers. I think it is important to let you know where you – where we all stand, in this matter. First, I'm glad you're working with Eugene, though I think you should look at it as temporary. Having something to do on a daily basis is a good thing, especially in these early days. However, it's not a business for a woman and it should be sold as soon as possible while buyers still see it as profitable. Also, you should be aware that Dwight had some debt before he died, and that debt has grown since his need for hospitalization has to be factored in. You can't expect that others will pay for his, um, indiscretions."

As gentle as Father is attempting to be, his attitude annoys me. Of course, I don't expect that others will pay for Dwight's "indiscretions." It's nasty of Father to bring that up, especially now, when Dwight has just passed on. "You just told me that the business is at its peak earning power. Surely it can earn enough to pay off a few debts."

Father abandons his search for whatever paper he wanted. He ignores my comment about the business and changes the subject. "The second thing we need to discuss is the welfare of your children. You think you can look after them by yourself, but you don't have any real concept of what it costs to feed and clothe three children. Their schooling alone will cost a fortune. Lucille and Earl have, in kindness, offered once again to take you and your children in. You are doing your best to deter all attempts to help you. You need to forget your own feelings and think about these children."

I feel anger. It's like an entity unto itself. How dare he!! We have dealt with all these things. Why does Dwight's death mean we have to go back over them again?

I get up from my chair, but before I can speak a single word, he stands to face me. "Sit down, Amelia. I am not here to fight with you, but I am going to tell you what I think." He towers over me; his very presence overpowers me. I sit down again.

"The third thing I have to say is that I'm alarmed by your disrespect for our beliefs. Your mother, rest her soul, would turn over in her grave if she heard the way you talk about God. We have been Presbyterians all our lives and

shall continue to be so. I hope I make myself clear on this."
He sits back down.

He seems to be waiting for a response from me. I
swallow my anger for now. When I don't speak, Father
continues, going back to his rant about money. "Dwight
still owes close to a thousand dollars on a loan he took out
to finance a Mexican land investment. It was a bad deal,
but it is coming due and will have to be paid. You have no
assets to sell. There may be enough profit from the sale of
his business to pay it off, but I am not sure."

I interrupt him. "I want to know what I'm left with."

Father opens his mouth and then closes it. "All right
if that's what you want. You have the house. You have the
business. That appears to be all of it. According to Eugene,
you will have the cash flow to meet your business payroll
for a while, but only if you bring in enough new business
to meet your demands. It means you will have to take only
a pittance for yourself. Probably less than your present
stipend."

"Then I shall have to learn to live with a pittance, shan't
I?" I know by my tone that I am being disrespectful, but it
just comes out that way. Father still thinks of my wages as
a stipend from the business. I don't think he understands
that I work hard for my wages.

He looks at me, stunned, then retorts, "Do you even
know what that means? It means you and the children
will live in this big house without Jane, without Manson,
without Dotty, without horses, without a carriage, and
with just enough food to get by. What will you do with
the children when you are working? Who will fix your

meals and buy you beautiful clothes? Who will pay for the children's schooling? Why can't you just do what I tell you? It will be much easier for you. And after an appropriate time, we will find you a husband."

"What? Why would I want another husband after what I have been through?"

"Well, you know what I mean. Look, Amelia, I'm explaining your situation to you. You have to put your children first."

"I am putting my children first! Even the thought of living with Lucille and Earl is just wrong. They are not parents. When Mother died, you didn't farm us out to other relatives! Don't you understand how I feel, given what you went through with us? Don't you have any heart for the children or for me?"

"Stop shouting. The whole neighborhood will hear you. You are as shrill as a witch and just as impossible!" He is shouting now. "I will return when you have calmed down and when I can talk some sense into you. You are impossible." He slams the door as he leaves.

I wait until I hear the horse's hooves fading in the distance before I cry. I cry for myself and my children. I am trapped in my own inabilities.

There's a soft knock at the door. It's Jane with the children. "We've come to get you for dinner," she says.

"I'll follow you shortly," I tell her. "I'd better wash up first."

She nods and then says, "I'm sorry for your troubles, Ma'am. I couldn't help but overhear some of the conversation."

"Thank you, Jane. I'm sure we can work something out."

After dinner with the children bathed and in bed, I wander back to the sitting room to sit for a while to think. Father left his briefcase behind in his haste to get away from our confrontation. I wonder what's in it. It's wide open, so I peer in. It contains a stack of official-looking documents and a large wad of receipts. Maybe they will shed some light on my predicament. Living alone with little money can't be much worse than living with Lucille and Earl. I console myself as I start to go through the papers.

The first paper is from The National Bank of the Republic. It has Dwight's name on it and says he borrowed $2000 in 1895. I find the receipt that says he paid that off in 1900. That can't be the debt Father was talking about.

I continue going through the documents. Most are everyday receipts or business correspondence, but I find an envelope marked "Confidential" and dated 1920. I pull out three sheets and stand transfixed. It must have just come to Father through the mail from Ada. It's a day-by-day account of Dwight's health for the days leading up to his death. As I read, I realize what agony Dwight must have gone through in his last days. The paper tells me he talked to himself constantly, he couldn't walk without support, he messed himself and his bed daily, and at the end he thought he was a general fighting some imaginary war. He eventually died of "general paralysis of the insane".

By the end, I am in tears. At least they didn't write syphilis on his death certificate. I wonder if general paralysis of the insane is any different. The last piece of paper from the briefcase is a handwritten copy of the obituary that has a note attached, saying that it will be appearing in the Salt Lake Tribune in the following week. I read the neat, scripted words in disbelief. It announces to the world that my husband has been laid to rest in Stockton, California. It gives his cause of death as the Spanish flu. I guess for us, this epidemic has served a purpose. Father has thought of everything. It's a good thing I snooped through his papers, or I wouldn't know what to say to people who ask why he died.

CHAPTER 19

Father stopped in at the office yesterday and announced that he would be coming to visit me tonight. I haven't talked to him since our last unhappy meeting. He didn't ask me if it was convenient; he announced it and without giving me a chance to react, he left. I remember the last time he did this he had arranged for a family meeting without telling me.

I'm not happy to see anyone right now. I've been gathering Dwight's personal effects and packing them away. I can't bear to have signs of him lying around the house. His picture is on the mantle. I'm packing it away for the children to have when they're older.

The children hear Father arrive before I do and run to greet him. George flings open the door as I come to the top of the stairs. Aunty Mary, Uncle Quincy, Lucille, and Earl step inside behind Father. I stop in my tracks, then proceed slowly down the steps. I should have known they would try again. I sigh. I can't help but wonder if this will just be another fight.

"Well, we are here," Father announces. He's smiling, and he walks towards me without removing his boots and gloves. He attempts to kiss my cheek, but I draw back and he steps away. "Are you still angry?" he asks.

I feel more resigned than angry. I have nothing to say to Father or to the rest of them. I know what they're going to say. They're all going to insist I do it their way. I know it. And I'm not. No matter what. They remind me of vultures the way they all push their way into my house, all laughing as if they are enjoying some private joke.

Jane appears and shoos the children upstairs once they have said their hellos. She seems to know when it's better if the children are out of sight. I can't imagine not having her around.

"Shall we all go into the sitting room? I presume you're not here for a social visit, but to discuss my life." Why do they think they can just show up?

Father nods and proceeds to the sitting room.

"You'll be surprised at what we have in store for you," Aunty whispers to me as she follows Father.

I glare at her.

"Don't worry, Dear. It'll be fine," she finishes.

Father has brought brandy with him and offers it to Earl, Uncle Quincy, and Aunty Mary. He must consider this a special occasion, or he wouldn't suggest drinking. I ask Dotty to bring glasses and tea for Lucille and me.

Once everyone is seated with their drinks, Father begins. He says the family has given great thought to my dilemma and have come up with an idea they want me to hear.

I break into his little speech even before he can get his ideas out. "I'm willing to listen to anything you have to offer," I tell him. "But I will never agree to live with Lucille – or anyone –and I will not give up my house. I will starve to death first."

"Amelia, must you be so dramatic? We are not the enemy."

"Then get on with whatever it is you have to say, so I can stop guessing."

Father's frown grows deeper. This time he's not going to bully me. No matter what.

He sighs. Then nodding to the men, he says, "Earl, Quincy and I have talked it over and we've decided that we can do something to help you." He pauses for a sip of his drink. "Instead of selling the house, Quincy has developed a plan to enable you to gain some income from it. He has drawn up a blueprint to divide the house in two. One side will be for you and the children. The other side you will be able to rent out. The rental will provide money each month. Houses are scarce in this area, and you should be able to ask a goodly sum for such an accommodation. The rental money can go on the debt until it's paid off." He smiles, proud of himself.

They all smile.

"Of course, it is just an idea," he finishes. "But one we hope you might agree is a solution to the problem of paying off the debt." He doesn't say Dwight's debt, and I understand that Dwight is truly gone. The debt is now mine.

This is a change of tactics. Father is asking me if I agree with their proposal. There must be a catch. "But it will cost money to make the necessary changes," I say. "How will I pay for that?"

"Earl and Quincy will supply the workers at no cost to you. They offer their help out of respect for Dwight – and of course to help you. I think it is a kindness on their part."

Earl comes forward and spreads a large drawing out on the table in front of me. He smiles at me and says, "This is what we think would work without too much trouble or inconvenience to you. First thing, we'll put the main wall through the kitchen and along the living room. That will divide the spaces. Then we can work on the other side of the wall, out of your way. It won't change much of what you have right now, except that the kitchen and living room will be smaller. It's the new side that will require work. It will need a commode and a couple of smaller sleeping rooms. Most of the work will be on the new side." He steps back to let me look at the drawings. The whole group is silent. They are waiting for my reaction.

"It looks like it would work," I say, though I'm quite confused by it all. "Why are you doing this? I don't want help out of pity," is all I can think of to say. This isn't like my family. I'm not used to them holding back.

Quincy comes to my side. "This is not pity, Amelia. I assure you. We –" His voice breaks.

Aunty continues for him. "Since you are so adamant about living your own life, we want to give you every opportunity to do that. That's all we mean by this. It would be our pleasure to give you this – this new space – as a gift."

Quincy slinks back to his chair frowning at his wife. I think he hates it when she speaks for him. Poor man, he doesn't stand a chance.

Father throws up his hands. "If it were up to me, I'd have you come live with me, since you're hell bent on not living with Lucille." He shrugs. "But I imagine you'd fight with me if you came back to my house. I think we'd not be a good pair, though I would love to have the boys around all the time."

Father continues, "I ask you; do you have some other suggestion that might be better for you and the children?"

Now they are all staring at me. Their faces are hopeful. They seem content to wait for me to decide whether I want this or not. At least they're not telling me what to do. Maybe this would be a good idea. With money from the house to pay off the debt, I might be able to survive without having to call on Father and others for anything.

I nod my acceptance. "It's a good idea. I can see it's best for the welfare of the children."

The relief in the room is visible. Everyone breaks into excited chatter. Quincy smiles at me and nods. "We'll start in a few days," he says.

Aunty and Lucille go up to say goodnight to the children. Later when the others leave, Father lingers. "I feel like a cup of tea before I go home," he says. "We should talk about a few other things."

Rather than disturb Dotty, I prepare tea for Father. Both of us drink our tea while we chat about the weather and the children's schoolwork before we set the cups aside. Father clears his throat and says he wants to talk about the servants. Whom we should keep and whom we should let go. He speaks about them as if they are all working in one household.

"I want you to keep Manson and Dotty for as long as they wish to work for us. I feel I owe them. They have been long-time loyal servants. I may borrow one or both in the coming years as I have the need. Dotty has turned into a good cook so I may use those talents here. I have talked to her about this arrangement, and she has agreed. She also says she can easily clean both houses without difficulty. I've decided to release the rest of my servants in the coming months. We'll find a way to keep Jane until Babe goes to school. By that time, George will be old enough to watch the younger children until you get home."

"I don't understand why you're letting all the servants go." I'm confused by Father's announcement. "Is there something you're not telling me?"

"Ah, Amelia, there are many things you don't know. For now, we won't discuss my reasons further, but let's just say it is time to be frugal. Your sisters have married well, so my worry over them is now alleviated. I need to keep what resources I have for future use. I must not fritter away what is there."

"Are you saying I am a burden to you?" I ask.

"No, of course you're not a burden. You're my daughter. I'm thinking about you and the children and what they will need in the future. It will be many years before they will be on their own. I want them each to have a good education. What you make in the business will never cover their educational requirements, so they will need additional funds to continue in good schools." The fact of Dwight's death is in the room, drawing us together even though neither of us mention it.

I don't have any other questions for Father. But something doesn't add up. I wonder about Father's real reasons for letting the help go. Father has never had a problem with money. He has his estate and his legal practice. He made money from all those land deals in Mexico. Yet, he is behaving as if he is about to go broke.

A few days later, Uncle Quincy is at my door with a small crew of men. "We are starting on the renovations this very moment," he says, with a smile. "They might be noisy," he tells me. "I have asked the men not to work too far into the evening so as not to disturb the children. We do want to get this project done as soon as we can so you can have access to the funds it will generate."

I thank him. I should feel more grateful than I do. But it is invasive – cutting my house in two. My space will be reduced to just over half the room I have now. The children will have half a playroom. Perhaps they can play outside more.

Two days after the renovations begin, Aunty Mary arrives unannounced. I'm getting ready for work, but she insists we talk.

"What is it, Aunty? What is so important that you have to talk to me right this minute?"

"Your father has asked that I bring you some news," she says. "I think you should sit down."

"Aunty, I don't have time to sit down. What is it? Just tell me!"

"All right, Amelia. Your father has informed me that Dwight's body is on its way here to Salt Lake City. He received a wire last night that it will arrive on the afternoon train. He asked that you be there to meet the train with him."

I cannot believe it. This can't be true. "But the obituary in the paper last week said he was already buried in Stockton. How can his body be arriving here? This makes no sense."

Aunty comes forward to hug me.

I step back, unable to accept her need for an embrace. "Haven't I put up with enough?" I spit out. "I want no part of this. How can Father insist I do this?"

"He's not insisting, Amelia. He's asking you to be there," she says, and then adds her own thoughts. "Your father decided that it wasn't proper for Dwight to be buried in Stockton, no matter what the paper said so he has arranged to bring him home to Salt Lake. Amelia, think about it. People will think it strange that a man's own wife wouldn't meet the train that is bringing his body home."

"Who knows except us?" I ask.

"Oh, Amelia. You should want to do this. He was your husband."

"I know he was my husband. But I am not going to meet the train. Father can do that."

"All right," Aunty stands and pulls on her gloves. "I will let your father know." She goes to the door. "You should also know that your father and I have decided that we will hold a gathering in honor of your poor dead husband. Now that we have the body, it is even more imperative that we do something. People are beginning to talk."

When I refuse to ask who is talking, Aunty continues, "Mrs. Bradley told me yesterday that she saw the obituary in the Salt Lake Tribune last week. She said it was sad that this terrible flu plague has taken one of our own. She mentioned that it was particularly distasteful when families didn't have funerals for their dear departed." Aunty tries again. "Everyone would like to help you mourn this tragic event. How can you expect to grieve if you don't provide an event? I want to offer you my home. You can invite as many people as you want."

"Thank you, Aunty, but I don't want an 'event.' I have already grieved. I don't need anyone's help. I know you're trying to be nice, and I appreciate that. But right now, I don't need this." A feeling of profound sadness wells up in my chest. I need to get out of the house. "No, Aunty!" I insist. "No. On both counts. I won't meet the body and I don't want a funeral."

"Oh, thank God, here's Manson," I finish as I hear the carriage approaching the house. I run for it, leaving Aunty standing in the doorway. It's a relief to climb into the carriage and be carried away from her. She won't understand – she can't understand how anyone can refuse to let her host an event. I know I haven't heard the end of this. I don't want a funeral or anything that brings back the memory of my life with Dwight. I relax a bit when I realize she probably can't have a funeral anyway due to the Health Department Epidemic Decrees.

Chapter 20

1923

Today is George's birthday. How can my solemn sweet boy be twelve years old already? Father's namesake. Dwight's son. My man of the house. Mother's grandson. It's interesting how those who are gone always feel close at times like this.

George is seated in the place of honor at the dining room table surrounded by his family and five of his school friends. Catherine and Eugene are here as well. I smile at the casual chatter of the boys as the adults seem to lean forward to listen. When it feels like enough talk time has passed, I retreat to the kitchen to get his cake.

It's been three years since Dwight's death and sometimes the memories still overwhelm me. "Amelia," I say out loud to myself, "don't let those memories make you too morose to enjoy this event." Not today. I take the cake into the dining room.

"The credit for the cake goes to Babe," I tell everyone. She may only be seven, but she's already a cook. I'll soon turn all the cooking duties over to her. She did this whole cake almost by herself."

Babe stands close to George in sisterly adoration of her big brother. She smiles proudly. "I made it just for you, Georgie."

George gives her a hug. "Indeed, Sister. You're such a clever little thing."

"I'm not little, Georgie. I'm big enough to make you a cake. So, I'm not little!" She stamps her foot.

We all laugh. George smiles at her. "You'll always be my little sister, with big emphasis on little." He knows his teasing will set her off.

Before the bantering gets heated, I interrupt. I've prepared what I want to say, but I'm not prepared for the emotion that overwhelms me as I look at my son on the edge of manhood. My voice breaks as I speak. "I want us all to toast this wonderful young man: George Deschamps. He has been a joy from the day he was born. May he have many more birthdays surrounded by those who love him."

Glasses rise, as much a blessing as a toast. George's friends raise their juice glasses and the adults, their wine goblets. George smiles, his eyes full of pride. He has had a good year at school and has been recommended for a full scholarship to the next level. A good thing. We no longer have funds to send him to a private academy. Father was distraught over the thought George would have to drop out and go to the public school in Salt Lake. Father thinks he gets a better education in a private facility. I don't see it myself. I think the public schools are fine. Besides David and Babe have no choice but to attend public school.

I light the twelve candles on the cake. "Blow out the candles, George," I tell him. "Or your wish won't come true."

Giving me a strange look, he says, "Don't be silly, Mother. I don't believe in wishes but I will blow out the candles." What an odd thing for a twelve-year-old to say.

As I cut the first piece and place it in front of George he exclaims, "Mother, the cake looks almost too scrumptious to eat!" George laughs, wide-eyed with amazement. The cake does look too good to eat – three thick layers of chocolate cake with nuts, figs, and raisins oozing out between the layers, covered in burnt-sugar frosting. George's favorite.

I serve the cake to the rest of the guests. The five boys grin their thanks and I tell them they can dig in. The sooner they eat, the sooner they're outdoors, and the sooner the adults can relax and get on with visiting.

In minutes the boys are excusing themselves. The house quiets as the last of them goes out the door, George calling to them that they are enough for a ball game. I can't help but admire their youthful energy.

Babe watches the troop of boys leave for the outside. I can see she wishes she could follow them. She sighs in resignation and announces that she wants to go and visit Tanya, the daughter of the family who has lived in the other half of our house since the renovations. The extra income has helped to keep us fed these past couple of years. The renovation idea was a good one and it brought Babe a good friend as well.

Once Babe goes next door, the adults finish their cake and tea, chatting. I sit gazing at the group: Father, of course, Aunty Mary and Uncle Quincy, Lucille and Earl, and Eugene and Catherine. They've all become indispensable. It's not that much has changed in the last few years but that I've come to feel less afraid that they might have more hidden plans for my life.

Father looks weary. He smiled all the time the young people were at the table, but I see now even adjusting his position in his chair makes him wince with pain. He troubles me. He says he is fine, but he has no energy. At seventy-three, he complains of arthritic aches in all his joints. It's been difficult for him since Dwight passed on, though the difficulty has had nothing to do with Dwight's death. After the funeral that only Father and Aunty wanted, Father seemed to lose his interest in work. It's a good thing he had turned the responsibility of his law practice over to a partner several years ago or that would have been additional trouble.

He scaled down his household. We said goodbye to Jane and Manson six months ago. They both found secure employment in Provo. They had plans to marry. I didn't see that coming. I haven't heard whether they did or not. I don't hear anything from them. I know the children miss them both.

Dotty is back with Father. Now that the children are older, he needs her more than I do. She is becoming his nurse as well as his housekeeper. I don't know how long that can continue. I asked Father Dotty's age the other day and he said she's sixty-six. I didn't realize she was that old. I know my grandparents took her in when she was ten, but I'm not sure when she came to live with us. She's just always been part of the household and age was never something I thought about.

When the conversation dies down, I stand up to gather the plates and cups. Having to give up servants has its pitfalls. I've learned to wash dishes and clean house. I find neither very satisfying, but I accept my fate. At least, between the house income and the small stipend from the business I can say I am succeeding in looking after myself and my children.

"I hate seeing you have to do this," Lucille says, assisting with clearing the table. "You know you don't have to do this. I'm sure Dotty would come and help you." Lucille has stopped offering to host all the family events – even my children's birthdays – at her house.

"It's not important Lucille," I tell her. "It's enough that Dotty looks after Father. She doesn't need to come here. I'm able-bodied. I can look after myself and the house. Besides, I have only half a house."

"Where is Dotty today?" Lucille asks. "She is usually with Father."

"She went to visit a friend. She told me she wanted Father to have time alone with his family, which I think is thoughtful of her. I do think of her as part of our family these days and I miss her."

Lucille nods and collects more plates before walking with me to the kitchen. It's strange that she doesn't quarrel with my saying that Dotty's a part of the family, but I keep that thought to myself.

"Thanks," I tell her. "I do appreciate your help, Sister."

"You're welcome," she responds. "I do have an ulterior motive. I want to talk to you about Father. Have you noticed lately how much he's aged? He seems to have no energy. He doesn't even come visiting and that worries me."

"I know," I answer. "He hasn't told me much about his health. He just chuckles when I ask and says, 'I'm just getting old.'"

Lucille continues, "I was so worried about him that I went to talk to Doc Parker. He says the same thing as Father does, that Father is just aging – and not to worry. Doc Parker is as old as Father is – so of course he says not to worry. That's all I could get out of him. He and Father are such good friends that he wouldn't tell me anyway. When I spoke to Father about it, he said he was fine, and told me not to bother the doctor with my silly worries. You know, Amelia, I offered to take Father into our house, but he said he didn't need any help and he didn't want to live with anyone but himself."

"That sounds like Father. Dotty takes good care of him. I'm sure if something was wrong, she would let us know."

Before Lucille can respond, the kitchen door opens, and we hear the ruckus as the boys return. George comes into the kitchen. "Mother, I'm ready for the rest of my party," he says.

I smile at the excitement on George's face. He's not too grown up to be excited about opening his gifts. I turn to Lucille, "Let's finish our conversation later. We seem to be holding up the party."

Lucille nods and we follow the sound of voices to the sitting room. We enter in time to see Aunty Mary and Uncle Quincy bringing in everyone's gifts that have been stowed in the hallway where George couldn't see them before the time was right.

Aunty and Uncle give him a large, brown, leather school case with silver buckles – perfect for his upcoming year in the private academy. He looks like a pint-sized lawyer. "It's real cow's leather," Aunty boasts. "It would cost a fortune here, but we got it in Europe for half the price."

Oh, dear God, leave it to Aunty to flaunt her wealth, especially when we're having such difficulties. Perhaps I should ask her for a loan for a year of living expenses. I bet that would go over like a pound of lead on a kite tail.

Ada's package from California comes next. George appears more intrigued by the stamps on the brown paper wrapping than by what might be inside the box. He examines the stamps in minute detail. Father coughs and grumps at him to "Move it along or I'll be dead before you open the darn box!" We all laugh. George dramatically rips the wrapping off the box in one swoop of his hand. He takes off the lid and peers in.

It's a beautiful quilt – birds and hunting scenes embroidered in green and blue tones – suitable for a young man. Ada has outdone herself. George reads the attached note aloud.

"Dearest George. I am delighted to hear you have passed the threshold of childhood and are on the brink of being a man. I want you to have something special, so you won't forget your old Aunt Ada who lives so far away. So, I made you a quilt. When you snuggle under it on those cold Utah winter nights, think of me. Have a happy birthday. Come and visit us next summer. You have five cousins you need to meet. They are anxious to get to know you.

Love from Auntie Ada and Uncle Clarence and the rest of the flock."

George, ever the proper young man, says, "It was very nice of Aunt Ada to make me a quilt. I'll write to thank her." He turns to me. "Mother, do you think I can go visit them next year?"

I can tell he's interested in going. "We might be able to arrange that, George. Perhaps we should all go. It's been a long time since we've seen any of them. I glance at Father. He's dozing in his chair.

George saves Father's gift for last. Aunt Mary nudges Father when George picks up the long narrow box. Father sits up in his chair, nods his thanks to her, and says to George, "No disrespect to all you other very generous people. But my gift is special. It's given when a boy becomes a man."

A look of understanding passes between George and Father. The gift isn't a surprise to George. He and Father know I will never approve of it. "A Winchester," George says as he opens the box. George's friends gasp, and then shout their approval. The adults burst into a round of applause. Why would anyone give a rifle to a twelve-year-old boy?

"Thank you, Grampa. That is the best gift," George says, his eyes shining. He walks over to Father and puts out his hand. Father takes his hand and puts his other one on top of George's smaller one and the two exchange a solemn handshake.

Father turns to me, "Now, Amelia, I know you're worried about George having a Winchester. But it's time he had the means to protect you and the other young ones. You don't need to be concerned. I'll take him hunting, teach him how to handle it in a safe manner."

Father means well, but I wonder how he will do that, given that he can barely lift the box that the gun came in.

"That's a good idea, Judge," says Earl, stroking the gun. "Every man needs a gun, and this one's a beauty. You're never too young to start knowing how to shoot and be safe. I'd be happy to help you teach the boy."

George smiles at Earl. "Thank you, Uncle Earl, I would like that very much." Father glances at me and nods, as if he heard the questions in my mind.

Lucille bends towards me as if to give me a hug but as she comes close, she says, "If it's any consolation, I think these men are crazy. A twelve-year-old doesn't need a gun, even if it is a Winchester."

I smile at her, glad to have someone on my side. Nevertheless, I have the feeling it won't do either of us any good to stand up against the men in the family, on this issue. I remember Mother's concern when Father went off hunting. She liked the meat they brought back, but she was always anxious until they returned. She told me about how her ten-year-old cousin went hunting one spring afternoon with the men and was killed by a shot through the head. One of the uncles mistook him for a deer. I think she imagined that would happen again when Father hunted.

When the party is over, George's young guests trickle out. It's been a pleasant time except for the gun. Father has been offered a ride home and as he leaves, he gives me a hug and whispers, "Don't worry, my dear. We'll take good care of George."

"Yes, Father, I know you will. That's what I'm afraid of."

He looks at me, exhausted, but smiles. "You women are all alike. Your mother used to hate it when I took the gun and went hunting. She always swore she'd never have a gun in the house. Guess she was wrong on that one."

When the time comes for hunting, we'll see who wins this one.

After Father leaves, Lucille suggests we have some more tea. "I have something I want us all to discuss," she says. George offers to settle Babe and David in their rooms and get them ready for bed. Eugene and Catherine offer to leave but Lucille tells them to stay.

We gather in the sitting room, and I serve tea and leftover cake.

"We need to talk about Father's health and his financial issue," Lucille begins.

"What financial issue?" I ask, confused. I don't know of any concerns more recent than the one that caused him to let the servants go.

"Father has put his house up for sale," Lucille announces. "Earl found out from a real estate client of his."

"What?" I exclaim. "That can't be possible." I turn to Eugene. "Has Father told you anything about this?"

Eugene sets his tea down. "This is the first I've heard of it. He has his own accountant for his personal financial

matters. He never said anything to me about his house."
Eugene looks serious and I know he is as concerned as
we are. I think Eugene admires Father more than he once
admired Dwight.

"It seems absurd that he would try to sell his house and
not tell any of us," is all I can say.

"Well," Eugene, ever the practical one, continues, "It's
not absurd if he wants to liquidate. Perhaps, he is thinking
of buying a smaller home?"

"But why wouldn't he confide in us?" asks Lucille.

"He has cancer," Aunty says, her tone betraying the
satisfaction she feels at knowing someone's secret. Uncle
shushes Aunty with a disgusted tone. "That information is
not yours to share, Mary," he barks.

I'm shocked. "Father has cancer? I didn't know he was
that sick. How do you know it's true? I can't believe it." It's
hard to know what to say. My poor father. Why wouldn't
he tell me?

Uncle looks at me and says, "About three months
ago, your father asked me to take him to see Doc Parker.
He confided in me what the doctor had to say. I made
the mistake of telling your Aunty his secret and she is
apparently unable to keep a confidence."

Aunty's mouth flies open, but nothing comes out. She
flounces out of the room in anger, or is it embarrassment?
It's hard to tell which. I've never heard Uncle speak to
Aunty in such a way before.

"I apologize for my wife's indiscretions," Uncle
murmurs, "but it's too late to be angry about it now." He
sighs. "We need to acknowledge the facts. Your father is

quite ill. Some treatment is available in California. It's very expensive. He's not as well off as he used to be. It seems he made a bad deal or two in Mexico – as Dwight did – and they both suffered financially from that. I think he wants to use the house money to pay for the treatment."

This is crazy. Father is ill, and he doesn't even tell me, his own daughter. "This family is full of secrets. It's maddening to me."

"What do you mean by that?" Lucille asks in a loud angry voice. "I don't think we have that many secrets."

"You can't be serious," Earl blurts. "Your family has more secrets than any family I have ever heard of. More secrets than you will ever know."

Unfortunately, Earl is right about that.

CHAPTER 21

I hear footsteps in the hallway and then on the stairs leading down to the kitchen. It must be Father stumbling around in the darkness, like he does when he's in too much pain to sleep. I drag myself out of bed and turn on the light. The clock says four. Good grief! I'll never get back to sleep worrying about him. I slip out of bed and put on my robe. One of these nights he's going to fall down the stairs – and then what will I do?

"Father, what are you doing up at this hour?" I ask, as I find him sitting on the landing of the stairwell, gasping for breath.

"I couldn't sleep." His voice is slow and laboured.

"I already figured that out. Are you in pain?"

"No," he answers, "Tired of being in bed."

"Want a cup of tea?" I ask.

"I think I'd rather have a snifter of brandy if we have such a thing."

I can't help but smile. Father was never much of a drinker. In fact, in his younger days, he would never allow it in the house. Now it seems no matter how sick he is, he's always up for a bit of brandy. In fact, Doc Parker told him it might be helpful to ease his pain. I can't help but smile.

I'm sure Mother would never approve, no matter what the reason. Guns and drink: two things she could not abide. I take his arm in mine and help him to the kitchen.

I pour the bronze liquid into a small glass and hand it to him. He reaches out to take it, but the tremors are severe, and he motions for me to put the glass on the table. I wonder if we will have to spoon-feed him before long. It's difficult to see him like this. His diagnosis came a year ago but there seems to be a different symptom every day

Father sold his house six months ago, just as Earl said he would and for all the reasons we spoke of back then. He used the money to start treatment in California for his sickness, but in a short time, it was clear the treatment wasn't working. In fact, he got worse. He became very depressed and returned to Salt Lake. In his weakened condition it didn't take much persuasion for him to move in here with me and the children. For all the trouble that has passed between Father and me, these days are different. Father has given up telling me what to do with my life and seems to enjoy my company. I must admit, I have come to enjoy his company as well. Like tonight, we sit and chat while he sips his brandy.

"It's nice here, Amelia. I don't say it very often, but I do appreciate your taking me in. More than anything I am grateful that you found a place for Dotty as well. She surprised me when she said she'd come with me to California and surprised me more when she agreed to come back to work for both of us here."

"Father, I'm surprised you didn't go live with Ada or Lucille. I'm sure their lives are more exciting than mine."

Father looks at me and smiles. "That's the precise reason I didn't go there. Their lives are way too busy for me. I wouldn't feel needed in either place. To tell the truth, I think I need those children of yours around me and I think they need some male influence around them. Perhaps I will continue to feel useful in my old age."

"You'll always be useful to us, Father. I just hope you and Dotty will be comfortable here for a long time."

"I think Dotty was a bit overwhelmed when you fixed her a room next to mine. It seems to be a perfect little place for her. I'm a little confused about how you made that happen, but she seems happy with it."

I smile at Father and watch him sip back his last bit of brandy. We made Dotty's room in what used to be my extra-large, closet. Now that there is little money for clothes, I don't need such a large closet. She can stay near Father and watch out for his needs in the night. Trouble is, she tends to sleep through his middle of the night wakeups, and I end up following him to the kitchen. Sometimes, I sit with him at the table, like now, while he talks about the old days. Sometimes, he prefers the sitting room where he'll choose a book to leaf through. There are times when the pain he suffers makes him grumpy. But with Dotty here to care for him through the day while I work, having him here hasn't been an imposition.

"I'm just happy that Dotty likes doing the cooking. It makes my life easier. I'm glad you talked her into taking a salary instead of just free room and board. She does so much for us these days," I tell Father.

"Yes, she does do a lot for us, and I don't think It's an easy job looking after me," Father says with a twinkle in his eye.

He has that right. Sometimes, he goes for days without having a conversation, even with me. Only a few of his old cronies from his judge days come by from time to time but sometimes when he's having a bad day, he tells them he can't see them. Those are his painful days. I'm told that's normal for a man with his disease.

"Well, Father, I'd appreciate it if you'd consider going back to bed. I'm never going to make it to work tomorrow if I sit any longer talking to you."

Father laughs and struggles to get out of the chair.

The next morning, I do in fact arrive late for work. "How is your father today?" Eugene asks. As usual, Eugene has arrived hours before me. He never seems the worse for wear. He says he enjoys the early morning hours because he gets more done when no one is around. How fortunate we are to have his services.

"He still manages to join us for breakfast, and he is able to drink brandy at four in the morning. I suppose that's positive."

"Oh, my goodness! Brandy at four in the morning?" Eugene responds chuckling. "Perhaps he is better off than we think."

"I think you may be right." I smile at Eugene. I like his amusing perspective.

"So, what's on the agenda for today?" I ask.

"Just some of the usual. I'm not happy about the order we sent to Chicago yesterday. I think there was some sort of mistake made."

Before I can ask what he means by that, a young, uniformed man comes in and stops at my desk. He takes a large envelope out of the leather bag slung over his shoulder.

He announces, "I have something for a Mrs. Deschamps."

"I am Mrs. Deschamps," I reply, curious.

He puts the yellow envelope on my desk, and I sign for it. The return address is Hyrum Smith Harris, Attorney at Law. I think I remember Dwight mentioning Mr. Harris, but I assumed he was another friend of Father's.

Inside the envelope is a letter folded in half and a small jewelry bag. I recognize Dwight's careful handwriting and the sudden shock of something so familiar takes my breath away. I open the letter with shaking hands and begin to read.

My Dearest Amelia:

I hope that, by the time you are reading this, you will be long past mourning my demise and be happily married to someone who deserves you. I hope you have chosen a man worthy to be the father of my children and one who will be able to make all your dreams come true. I shall attempt to look over our children from wherever the good lord has decided I should go. I am certain, that by the time you finish reading this epistle you will know for sure that I belong nowhere but in hell.

I am afraid my life was always tinged with the elements of sin and for that I make no apologies. It was what was handed to me. I wanted to be a good and faithful husband to you, and I hope I succeeded at least in that. However, it was an additional act of what some church officials might label as mortal sin that brings me to the conclusion of this letter and its reason for existence.

A great deal of thought has gone into the idea of whether to divulge this information to you, and I have decided that it is best for all involved that someone know what transpired in the days after the attack on you in Stockton, California. Your father has sworn me to secrecy, but I am sure if he is still on this earth when you read this that he can verify the events that took place.

I wish to confess that on the day following your attack, your father and I combed the bars, hotels, homes, and fields of Stockton to find Sam Goutière. We came upon him in one of the many ale houses in Stockton; from there your father and I removed him and rode with him into the desert. He arrived there unconscious. We stripped him of his clothing and left him to die. In the years since, I am aware that his parents have searched for him, but he has never appeared, nor have his remains ever been found. Your father was in favor of shooting him, but I was able to stop him from doing that. We left him without water or food or clothing.

When you became pregnant from that attack, I waited and watched for that child to be born. When it was, we knew that a terrible injustice had been done. That was no child of Sam's. Perhaps if your Aunt Mary is still on this earth, you should ask her what really happened to that child.

Now I have left you with a dilemma, and for that, I again apologize. Your world is so filled with secrets that perhaps this letter will give you answers to some things you must have wondered about for a long time.

Also enclosed with this letter you will find a certain trinket. I found it on the dresser in your hotel room the night of the attack on you. Sam's name engraved on the ring is what prompted our anger. It's been a burden for me all these years.

Know that I shall remember you with love until the day I die, and perhaps beyond.

Dwight

I drop the letter onto my desk. I open the bag and the ring on the chain that Sam gave me falls into my hand. I'm numb with shock and anguish. Why would Dwight write such a letter? I examine the ring and put it back in the bag. Long ago it was such a precious thing. Why would Dwight tell such a story? It cannot be true.

But in my heart, I know it is true. All these years I wondered why the mention of Sam's name brought such angry responses from both Father and Dwight. But I never thought that Sam could be dead. I thought he had just ridden away; that he didn't want to get involved. How could my father have done such a thing? From the beginning I told Father it wasn't Sam, but he didn't believe me until my baby was born and then it was too late. Sam was an innocent man. Dear God, now what do I do?

I look up and realize Eugene is staring at me with concern. "Are you alright? he asks.

"No, Eugene, I'm not." I hand him the letter. Maybe he will have some insight into what I should do with this.

I watch as he finishes reading. His head is shaking from side to side. "Ah, Amelia, what can I say? What can I do?"

"Eugene, how could Father do such a thing? Moreover, how could Dwight participate and then keep such a secret? How can my father live with himself?" I feel the anger building inside me. "What did Dwight mean about my poor dead child? This is all too much." I stand up. but Eugene holds up his hand.

"Amelia," he says, his voice calm. "Come sit down. You must think, my dear. Think before you act. What will you – what will we do about such a thing as this?"

"I'm going home to confront Father. Then I am going straight to Aunty's. They both have a lot to tell me, a lot to answer for. Oh, my god. I can't believe any of this." I sit down again. I pick up the letter, but the words are blurry through my tears.

"Amelia, we will close the office," Eugene says. "You must give yourself time to calm down before you confront your father or your aunt. You don't want to say something you will regret. We need to think about this. This is serious business."

"I need to go home now!" My voice rises. "I have to talk to Father. I must, Eugene. I have to know what he has to say."

"Catherine is very good at understanding things like this, Amelia," Eugene says. "Why don't we go and talk with her? She might have some ideas as to how to approach your father. If we don't handle this in a proper manner, your father and his reputation could be ruined. We don't want that. Please come home with me. You are troubled, and I don't blame you, but now is not the time to confront anyone about this. There could be serious ramifications."

Through a cloud of shock and disbelief, I see Eugene's point. Angry as I am, it would be terrible for Father to spend his last year under a cloud of gossip and disrespect, even if he deserved it. He's still my father. I wouldn't want him put in prison, especially now that he is so sick.

I nod to Eugene. "If you think it's best then I'll come with you to talk to Catherine."

"She'll be pleased to see you, Amelia. I know she can help." He brings me my cloak and reaches for his coat. "We should go now." Eugene says. He and Catherine live just a few blocks from the office. If nothing else, the walk will do me good.

As we walk, Eugene says, "You know that Catherine enjoys your children. She enjoys looking after them when they come home from school. She always says how well behaved they are."

I stop walking and turn to Eugene. "I know you're trying to distract me, but it won't work. I must talk to Father. I must get to the bottom of this. Catherine has enough to do without having to deal with my problems. I should go home."

"Amelia, Catherine will be more than happy to see you. I don't mean to put her nose in your business, but I think she would be a good person for you to talk to about this, her being a woman and all."

I sigh. It's hard to refuse Eugene. He's right. I do need a friend. I think of Eugene as my friend, but there are times when I need a woman's view of things.

When we get to the porch, Catherine comes to the door, looking surprised. "For heaven's sake, come in, come in," she says. "How delightful to see you, Amelia. What a nice surprise."

Catherine hangs my cloak and hat in the closet next to the front door, and I follow her into a large sitting room filled with plush chairs and settees. Small tables in the corners are covered in bright-colored, crocheted doilies held down by tiny ceramic figurines. Those are the only feminine touches in the room. The rest of the room is filled with bookshelves holding heavy leather-bound volumes of every size and shape. Eugene is proud to explain how he likes to present the volumes on the shelves based on their size and color rather than their title or author. He claims that by doing it that way, the room appears to have less clutter. Looking at all these books reminds me of Father and why I am here at all.

I sit down next to Catherine on a small couch and she asks, "To what do I owe this visit?"

"Catherine," Eugene starts. "Mrs. D. has received a letter from the past. She –"

"It's all right, Eugene," I interrupt. "It's better if I explain." I pull the letter out of my pocket and hand it to her. "I received this letter today. Dwight wrote it a few years ago, but I received it from his lawyer just today. It's so disturbing that I had Eugene read it. I thought he might have some insight as to how I should handle this."

Catherine takes the letter from my hand. After reading it through, she folds it and slowly places it back into its envelope. It seems like an eternity before she says, "Oh dear, how tragic for you. How tragic for your family."

She moves closer to me and puts her arm around me hugging me to her in a quick, but warm embrace.

"Oh, Catherine," I say, my voice louder than I intend it to be. "I'm so angry – and sad."

"You have the right to be angry," she replies. "Is Sam someone you knew well? I'm not sure what I'd do if I were in your shoes. What a terrible shock it must be for you."

I suddenly have the feeling that Catherine knows more than she is letting on. How could that be? She doesn't ask me any details as to what really happened, and I wonder if I should try to explain the whole story. On second thought, I'm too exhausted to go over all that again.

I ignore her question about Sam. How would I explain Sam? Instead, I tell her "As much as I hate the thought of what I might find out, I need to know the truth. My dilemma is that Father is so old, so fragile. I'm afraid to ask him about this in case it's too much for him. But I don't know how else to find out the truth. There isn't anyone left to ask."

"What about your aunt?" Catherine asks when I fall silent. "The letter seems to indicate that your aunt was involved in all of this in some way."

"I don't understand that part at all. Aunty was involved in delivering the child, but how would she know about anything else?"

Catherine looks at me for a few seconds and then says, "Well, from reading this letter I surmise that Dwight thinks she knows something about the father of the child – and maybe more than that. Maybe Dwight or your father told her more. I'm just guessing, but knowing your Aunt Mary, I bet that she knows more than most about this whole story."

Confused, I ask, "I still don't understand. The letter doesn't say anything about how the child is tied to Sam, does it?"

A look of understanding passes from Catherine to Eugene and Eugene nods as if passing on permission for some great confession.

When Catherine doesn't speak, I ask, "What are you trying to tell me?"

Eugene takes over saying, "Dwight confided in me that you had been the unfortunate victim of some terrible crime in Stockton. He said your father was quite certain that one of his work companions was to blame although he himself was not convinced. Dwight told me that he and your father had taken care of the culprit in their own way. I didn't question him further. I assumed he meant he went to the sheriff. He later confided that he realized your father was mistaken when your child was born dark-skinned."

"Oh no! I can't believe it!" I look from Eugene to Catherine and back again. All these years, Eugene – and Catherine – have both known my secret. "I didn't know you were privy to all this. I suppose I should be embarrassed but I feel relieved that you know. I do have one question. Eugene, why would my husband tell you all this?

My father's wish was that we must never talk about it with anyone outside the family."

Eugene smiles at me. "Dwight and I worked together for enough years that we developed a rapport. Sometimes Dwight didn't have the best judgement when it came to business decisions or investments, so I often helped him out. I know I'm but an accountant, but Dwight trusted me, and I think that's why he told me the things he told me. I hope you understand what I'm trying to say. I would never betray this confidence. Yes, I told Catherine but she's my wife and I tell her most everything."

I nod. "Yes, I see that." At least there is someone I can go to and not worry about hiding my past.

Catherine interjects, "Don't worry Amelia; I will never say anything to anyone. You have my promise about that."

I smile at her. I believe her.

"Now I think we all need a cup of tea and some sweets," Catherine says, smiling. "You two chat and I'll be right back."

While we wait for Catherine to return, Eugene turns to the subject of his books. I have the feeling he is trying again to distract me from the earlier conversation. He is excited over his recent purchase of a new volume. It's the latest in a series of murder mysteries. I am surprised by this revelation. "Oh, Eugene," I tell him, "I thought all these volumes related to work."

"Well, yes, I suppose many of them do, but if the truth be known I love a good mystery," he responds enthusiastically. "I especially like Edgar Allen Poe and his grisly tales. They must appeal to my darker side."

I smile at Eugene's excitement. It's not something I would attribute to him. I wonder if he has answers to all the mysteries in his books. I shake my head. "Eugene, how many books do you have on all these shelves?" I ask.

"At last count there were 945."

"Yes, 945 books and counting," says Catherine returning from the kitchen with a large tray of sweets and tea. She laughs. "This man does love his books. He guards each one as if it is worth a king's ransom." She laughs again. "They probably are. I never ask the price."

She sets the tray of pastries down on the table. "Help yourself, I made them," she says, full of pride. They do look delicious. I reach for one of the smaller ones – more not to be rude than out of hunger.

She pours tea for each of us and points to the milk and sugar. "Oh, in case you would like something stronger than milk or sugar, we also have rum." She picks up a small flask of the brownish gold liquid and offers to top up our tea. She smiles as she pours some in Eugene's cup. "Rum and tea. The perfect combination," she declares. She turns to me. "Would you like some as well? It might help to take your worries away."

"Yes, Catherine, I think I would." She pours a small amount into the tea, and I bring the cup to my lips. The tea is warm and smells of alcohol. I wonder how much I would need to drink to make my sadness and my anger go away.

I'm grateful that no one talks. We just enjoy the food. I sense they are giving me time to think about what to do before resuming the conversation.

When the food and drink are finished, and there's nothing left to do but talk, I tell them, "I wish I didn't have to talk to Father about any of this, but I need to know the truth. I do. I can't let this go. I can't just decide to believe it isn't true. If I don't find the answers, I will always wonder. I can't just forget about it."

I turn to Catherine. "The problem is I don't know how to talk to my father, Catherine. I'm afraid I might cry. Oh, God, to cry would be the worst. Father hates it when I cry. When I cry, he tells me I am being hysterical. I hate it when he says that."

"I'm sorry, Amelia. It sounds like you and your father have a difficult time of it. Perhaps I might make a suggestion?"

I nod, hopeful.

"What if you have your father read the letter and then ask him about it? Try to approach out of compassion and not in anger. If this is true, think of what he has been carrying all these years. He might be relieved to tell you about it."

"Do you think that's possible? Oh Catherine, I'm afraid of what he might say either way. What if it's true? What if my father really did murder Sam?" I blurt out Sam's name without thinking. My hand flies up to cover my mouth. I hope she doesn't ask about him.

"Well, if he admits it, you'll have to deal with that fact at that time. But maybe consider another question. How do you know any of this letter is true? What if it is just the imagination of a sick man who was out of his mind at the time?"

Eugene who has been sitting in the chair across from us, interrupts Catherine. "According to the date on that envelope, Dwight gave that letter to his lawyer before he left for the hospital in Stockton. I don't think he was that sick in his mind then."

"Well, it's something to think about." Catherine says. "Sometimes you can't tell about the state of someone's mind by looking at them." Catherine is trying hard to be helpful. She looks at the positive side of everything. I would like to be like that.

Turning to me, Catherine asks, "Would you like us to take you home now? I can see that you need to talk to your father to get any peace at all. Realize that what he has to say may cause you even more pain."

I nod. "Yes, I would like to go now. The children will be home from school soon and it would be nice for us to be there when they arrive."

"I'll bring the motor car around and give you a ride," Eugene offers. "Perhaps we can visit the children while you talk to your father. Would that be all right with you?"

"I would appreciate that," I tell him as he leaves to ready the motor car.

"You have a motor car?" I ask Catherine.

"Yes," answers Catherine. "Motorcars are Eugene's new interest. He bought it just a month or so ago. Eugene is convinced they are much cleaner than horses."

"But aren't they expensive?" I ask.

"Maybe a bit, but their price has come down dramatically from when they were first available. Think how much a horse costs, and you have to hire someone or have servants to look after them."

I never thought of it that way. It causes me to wonder why Father never bought a motorcar. They have been on the road for a long time now, but he never made a move to purchase one.

CHAPTER 22

My train of thought is interrupted by a loud moaning sound followed by a guttural beeping. "That'll be Eugene. That horn always makes me smile. Let's go." says Catherine, holding out my cloak and gloves.

On the street is a large black vehicle, with a silver grill and a funny copper winged ornament on the hood. Eugene leaps out of the driver's side and opens the back door for Catherine and me. I step inside and slide across the leather seat. This is more comfortable than the carriage I'm used to. Once we are both seated, Eugene takes the driver's seat, and we move off in the direction of my house. It is quite the sensation driving down the street in one of these. Not as bumpy as a carriage.

"How do you like the ride, Amelia?" Eugene asks me.

"It's very nice, Eugene. Luxurious."

We pull up to the house just as the children are coming home from school. They run up to us and are excited to see their mother get out of a Model T.

After all the oohing and aahing, Eugene asks them, "Children, would you like to go for a ride?" Hoots of joy and big grins tell me they would like that. He nods to

Catherine. "You go with Mrs. D. and I'll take the children for a ride."

As we hang our outdoor clothes in the closet, we meet Dotty carrying a tray with a bowl of stew and some brown bread on it. It smells wonderful.

"Hello," she says, smiling, "I'm taking some food up to your father. He doesn't feel well enough to come downstairs today. There's enough left for your supper. I'll sit with him while he eats and then come down and serve if you like. He doesn't seem to eat much unless I am there to oversee him. The children should be home any moment."

"We met the children coming in," I tell her. "They've gone for a ride in Eugene's motor car. They should be home in a while."

"Thank you for telling me," Dotty says.

I turn to Catherine. "I think I should wait until Father has eaten before I talk to him."

"Good idea," she answers. "I'll wait with you."

We make ourselves comfortable on a large couch in the sitting room. "I want to thank you, Catherine. I appreciate your kindness. It helps to be able to talk to someone about this and not have to feel I'm being judged."

Catherine nods and smiles, patting my arm. "My dear, I'm sure it will all be fine. I am just wondering what your Aunt Mary has to do with all of this. It sounds like she has a lot to account for. Maybe even more than your father."

Aunt Mary. I've been so concentrated on talking to Father that I have forgotten what the letter said about her. It intimates that she did something to my baby. I don't even want to think about that possibility. The baby died. What more can there be? "I'm going to fix a pot of tea," I tell Catherine. "Want to come and help me?"

We drink our tea and talk about the weather while we wait for Father to finish his supper. The subject of our visit lies heavy between us, but we don't discuss it further. In what seems like a long time, we hear Dotty coming down the stairs. That is our cue to visit Father but when we meet Dotty in the hallway, she is carrying a tray that doesn't appear to have been touched. As she passes us, she says, "He's feeling particularly ill this evening."

I turn to Catherine. "Maybe I should put this off?"

Catherine shakes her head. "There will never be a good time to do this. I think you should go and see what he says."

I hesitate, but Catherine encourages me. "Go on," she says, "I'll be here when it's over."

She's right. I must do this. I still can't believe that any of this is real. Perhaps it isn't. Perhaps I'm just having a bad dream and I'll awaken at any moment.

As I approach his room, the edges of the letter seem sharp between my fingers. How can words be so hurtful? I could turn around and go back downstairs and forget all this. I could pretend that it's the scribbling of a madman and means nothing. But I don't. I knock on Father's closed door.

"Come in," says Father. He has a cough again. He gets sick often these days. It's like he can't abide even the air in the house. I feel guilty coming to him like this.

"My dear Amelia," he says, smiling as I enter. He's sitting up against a pillow in the middle of his large bed. He looks fragile and old. "I'm sorry I couldn't come down for dinner tonight. I'm not myself this evening." He coughs, a deep guttural sound. I have the urge to take a few steps backwards, but I don't. I stand my ground next to his bed.

"It's all right, Father. I noticed you didn't eat very much. I'm sorry you aren't feeling well."

"I ate enough," he tells me. "I don't require much food these days, I'm afraid. But how was your day?"

"Actually Father, today was rather distressing."

"I'm sorry to hear that," he says. "Come and sit closer. Tell me what's going on."

Why didn't I just blurt it all out before he had time to be concerned for me? I take a deep breath and pull a small chair closer to his bed.

"I received this letter. It is the source of my troubling day," I say, pushing the letter into his wrinkled and trembling hand. "I want you to read it and tell me what you think."

He looks at me and then down at the letter, confused. "All right, but I shall need my pince-nez for this exercise, dear. Could you hand them to me, please?"

I find his funny spectacles on his armoire. I hand them to him, and he snaps them onto his nose with tiny pincers attached to the nose piece. They look uncomfortable. I've seen him in this contraption before, but tonight it just makes him look even older and sicker than he is.

"Now, what is this that it's so important you want me to read it now? Why can't you just tell me what it is?"

"Please, Father, just read it. I don't know how to tell you about it."

He sighs and begins to read. The farther he reads, the more his hands shake. As he gets to the bottom, the letter flutters to his lap. I pick it up and put it in my pocket.

"How in God's name did you come by such a letter?" he asks, eyes moist and wide.

"I want to know if what Dwight says in that letter is true. Did you and Dwight – do away with Sam like Dwight says?"

"What? No! Of course not! What kind of a man do you think I am? It's all lies. Every word of it. Good Lord, Amelia, I'm a judge! Why would Dwight say such a thing? I can't believe that Dwight would write such an epistle." He pauses and then he exclaims, "He must have been mad. You know at the end he was hallucinating. Yes, that's got to be it, he was mad by then. He could say anything in that state."

"Father, according to the date on the letter, he still had long periods of lucidity when he wrote it. He was sick, but he wasn't insane. His words aren't the words of a madman. Even his script is smooth and well written. He wrote it before we sent him away to California. He carefully dated it and gave it to his lawyer to send to me choosing a time he thought would be long enough after his death that it wouldn't be so traumatic. Those are not the signs of a madman."

"I don't know what to say. Do you think I am capable of such a thing? I suppose you think your Aunt Mary is capable of something equally horrific. There's nothing to say about any of this, Amelia. Except it isn't true. I wouldn't kill anyone. I was angry – but not angry enough to kill."

I stand staring at my father. He stares back at me, his expression defiant. Catherine's words about compassion come back to me. "Father, I believe you. I believe you didn't kill him. Just answer me one thing. Did you and Dwight take him into the desert and leave him there?"

"No, no, of course not." He pauses and then continues, "I mean – I mean ... God, it was a long time ago! My mind doesn't work well these days."

I sit down on the edge of the bed. "I'm trying not to judge you, Father. Only God can do that. But I need to know what happened to Sam. Dwight says you beat him, took his clothes, and left him to die in the desert. Is that how you remember it?"

"No, no, I don't know. I don't remember." He pauses, and sighs. I can see his pain. His eyes are watery. I wonder if they are tears or just the mist of sickness and old age. This hurts too much. I need to leave. Just as I am about to head for the door, he struggles to sit up more on his pillow. He asks for another pillow behind his back, and I bring it to him.

When settled, he looks at me and I recognize a kind of resignation in his voice as he says, "I'm too old for this, daughter, but I know you need to know the truth, so I will tell you what I know. At first, I believed Sam did that to you. I wanted to kill him, but I didn't. I know I didn't. Maybe he isn't dead. Show me the body. Even his own family doesn't know if he's dead or not."

He is interrupted by a fit of coughing that goes on for several minutes. I reach for a handkerchief sitting on his night table and help him wipe his mouth. Dotty knocks and then comes in. She walks to the bed and sits next to him, plumping his pillows and wiping his brow. I stare transfixed. There is an intimacy between them.

"I can't talk anymore. Please leave me, Daughter. I can't talk anymore." His hands are shaking more now. His brow is furrowed, and his eyes beg me to leave him alone with Dotty. She holds his hand and is trying to calm him

Before I leave, I bend over him and whisper I love him, kissing his wrinkled cheek. I can't explain this gesture. It's not something I say very often to Father, but it feels like the right thing today.

"I know," he whispers back. "But I wouldn't blame you if you didn't."

I pull the door shut behind me and make my way down the stairs. As I reach the landing, I feel sad and euphoric at the same time. At the bottom I sit on the steps to think about what Father has said and how I feel about it. Is this what real love is? When you love a person even though they've done despicable things? When you forgive and go on caring? I feel Dwight's presence, and remember I never got the chance to tell him goodbye. My thoughts about Father and Dwight are all intermingled tonight.

The noise from the sitting room catches my attention and I follow the sounds. The children are back from their ride with Eugene. He looks comfortable sitting at the table helping David with his schoolwork. Catherine is drinking tea and chatting with Babe. It's a charming scene, much better than the one I left upstairs.

Catherine gets up and puts her arms around me, asking, "How did it go?"

I move out of her embrace and grimace. "I'm sad, but It wasn't as bad as I thought it would be."

"Did he own up to any of it?" Catherine asks as she moves back to her seat.

"What are you talking about?" asks David, looking up from his schoolwork.

"Oh, nothing of interest to you, David. Just old people talk," I answer.

"Sounds serious to me," David continues. "You said you're sad Mama. Why are you sad?"

"I'm tired is all. Just tired."

"I don't think so, Mama. You look sad."

Eugene intervenes with a question from David's schoolwork and they both turn back to their project. David knows me too well. He always seems to sense how I feel about things. I must be more sensitive around him from now on.

Catherine and Eugene stay for dinner to finish the food that Dotty prepared earlier. They linger after the children are off to bed.

"Did your father offer you any explanation?" Catherine asks, resuming our conversation.

I tell her the basics of what Father said and she listens. "I felt sorry for him. Honestly, Catherine, he is frail and old. What is the use of any of this? I realized halfway through that no matter what he might have done, I forgive him."

"That's good, Amelia. Forgiveness is healing. Did you tell him that?" Catherine asks.

"No, I just told him I love him. It seemed the right thing to do."

Catherine moves close to me and puts her arm around my shoulders. "Good for you," she says, "and telling him you love him is also good for the soul."

I tell her and Eugene again that they must never tell anyone about any of it – what happened to me or what my father and Dwight might have done. They both promise. I trust them, but I feel better having reminded them.

"What about Aunt Mary?" Catherine asks when there's a pause in the conversation. "Did he say anything about her part in this? What exactly is she accused of?"

I don't speak. After a long pause, Catherine says, "It's all right if you don't want to tell me. I understand."

"It's not that I don't want to tell you Catherine; it's just I'm not sure I know how."

"Well, take your time. Whatever you say will never leave this room."

I nod. "I don't think my child died a natural death."

Catherine sits wide-eyed and upright in her seat, a look of sad disbelief on her face. Eugene is sitting close to her. He puts his arm around her in comfort.

"That is a serious accusation. Are you going to discuss this letter with your aunt?" Catherine asks.

"I have to," I answer. "Visiting Aunty will be my next step."

Catherine nods and adds, "We will go with you if you like, Amelia." Eugene nods.

***

A few days later, on a Saturday afternoon, Eugene and Catherine arrive to pick me up in their motor car. Eugene comes to the front door and steps inside. "I just want you to know I sent one of the workers from the factory to inquire of your aunt whether she would be home today and could see us. The worker says she would be delighted to have a visit."

"I wonder if she will be so delighted to see me when she finds out what I want to discuss with her," I tell him.

"Amelia, it's best that she doesn't know beforehand."

I laugh, "I was just making a sarcastic remark, Eugene."

"Oh, I see," he replies, smiling, "I'm afraid I'm not very good at sarcasm."

We walk the few steps to the motor car. Catherine is sitting in the front seat under a blanket and welcomes me with a smile as I slide onto the back seat. She turns to face me, and I smile back at her. "It's good to see you smile today," she tells me. "I was afraid you might be having a difficult time recovering from the talk with your father."

"I peeked in his room to see him this morning, but he was sleeping so I haven't really talked with him since our last discussion. He hasn't left his room since then either. It's probably just as well. According to Dotty he hasn't slept well since then. I think I've caused him quite enough pain for now."

"But how are you feeling about everything by now?" Catherine asks.

"I don't know how I feel, Catherine. Sometimes, I'm overwhelmed. Sometimes, I'm sad. Sometimes, I'm angry. I don't even want to visit Aunty today. I almost don't care what she has to say. No, that's not true. I do care. But it's so sad to think about and it was so long ago. I've tried hard over the years to put it out of my mind. This just brings it all up again."

"Haven't you ever wondered what happened to your child?" Catherine asks.

"I assumed that he died as soon as he was born. It was a difficult birth. Aunty was distraught at the sight of him. Dwight was too – he told me that. I assumed there was something very wrong with him. Aunty wouldn't let me see him right after he was born, and I was so worn out that I never asked again. By the time I wondered, he had already been buried."

"How awful. What a terrible thing to go through," Catherine says. She has such a compassionate way about her. I'm glad she's here with me.

"I guess it is a terrible thing to go through, but I've often thought a child conceived under such circumstances shouldn't live anyway. I thought his dying was an act of God."

A look of horror crosses Catherine's face. "God wouldn't do such a thing, Amelia. He loves all his children, even those conceived in violence. He doesn't cause such tragedy for his children."

I'm not in the mood to argue religion with Catherine. Her statement startles me. I think this may be one subject we can't share in the future.

Aunty greets us by flinging herself out the door dressed in a black blouse that sparkles and a long shiny black sateen skirt with a fuchsia sash. I can't help but smile at her outfit. No matter what the occasion she always looks like she is ready for a fancy party.

"Come in, my dearies," she exclaims, folding me in a tight hug and planting a wet kiss on my cheek. "Catherine and Eugene, this is indeed a pleasure to see you two again. It's been a while since I've seen you. I think it was George's birthday, if I recall correctly. Welcome."

"Thank you, Mary, it's a pleasure to see you again," Catherine states, though I suspect she's not quite as sincere as she sounds.

Eugene nods to Aunty, and then tells us, "I'll leave you two ladies here and return in an hour or so to pick you up."

"Thank you," Catherine says and nods to him. They must have planned this beforehand. I wish he would stay, but I can understand why he would think it better to leave us women to talk on our own.

We take off our outer clothing and Aunty leads us to the sitting room sending orders for hot drinks and sweets. I take a comfortable-looking chair next to Catherine and try to relax. I would rather not be here. Aunty is in such a good mood. She is as flamboyant as ever, but she seems happier than I've seen her in a long time. My questions will change all that.

We chat about the weather and how cold it is. Did I know that Edith Young had a baby girl? I didn't.

"To what do I owe this visit?" she asks as the servants bring in trays of cheese and bread and sweets. "Since you sent me a notice of your visit, am I to understand you have some exciting news you want to tell me? You haven't decided you want to marry again, have you?" she asks with a twinkle in her eye. "If so, I might know someone I could match you up with."

I nearly choke on my tea. "No Aunty, nothing like that." Not knowing what to say, I blurt, "These sweets are very nice. Where did you get them?"

She chuckles, "My new chef made them." The room grows quiet and after a long sip from her cup, Aunty turns to me and asks, "Tell me your news. If not a plan of marriage, then what?"

I take a deep breath and turn to Catherine. "If you don't mind, I'd like to speak with Aunty alone."

"Of course, Amelia. I'll go to the kitchen. I'd like to talk to the chef about his wonderful sweets." She gathers up our dishes as she leaves and smiles at Aunty as she passes. I wonder what she's thinking.

Aunty looks puzzled. "I don't understand. Is this a personal issue?" she asks.

"Yes, Aunty, it is," I answer.

Aunty moves her chair closer to mine.

"Aunty, something has been brought to my attention and I want to ask you about it."

Aunty looks at me and nods.

"I'm not sure how to bring this up," I stop and take a deep breath. "Aunty, I need to know what happened to my baby that died."

"Oh, my goodness!" The words pop out of her mouth and her eyes grow round. "What – Why are you asking about this now?" she asks. "Why now?" she repeats, as if I didn't hear her question the first time. "Whatever has brought this on now, dear child?"

"I am not a child. It's a simple question. What happened to the baby? It doesn't matter what has sparked the question. All that matters is that you answer it. I want the truth, Aunty."

"Of course, you do, dear, and I will give it to you. There is nothing mysterious about it. The baby was born dead, and I sent it to the undertaker." She moves away from me as she speaks, turning her head as she shifts her position.

"No, Aunty. That's not what I want. I want the truth. That was the story you told at the time. But I know there is more to it than that."

Aunty looks at me. Her eyes go dark and what softness was in her demeanor is now gone. "The real truth?" she asks, "You want the real truth?"

I nod. "Yes, Aunty. Please."

"The baby was born. I looked at it, and I did what I always do when a baby is born that isn't quite right, if you know what I mean."

"No, Aunty, I don't know what you mean. What do you mean by 'isn't quite right'?"

"Well, you know, has a deformity or is too weak. You look at the little thing and you know it's just not right. Like a mental deficient."

I feel chilled to the core. "What I always do when a child isn't quite right." All of a sudden, I realize we are no longer talking about just my child.

"I do what other midwives do. We kiss their little heads and then lay them naked in the snow until they stop moving. In the summer, we find other ways. God doesn't want them to live, and he always takes them quickly. Can you imagine what a burden they would be to their families? It's an unpleasant job that someone needs to do."

The breath has nearly gone out of me when she pauses. I want this to be a dream.

"Aunty, was my child a mental deficient?"

After several moments of silence, Aunty answers, "No. But some might think it was even worse than that."

"What then? What was wrong with my child that you had to dispose of him?" I want to say murder, but the words won't come.

She moves closer to me and looks into my eyes. "My dear naïve child! I did what I did out of love – it was the most merciful thing to do. I knew your life would be so much easier without that child. And it has been. No child brought into the world as a result of such a terrible circumstance should live. Think if it grew up. You would blame it for your pain, and it would never understand why you didn't love it. Besides, these children always become criminals."

I put my head in my hands. A few moments pass before I can look at Aunty. God, what am I going to do now?

Aunty continues. Her words tumble out as she tries to convince me of the rightness of her actions. "You have other children, and they are beautiful. If that poor thing had lived, it would never have fit in. It was, it was – it was very dark-skinned. Everyone would have asked questions. It would have been a very bad mark on your family. You must admit, that would not have been good for your family."

That poor child, my poor Aunty, poor me. I discover a piece of myself that has been missing for a long time and now has been found. I might die in my misery. I must get out of here. I stand, trembling. All I can say is, "God help us all."

Aunty gets up when I do. "What is that supposed to mean?" The self-righteous tone of her voice shocks me.

"It means just what I said. God help us all – especially you, Aunty. Don't you know what you have done? Don't you see the wrong in all of this?" I step away from her as I speak. I have to get as far away as possible from her, from what she's done – to my child, to other children.

Anger flashes across Aunty's face. Her jaws clench and she trembles, taking a step towards me. I step back some more. She sucks in a rasping breath and raises her voice. "No, Amelia, I don't. You should thank me for saving you from a lot of heartbreak. It's over. I'm sorry that you are upset, but I can't do anything about that. I can't bring that child back and furthermore, I wouldn't if I could."

She can't bring the child back, but how can she not feel some remorse for its loss? How many mothers have suffered the loss of a child because of her misguided actions? I never want to see this woman again as long as I live. Then, I hear Catherine's voice in my head. "Compassion, compassion," it repeats.

I leave without saying anything more. Catherine is standing in the hall. She puts my cloak around my shoulders, and her arm stays around me. Out of the corner of my eye, I see Aunty sitting in her chair with her head bowed.

CHAPTER **23**

1927

Early in the morning on the first day of the new year Dotty wakens me by bursting into my room in great distress. "Oh, Missus," she says, out of breath, "You must come. Your father has fallen. Please come. Hurry!"

"Oh, no. What happened?" I ask frantically trying to throw on my dressing gown. I follow her down the hall to Father's room where I find him on the floor moaning in pain.

"I couldn't lift him," Dotty wails. "I tried, but he's too heavy for me."

Dotty's panic matches my own. I kneel by Father's side and put my ear to his chest. Is he breathing?

"It's okay, Amelia. Not dead yet," he mutters as he tries to push me away. I snap up at his voice.

"Father, how can you joke?" I say, annoyed at first. But my voice softens as he moans again.

"Where does it hurt?" I ask as gently as I can.

Father struggles to sit up, but he winces and slumps back to the floor. "Shoulder," he whispers. I try to help him up, but everything I do causes him more pain.

I'm about to send Dotty for George when George appears at the door, bleary-eyed and confused. "What's all the noise?" he asks. Then he sees Father. "Oh gracious, what's Grandfather doing on the floor?" George scoops Father off the floor as though he weighs nothing and lays him on the bed.

How thin Father is. In the past few months, I've seen him only under thick quilts and heavy bed clothes. It hadn't dawned on me how fragile he has become. "I'm calling Doc," I say.

"I don't need a doctor. I am fine," I hear Father murmur as I leave the room.

I ignore him and go downstairs to the telephone. Doc Parker's wife says that he's out on a call. I tell her to send Doc to us as soon as he arrives back and that it's urgent.

When I return to Father, his eyes are half shut, and his breathing is laboured. Dotty is sitting next to him holding his hand. Her eyes are closed. Their lips are moving in sync though I can't hear any words. I'm tempted to interrupt but think better of it. I watch and wait.

After a minute or so, Dotty raises her head and opens her eyes. "We were asking for God's help," she tells me.

Father opens his eyes as Dotty finishes, "I'm helping Dotty pray," he says. His voice is weak, but I can still hear the humor in it. "Though she seems to do just fine on her own." As he speaks, Father's words get clearer and firmer. That must be a good sign.

"It's okay. We need all the help we can muster right now," I tell them. "Praying is a good idea. The doctor will be here soon."

Dotty smiles at me and turns to Father. She strokes his hand as if that might ease his pain. There's that intimacy between them again. Mother should be doing that, not Dotty. The thought slips into my mind, though Mother died more than twenty years ago. Father smiles at Dotty's attention to him and covers her hand with his own.

I should be grateful to Dotty for the way she cares for Father. But the gratitude doesn't come, and I go to wait for Doc. Father doesn't seem to need me anyway.

I must keep myself busy until Doc gets here. I go to my room to wash my face, brush my hair, and get dressed. I resent how much time it takes to look after long hair. Maybe I should cut it into one of those new bobs. They're so fashionable these days.

By the time I get downstairs again, more than an hour has passed and I hear a motor car stop outside the front door. I remember Doc's fine roan-colored horses and black carriage. Now he drives a black motor car. Black, the color of death.

Once inside, Doc sets his large black bag on the floor while he removes his hat and coat. "Ah, Amelia, how wonderful to see you again. It's been a while," he greets me. "George says your father has had a fall."

"Father says his shoulder is causing him pain. I apologize for calling you out, but he seems so fragile and I'm afraid for him."

Doc Parker smiles at me. "Calling me is the right thing to do. Falls are never a good thing for us old people. I'll go up and examine him." Sometimes I forget that Doc is my father's age. He seems to have endless energy and boundless good spirits.

I settle myself in a comfortable chair in the sitting room. Why is there so much sadness? Why must people suffer so much? My mind is filled with the woes of the world.

David and Babe come down the stairs still dressed in their pajamas, their faces showing concern and fear. "What's wrong with Grandfather?" Babe asks. "Is he going to die?"

I should tell her the truth – that I don't think he has much life left in him. But how can I tell her the truth when I can barely admit it to myself?

"Doc is still with Grandfather," George responds to Babe. "Dotty's waiting just outside his room." He grins, attempting to be funny. "It seems that all Grandfather needs these days is Dotty." He laughs, but stops when he sees I don't find it funny. I wonder if he is as uneasy with that situation as I am.

"How would you like to get something to eat?" I ask the children. "It's been a long morning. Would everyone like that?" I ask, hoping for some diversion.

"I can always eat," David tells me with a grin. At least one of us has cheered up.

The other two nod and I go to the kitchen. I'm not in the mood to cook porridge or anything for that matter. Instead, I put bread, cheese, and part of a lemon pie left from supper on a tray and pull some plates down from the shelf. Who cares if it's not breakfast food? I boil water for tea. Babe comes in, asking if I need help.

"Yes, that would be nice," I answer. "Carry the food and the plates into the other room and I'll bring the tea and its fixings."

The children laugh when they see pie for breakfast. I'm glad it brings them some brightness in a day that could be difficult. Over food the children start telling stories to each other about Grandfather. One of the tales is quite funny and it fills my heart to see them laugh so uproariously, especially at a time like this. Maybe it's their way of coping with their fear.

Doc Parker comes downstairs. "Amelia," he says, looking tired and less than cheerful. "I need to talk to you about your father."

The children turn toward Doc Parker with anxious faces.

"I'd prefer to talk to Doc Parker alone." I tell the children. Find something to do outside. I'll come and let you know about Grandfather as soon as I finish talking with Doc."

"We're not children," David retorts. "Every time something happens in this family, we get sent away."

I'm surprised by this outburst from David. He is usually my compliant child. He's probably right about being sent away when there's bad news. I keep thinking of them as babies.

George interjects good naturedly in a weird British accent, "We'll all go outside for a while. I'll tend to these underlings." He laughs as he says it. David and Babe frown at him and make funny faces, but he pays no attention and playfully herds them out the door. George always comes to my rescue.

"Thank you, George." I call after him. He turns back and smiles his now-you-owe-me-one smile.

I turn back to Doc Parker who has taken a seat at our dining room table.

He sighs. "I am sorry," he says as he takes the cup of tea I push toward him. "The situation is more serious than I thought." He takes a sip of tea, then continues, "The cancer in your father's lungs seems to have gotten worse. That's why his breathing is so laboured. The cancer is taking his life, Amelia. I am sorry, but there isn't much I can do except offer something to lessen his pain."

"Oh no. I knew he was slowing down, but I thought it was just a part of being old. What about the fall?"

"He's quite bruised, but I didn't detect anything broken, which, given his fragile condition, surprises me. He's in good spirits. He was joking with me. This disease seems to be progressing at a pace faster than I had hoped." He sighs again. "He likely won't live more than another month or two at the most. I'm sorry, my dear." He pauses for a moment. He rubs the back of his neck and I suspect that he is close to losing his composure. He and Father have been friends for many years.

"I'm sorry to have no good news," he says, putting his hand over mine. "You have seen much sorrow in your life, haven't you, Amelia?"

I nod. I'm sad, but somehow, I feel tired more than anything, not teary. I want to lie down and sleep. I wonder what the children will say.

"Yes, well. Good then," Doc Parker says in parting. "I'll come by every day from here on and give your father something to ease his pain, though I suspect I can teach Dotty to do that. He's very lucky to have such an attentive nurse. I'll see how it all goes. See you tomorrow. I can show myself out."

I see him to the door anyway and as it closes, the children return. "Come with me to the sitting room," I tell them. "We need to talk."

They're quiet. I'm sure they have some grasp of what is going on. "The doctor says Grandfather's very sick. He has a disease called cancer in his lungs. We need to help him rest as much as possible. Do you want to ask any questions about this?"

"Is Grandfather going to die soon?" David asks me. He's on the verge of tears.

I nod. "Yes, David, I'm afraid he is. Our job is to make these last months as comfortable for him as we can."

"I'm going to visit Grandfather in his room every day," Babe announces. "Every day when I come home from school, I'm going to say hello to him. When he dies, I think I'll be sad."

"Babe, you have such a way of saying things," George tells her.

"What's wrong with what I said?" she's defiant and ready to cry at the same time.

"You're our funny little sister, that's all," David says. "You're awfully blunt. If you stay that way, nobody will ever want to marry you."

"David don't say that to your sister," I tell him, surprised that such a comment came from him. "I'm surprised you think that about girls and whether someone would marry them or not. I suppose you think girls are dumber than boys as well."

"Of course, they are Mother. That's a fact," he tells me, smiling. Then he adds, "I'm making a joke, Mother." He raises his hands in defense. "I would never think you were dumber than a man."

"Thank you," I mutter. "In the future I hope you will be more careful with your jokes. Sometimes, they aren't as funny as you think. Do you understand?"

He looks at me, and then puts his head down sheepishly. "Yes, Mother." He gets up, comes to me, and offers a hug. I gather him into my arms like I used to when he was a small child. It's good to feel the warmth of him. I need him. I need all my children, especially now. "We need to work together and help Grandfather as much as we can in the coming days. He might not be here much longer, so we need to keep him as comfortable as we can."

"I wonder what it feels like to die," Babe says, as she snuggles up to me on the chair for her hug.

"I don't know, Babe. I don't know."

"Will you be sad when Grandfather dies?" she asks.

"Yes, we'll all be sad. He has had a good life, but it will be sad." I hug her close to me.

When I return to work a few days later, Eugene is at the office door. "Good to see you back," he tells me. "How's your father?"

I take off my coat and boots and tell Eugene about Father's fall and the doctor's visit.

Eugene nods. "He didn't look well to me the last time I saw him. He confided that he was not having a good time of it. Such a diagnosis is more ominous than I had expected. It is a sad time indeed." He studies me for a moment. "Is there something I can do to ease this time for you?" he asks.

"You could pay a visit to Father. He seems to want people around and he still has a sense of humor. Thank God, he has Dotty. She's an excellent nurse." I'm trying to be grateful. "She watches over him like a mother hen with one chick."

"I'll be glad to visit the judge. He's always treated me well and his kindnesses are many. He was a good man."

"He is a good man," I correct Eugene. It's such an unusual occurrence for me to be correcting him. It has always been the other way around. "He isn't dead yet," I remind him.

"My apologies. You are correct. It'll be a terrible thing when he passes on. I can't imagine it." Eugene looks very solemn. We stand there, neither of us able to get to work.

"I don't want him to suffer," I say. "The doctor comes every day to give him medicine for his pain. He's thin and he's having a difficult time eating and he fell out of bed. Did I tell you that he fell out of bed?" I look at my hands: they're shaking. Listing all the things that are happening to Father has made me realize how sick he is. Today, his suffering is mine as well.

"Yes, Amelia, you told me," he says. His voice is gentle and he's smiling.

I look into the caring face of my wonderful friend and wonder how I ever thought he was odd.

***

It's been three months since Father's prognosis and winter is changing to spring. It hasn't been an easy time. Along with Father slowly fading away, George has gone off to university, so there is an emptiness in the house we are all trying to get used to. The sun is just coming up and the light streams in the windows as I pass by Father's room on my way to breakfast. The light cheers me. Dotty is fussing over Father, trying to adjust his pillows.

"Can I help?" I ask her as I approach the bed. "What are you trying to do?"

"His breathing is weak today," she replies. "Let's lift him so he's sitting up a bit more. That'll help him breathe easier."

I place my arm around Father's back and attempt to ease him farther up on the bed while Dotty slides more pillows under and around him. It must be an awful thing for him to be so dependent on us. He doesn't respond when we move him or when I reach for his hand and hold it for a moment. I hope it means he has no pain.

"Now, you ought to feel better. Won't be such an almighty struggle to get some air into you," Dotty tells Father, patting his shoulder. He opens his eyes and looks at her, a slight smile crossing his lips. He moves his head to look at me, but I see no sign of recognition.

"He doesn't know me," I tell Dotty.

"He knows you, dear. Just the same way he knows me. It's the medicine. Makes his brain all foggy. He's been in and out of his head all night. Now his breathing is making a racket. Hear that? Hear that nasty rattle?"

I nod. "It's frightening, Dotty. Why is it like that?" I ask.

Her eyes are sad as she says, "It's a sign he's got little time left. If the children have something they need to say, they ought to come and say it as soon as they can. He may not react to them, but I think he knows inside what's happening. Hopefully, he'll last until they get home for lunch."

"You know a lot about this business of dying, don't you?" I ask. It's more of a statement than a question.

"I've seen some in my life. It's a thing, like birth. Certain things happen in a certain order and then it's over. Birth is usually a happier time than dying." She shakes her head, as if to rid herself of some long-ago memory.

I'm startled by the clarity of Dotty's explanations. Talking was never her strong suit. She's begun to talk more since she took on Father's daily care. It's as if she now has something to say. What would I do without her? I'd have to hire someone else, and I know Father wouldn't like that. Or I'd have to take care of him myself. I don't want to do that. I don't think I could do that.

"I appreciate the care you give Father, Dotty. You have been a great help to my family. I want you to know that." We're standing one on each side of Father's bed as I say this to her. Father doesn't seem to be aware anyone is nearby.

A look of surprise crosses Dotty's face and she seems embarrassed. "Thank you. He's always been kind to me. It's right that I should give back."

Before I can speak again, Father opens his eyes and raises his arm off the bed. It's a small gesture and it startles me. His lips move, and he calls my name. His voice is so faint that I almost can't hear him. "Amelia."

I bend over him and feel his hand caress my face. "I love you, dear Daughter. Take care of your beautiful children. I'm sorry for the wrong I caused you. Pray for my soul."

"Father," I tell him, "I forgive you. I love you. Are you in pain?" I take his hand in mine and hold it to my face.

"No," he mouths. Then he whispers, "I'm just tired, dear. I need to sleep."

I sit by his side holding his hand in mine until he's fast asleep. When I return, will he be gone? I sigh and tell him again that I love him, even though this time he gives no sign that he hears me. The sadness is overwhelming. I let go of his hand and turn towards Dotty. I look into her eyes and feel close to tears. I shake them off.

"Dotty, it's time for me to get to work. Let me know if his condition changes, please. When the children get home for lunch, perhaps you can tell them to talk to him and say what they need to say."

"I'll tell them. And I'll let you know if he gets worse. This morning, when he was in his right mind, he asked to see Mary. Why, I don't know, but I'm passing his request on to you. He asked and he was very firm about it."

Aunty. I haven't thought of her since my visit and my decision that I would never speak to her again. I should tell her that Father will soon die. But the reaction she had to his diagnosis makes me reluctant. She told Eugene that she was going to insist I dismiss Doc Parker and use her doctor instead. She said she was going to arrive on my doorstep and insist on taking over his care. Eugene was able to deter her. She is too impossible and I'm not going to deal with her, especially now. I do wonder though, what is so important to Father that he wants to talk to Aunty before he dies.

"I'm not going to tell Aunty anything until my father passes on, Dotty." I wait for her to protest.

She sighs. "I understand. I had to pass on what he asked."

"I know. Thank you," I tell her. "Would you rather I ask her to visit?"

"No, no, no. If you ask me, I don't think it would be a good idea." Dotty's voice rises and her eyes dance with fire. She glances at Father to be sure she hasn't disturbed him.

I chuckle at the vehemence of Dotty's reply. "You're not fond of our Aunt Mary, are you?"

"It's not my place to like her or not like her, but she's not my favorite," she replies. Her voice is demure again, but the fire is still visible in her eyes.

"Dotty, regarding Aunt Mary, you and I agree. Neither of us wants to deal with that witch."

Dotty puts her hand up to her mouth. My words have surprised her. She nods her agreement and turns back to Father.

Once I arrive at the office, I telephone Lucille about the worsening of Father's condition. Lucille says she will come soon. I send Ada a letter by Special Delivery. They have chosen not to have a telephone until the service in their area is more reliable.

I return from work early in the evening and find David reading in the sitting room by the fire. He stands as I come in and gives me a quick hug. "Hello, Mother. Did your day go well?" he asks. Such a proper greeting for such a young boy. He almost sounds like Eugene and it cheers me.

"Yes, David, it all went as usual. Nothing special." I pat his cheek.

"Dotty told us to talk to Grandfather today and say whatever we wanted. She said he might die soon."

"She said that?" I ask, surprised at such frankness.

"Maybe not in those exact words, but I figured out it's what she meant," he says. Such wisdom from my boy.

"What did you tell Grandfather?" I ask, curious.

"I told him I love him. But I don't think he heard me. Dotty said he heard us, but he's too sick to answer." David pauses, and then with a worried frown, asks, "Do you think he's going to die?"

I sigh, "Yes, David. I'm afraid at some point we all have to die, and, yes, I think your grandfather is getting to that point."

David blinks his big hazel eyes. I can see his tears. "What's heaven like?" he blurts. He sits down again and looks up at me.

"I have no idea." His face falls at my answer, so I tell him, "I've been told it's a beautiful place with streets of gold and angels flying around – but nobody knows for sure."

David sits for a moment, deep in thought. Just as I think he's finished talking, he says, "I hope he goes some place nice like that. Mother, do you think there is a heaven?"

"I hope there is – for your grandfather's sake." I want to say I don't think heaven is a place. I want to tell him that I think heaven and hell are right here on earth. I want to tell him lots of my other beliefs, but I fear it's too late for that. I've not taken the time to teach any of them religion. I can't abide the teaching of guilt and the benefits of a judgmental god to a small child. It doesn't feel right, so I'll make up things that I think will be useful in getting them through this.

"Mother, do you know a prayer we could say to help Grandfather get into heaven?"

"David, where are all these religious questions coming from?" I ask.

"Aunt Lucille said we have to pray for Grandfather, so he doesn't go to hell. She says you get burned in hell."

I sigh. "Let's forget what Aunt Lucille says, shall we? She doesn't have any better information about heaven and hell than anyone else does." I take a deep breath. "Your grandfather was a good man. Let's leave it at that. Okay?" The look on his face says he's not satisfied by my answer, but he says nothing more. "Go finish your schoolwork before dinner," I tell him, and he heads to his room.

I climb the stairs to check in on Father. When I pass Babe's room, she's reading. She drops her book and runs to me for a hug. "I had a nice day, Mother," she tells me. "I got to kiss Grandfather and he smiled at me."

"I'm happy for you, honey," I tell her. "Did he say anything?

"He touched my hair and said I'm a pretty girl."

"Well, he's right about that. You are a pretty girl."

"Oh, Mother, you're funny."

We are all subdued this evening. The children go upstairs earlier than normal. Dotty and I take turns sitting in Father's room. His breathing is raspy and ragged. At Dotty's insistence, I go to bed, but it's well after midnight before I can fall asleep.

I sleep until Dotty opens my bedroom door. It's midmorning. "Missus," she says – and I know what has happened. "It's your father. He's passed on."

She steps back and lets me go into Father's room first. All I hear is silence. The raspy breathing has stopped. Father looks peaceful.

Dotty whispers, "All's quiet now. His time was up. So, he left. I fell asleep and I woke with a jump when I heard the silence – and he was gone. He picked a time when I was asleep, so he could continue his journey alone. Lots of dying people do that. Did you know that? It's strange, but that's what some people do."

I sit next to his bed, put my head in my hands and cry. The tears are more of relief than sadness. This feels like such a long time coming. Dotty stands quietly, patting my back and telling me what a good man he was.

I look up when I hear Doc Parker's voice at the door downstairs. Dotty must have called him earlier. He lets himself in and comes up the stairs. I get up from my chair by the bed and move to the other side of the room so he can attend to Father. But, by way of greeting Doc walks over to me and pats my arm before attending to Father. I feel his sympathy and his sorrow. He examines Father methodically, holding his wrists and then touching his neck. He takes out his stethoscope and listens to Father's chest. He nods at Dotty, and they remove the pillows that propped Father up so he could breathe.

Doc Parker explains as he works, "Once someone has died, he has to be laid down flat. if we leave him bent like he is, he'll stay like that – and we won't be able to transport him to the undertaker." He smiles in apology.

Dotty comes to me, placing her arms around me in a comforting hug. "I'm sorry, my dear," she says, "Sorry. It's hard to lose a parent – and now you're an orphan. No matter how old we get, it's still hard to be an orphan." She pats me on the back as if I were a child.

I'm surprised at the word "orphan." I never thought of Father's death as making me an orphan.

"I'll call the undertaker," Doc Parker interrupts in his matter-of-fact voice. He puts his hand on my shoulder and his voice is now gentle as he says, "He's better off, my dear. I'm sure he's no longer in pain. You must think of it that way." He glances back at the bed where Father is. "I have another visit to make. I'll show myself out."

I nod. I'm heavy with exhaustion, or is it relief? The worry is over.

Dotty and I sit by the side of Father's bed talking about what a good man he was and how the children will be sad. We move only when the undertaker arrives in his black carriage. Odd that he still uses a carriage for this chore, a black carriage and four black horses. How symbolic.

The telephone rings and I answer it. "Hello." It's Eugene, wondering where I am. "Are you all right?" he asks.

"No Eugene, no, I'm not all right. Father has passed on just now. I won't be in to work."

"I had a feeling," Eugene answers. "I had a feeling. Can we do anything?" He doesn't give me any time to answer before saying, "I'll call Catherine. She'll want to know." Then he stammers, "I shall miss him. I'm sure you shall miss him as well. I mean – many people will miss him. I shall call Catherine." He hangs up with no goodbye. I can't help but smile. He will forever be my very strange Eugene. In his own way he will help me, of that I can be sure.

I return to Father's room in search of Dotty. She's sitting in the chair by the side of Father's bed, even though they have taken him away. She looks lost.

"I'm sure you must feel very sad," I tell her. It's clear that she is grieving as much as I am.

"My heart is happy he's flying free," she says, after a moment's pause. "His suffering wasn't too much and I'm glad for that. Now you'll be busy. A funeral to plan. Lots of people to tell. Remember to take care of yourself."

"You too, Dotty. It's important we take care of ourselves. What will you do now?" I ask.

"Oh, I suppose I will have to leave. I will find employment somewhere else. My time here is done. Your father doesn't need me anymore. The children are old enough – " she breaks off.

"Stay just a bit longer, Dotty," I urge her. "I don't think I can get through this without you. Besides, what about the funeral?" I see Dotty consider what I've said. I didn't mean to be too personal. Maybe she's feeling her place. I take her hands in mine. "I'd be very grateful if you'd stay on at least until that's all finished," I tell her.

She nods and smiles. "Okay. That would be nice. I can do that." Her eyes glisten with tears.

"Thank you, Dotty," I tell her. "Now we should both get to work. I must tell Babe and David. I must call George and tell him to come home. I hate to interrupt his studies, especially when he's so new at the university, but we need him. I must call Lucille, and send another Special Delivery letter to Ada, and call Aunt Mary and Uncle Quincy. I must let all the people who knew Father know. I wonder if Eugene has a list of his colleagues, I think we should call—"

Dotty puts her hand on my arm. "It sure in heaven's name all will get done. I'll fix you a cup of tea. We'll make a list. But first you need to sit and rest a bit." She pats my arm. "Come with me," she says.

I nod. I follow her downstairs like a child. She directs me to sit in the dining room and she brings me tea. "Here, this'll help." When she places paper and pen in front of me, I write down the people who need to be told. Dotty returns to the kitchen. I'm comforted by the sounds of her opening and closing cupboards, making the ordinary noises of cooking.

At lunchtime, David and Babe dash through the door, full of exuberance. They raced each other home. Their sudden energy overwhelms me. Before I can stop myself, I shout at them, "Hush you two, I can't bear your noise."

They both stop and stare at me. "What's wrong, Mother?" Babe and David both ask. "Has something happened?" Then, they fall silent and look at each other. "Is it Grandfather?" they ask.

I nod. My intentions were to tell them in a more gentle way, but their boisterous entrance knocked me off balance. "Yes, my dears, he passed on this morning."

"Oh Mother, that's sad," blubbers Babe. She breaks into loud sobs, hugging me tightly. David puts his arms around both of us and we stand like three intertwined ivies, clinging together in our grief. I don't know how long we stand like that. David is first to pull away.

Dotty comes in with a tray. "Lunch," she says. Babe and David sit down next to me and let Dotty serve them soup. She places a bowl in front of me as well.

"Dotty," I call as I pick up my spoon. "Bring your soup in here and have lunch with us. We need to be with each other today."

Dotty returns with her soup. We sit in silence, each one eating so the others will eat. As we finish, the smell of fresh baking wafts over us. "I smell cookies," says David. Dotty gets up and is back in a minute with a plate of warm cookies.

"I love you, Dotty," Babe says as she reaches for a cookie.

"Me, too," David echoes.

"We're lucky to have you, Dotty," I add. Again, a sense of appreciation spreads over me. I mean what I said.

CHAPTER 24

Death brings with it a whole litany of things to do. I'm grateful. Planning Father's funeral will leave me little time to be sad or to think about what I've lost.

Eugene and Catherine arrive at my house the evening of Father's death bearing gifts of apple cake and berry jam. While Dotty takes the treats into the kitchen, Catherine holds me in a tight hug, and whispers condolences in my ear. She steps back and nods to Eugene as if encouraging him to hug me.

His hug is both brief and awkward, but he manages to whisper, "May he rest in peace." These two people are different from each other in many ways. Yet each provides me with a small ray of sunshine in this dark time.

Eugene and Catherine chat about the weather as they remove their coats and hats. I usher them into the sitting room and make a quick trip to the kitchen to ask Dotty to make tea to go with the cake.

Just as I rejoin my guests, Babe and David come clamoring down the stairs, curious as to what all the noise is about. They greet Eugene and Catherine with quick hugs.

"Dotty is in the kitchen cutting up the cake that Catherine's brought. If you talk nice to her, I'm sure she will cut you both a piece," I tell them.

At the mention of food, David's face breaks into a wide smile. "Gee, Mother, that would be wonderful." It's good to see the children smile at such a sad time.

"We'll eat it in the kitchen," Babe tells us as she follows her brother out the door adding, "So you can talk."

"My goodness, they're growing up fast," Catherine says, looking pensive. "I see them quite often, but I still can't keep up with how mature they are. Makes me a little sad."

I nod. "I know. They'll both be gone soon, just like George, before we know what has happened."

Catherine's sigh is as big as mine. We smile at each other and she asks, "Amelia, is there anything Eugene or I can do to make any of this easier for you?"

"I'm not sure, Catherine. I'm having a hard time sorting out all that must be done."

"If I can help you with that sorting, I would be happy to assist," Eugene interjects. "Your father appointed me as executor of his will. As such, I am supposed to answer any questions you might have. We don't have to talk about this just now, but I thought I should remind you, in the event you want any information."

"Yes, Eugene, I remember Father telling me that quite a while ago. The will is at the lawyer's if I'm not mistaken."

"Yes, it is. But I have a copy as well. Your father wanted to be certain it would be easy to find, so he stored a copy with me and one with his lawyer, Johnathan Stewart. He went over it with me a month ago to be sure it was up to date. Mr. Stewart wants to have an official reading in a few days."

"So soon? It's hard to think about things like that right now, Eugene. I haven't had time to inform as many of the people about Father's passing as I should have with all there is to do."

"I can imagine that would be difficult," Catherine says. "Eugene and I can help you with that if you like. It might be easier for us. Just give us their names and addresses and we will send them a note on your behalf."

"Oh, that would be wonderful." I feel relieved to have that one task taken off my hands. I sigh. "The one who troubles me the most is Aunt Mary. I should let her know in person, but I don't think I can face her right now.

"If you need me to do that, I will," Eugene says, though I detect a reluctance in his voice.

"I know it's a lot to ask you," I say by way of apology.

"No, I'm happy to help out," he says. "I know how difficult such a meeting would be for you."

Dear Eugene, he always has a way of saying things. "Yes, it would be, Eugene. Even if you do tell her, she may still come knocking on my door. Though I will say, since we had our confrontation, she has stayed away."

A small smile appears on Eugene's face. "Perhaps she will continue to keep her distance," he replies.

After a soft knock at the door, Dotty enters bringing cake and tea. "Would you like me to serve?" she asks.

"Yes, Dotty. Please do." Our conversation hangs in the air until we are served. "Thank you, Dotty. Just leave the teapot. I'll bring the dishes out later."

Dotty shuts the door behind her, and we resume our conversation.

Catherine adds, "Would you like us to make it clear to Mary that she's welcome only at the service?"

I sigh. "Where Aunty is concerned, I'm not sure anything you have to say will hold her at bay, if she puts her mind to it."

"We understand," Catherine says, speaking for both of them.

"I have one more thing I want to ask you," Eugene says, finishing a bite of cake. "Did your father go over his will with you and your sisters before he passed on?"

"No, he never talked to me about a will. Maybe he said something to my sisters, but they've never said anything to me. Why?"

"Well, he drew up a new will just a few months ago and he said he was going to discuss it with all of you. I was hoping he had explained to each of you himself why he has done what he has done with his estate, so you would understand."

"That sounds ominous," I laugh to break the seriousness of Eugene's expression and then ask, "What possible things would he have to explain?"

"Well, to tell the truth, there are several things to explain."

Catherine frowns and interrupts him. "Eugene, maybe we should come back to discuss the legal matters. I thought we were coming here to express our condolences, not to talk business tonight. Shouldn't we do this another night?"

"Catherine, it's all right. Really it is," I say. "In fact, I would rather get it over with. I'm going to have to face this business sooner or later and it might as well be now."

Eugene looks at me with concern. "Are you sure?" he asks. "I should have been more thoughtful. I'm sorry."

"No, go ahead. I'm fine to talk about this now."

"I brought a copy of the will with me today in the event you might have questions." Eugene heads into the hall and returns with a small satchel. He sits across from me and removes a small stack of papers from the satchel and pauses. "I'll read you the relevant parts." He clears his throat, sighs and says, "Your father loved you. You know that."

"Yes, Eugene, I know that." I think he did anyway.

Eugene studies the paper and then explains, "He says that his estate is to be divided four ways."

I sigh. Here we go again. Father and his surprises. It never ends. "Four ways?" I ask.

"Yes, four ways."

"Eugene, there are three of us. Who in the world is the fourth?"

"It says in the will that the fourth portion is to go to his nurse-companion, Dotty."

Dotty? Oh, my goodness! She was with him for many years but nurse-companion? What will other people think of him leaving money to a servant?

"Eugene, how much actual money are we talking about?" I don't care if I sound crass. This is embarrassing. What was my father thinking? Wouldn't he realize how scandalous this would be for us?

"I am still working that out with the lawyer," Eugene answers. "Your father held much of his estate in property and some of that property has to be evaluated, sold and then split. It will be a while before we know the monetary value for sure. Some of the property is in Mexico which makes the evaluation even more difficult."

"I'm afraid I'm shocked by this. Eugene, do you think it's fair that he would treat a servant the same as his own children? I thought he would provide for his grandchildren before his – his nurse-companion. I'm having a difficult time with this."

"Yes, I can see that, and I understand your concern," Eugene tells me. "I believe the judge thought his estate would be worth more than it probably will be. When he talked to me about it, he said he would leave an equal amount to each of you girls. He knew you and Ada would share with the children."

Eugene continues, "I know it's hard to hear, but I am of the opinion that Dotty was more than a nurse to your father. He often referred to her as 'my companion.'"

He's right. It is hard to hear. If I'm honest, I think I knew all along. In my heart, I know she deserves whatever Father wants her to have. I must try to be grateful to her. I'm not sure how I'm going to tell Lucille and Ada. It might help that neither of them needs the money.

"There's something else you should know," Eugene interjects.

"Oh no. Not another surprise," I say. My head is still reeling from the last one.

"Well, it's about Aunt Mary. She made him a loan a while back when he was having cash-flow problems, and he promised to pay her back with interest. He has made a provision in his will to cover that."

Given what Aunt Mary did I don't want her to get anything, but the loan is between Father and her. I decide not to fight about it. I'm tired. I want to stop talking about this.

"You should also know that it was the judge's wish for the funeral to be in Salt Lake City where all his colleagues are. He has also left instructions to ship his body back to Pennsylvania so he can be buried next to your mother. I remember him telling me that he would like it if you and Lucille accompany his body."

"Of course, he would Eugene, of course he would," I tell him, my voice dripping with sarcasm. "This seems complicated to me."

"I don't think he meant it to be complicated, Amelia. I think he just wanted his family and friends in Salt Lake to have a chance to mourn his passing. I do know he was adamant about being buried next to your mother. Catherine and I can help you make the arrangements tomorrow. Your father did make provisions for this extra travel, so you don't have to worry about the cost."

"It's not the cost that bothers me. I'm not fond of train travel, Eugene. It's arduous and I have to leave the children alone for a long period of time."

"You could take them with you," Eugene offers.

"They cannot miss that much school."

"We can talk about this tomorrow when we meet to make arrangements," Catherine says, rising from her chair. "We must be on our way, Amelia. I know you must be tired. Today has been a difficult day for you."

I see them to the door and hug them both. No matter what the future holds, I will always be grateful for their support.

***

Ada and her five children arrive three days before the Salt Lake City funeral. The house buzzes with the children's laughter and echoes from their footsteps on the stairs. The door is opening and closing to let children in and out. The hallway is filled with boots, coats and miscellaneous wrappings. It's March, but it's still cold.

I've not had much contact with Ada in the past years and I find her blustery and domineering. Her body has grown rotund since the last time I saw her, and she moves with the gait of a person much older. It's as if she's unable to will her legs to propel her anywhere. Her husband dotes on her, bringing her whatever she asks for. She winces in pain when she is required to move around, but after a day of watching her, I note that she only winces when her husband is present. When he is gone, she appears perfectly normal.

I give George's old bedroom to Ada and Clarence, so they can have a quiet place to sleep. We manage to get Ada up the stairs to bed, but it takes her five minutes to make the trip. I am told by one of my nephews that she never goes to the upstairs bedrooms in her own house.

When George comes home from university, he can share David's room. The boy cousins are old enough to sleep on mats on the floor in the sitting room and the girl cousins stay with Lucille and Earl. Lucille is delighted to have these young girls all to herself. I'm not sure the girls are very happy to be separated from their family but, though reluctant, they didn't refuse. I rather like Ada's children. They are polite and well-mannered.

Since Ada's arrival, we've had several meetings concerning the setting for the Salt Lake funeral and details for the trip back east for the burial. Father requested a service at the First Presbyterian Church here in Salt Lake. Two days before the funeral, Eugene and Catherine transport me and my sisters to the mortuary to pick out a casket suitable for the funeral and for transport. We select a large one made from maple with a white velvet lining. The funeral director keeps saying we should have black lining, but when I ask him why it must be black, he has no answer. I tell him I couldn't bear the thought of Father draped in black and then being placed into the black ground. He frowns at my reasoning but agrees to the white lining. I think he just wanted us to pick the black one because it is more expensive.

Lucille was a worry for a while. She didn't take Father's passing well. For the first few days after his demise, she cried at the mention of his name and even took to her bed for a short period. I've always thought of her as the strong one, but it seems she does have her weak moments. She did manage to get herself together enough to help organize the food for the funeral but slumped again. For now, I can't worry about her. I need to worry about myself. I have taken it upon myself to write up small stories about Father for each of us to read in the pulpit. I'm not certain any of us will be able to get through even a few of the words.

The biggest surprise I got was when my sisters sat through the reading of Father's will and accepted it without any big disagreement. I thought they would be appalled at the thought that Father would leave money to a servant. It didn't seem to bother them at all. In fact, they both agreed that Dotty deserved every penny she got for looking after Father. Sometimes I feel like I don't know my sisters at all. They were more distressed at the thought of having to figure out how to transport Father's body back to Pennsylvania than at anything else.

Father worked with many well-known people when he was on the bench. Eugene has been able to contact several of them and they agree to speak about him at the funeral. I am certain having such illustrious people speak at his funeral would please Father.

On the day of the funeral we gather in the family room of the church to await our place in the funeral procession. I see no sign of Aunt Mary. I was certain she would want to join us for the procession or at least sit in the same area. Maybe she has given up trying to be a part of our family.

The First Presbyterian Church has been here a long time. It was built in the 1860s and has a huge congregation. It's the church I remember from my childhood. It has a feeling of peace throughout. The stained-glass windows are particularly beautiful. As we begin our walk down the church aisle, I am consumed by the holiness and the sorrow. I fight for control of my tears. I will miss Father. He was such a force in our lives.

We are seated in the front pew: me, George, David and Babe along with Lucille and Earl. Ada and Clarence and their five children fill the pew behind us. I ask Dotty to sit with us, but she declines. She says there is room for her in the back with some of the servants that used to work for Father. Maybe she thinks it's not her place to sit with the family.

Ada leans up to whisper in my ear that she doesn't like sitting behind us. She says she feels like people will think Father didn't love her as much as he loved us. I whisper back to her, "Nobody thinks that way, Ada." Poor Ada, she says the craziest things, but the tone of her voice tells me she is upset by this. The mortuary person standing at the head of the aisle hears us talking and asks if something is wrong.

"Yes," I tell him. "My sister isn't pleased at having to sit behind us. I don't see why she can't move up here with us. There's plenty of room."

He frowns at me and then at my sister. Hesitating, he says, "As you wish, ma'am," then motions for them to move to the front next to us.

Some members of the congregation are beginning to stir, turning to look at what the commotion is about. I feel my face grow red with embarrassment. There always seems to be some sort of theatrics when my sisters are around.

It takes two hours before all the talking is done. Many people stand up and speak about Father. I am exhausted by all the information and at the same time renewed.

Everyone says he was a good man, one of the best, and I agree with that. After the last person speaks, the minister says a prayer for the soul of my father. I have a new sense of pride in all he did. I never had a true sense of his fame until now.

The music sounds. Our family rises and I'm sure we all walk with a little more pride for our father than we had going in. People stand as we move down the aisle. Since there will be no burial today, everyone will join us at a nearby hotel for a reception. Neither the church basement nor Lucille and Earl's house is large enough to accommodate all of the people who have come to the funeral.

The plans for carrying out Father's wishes about being buried back in Pennsylvania have been finalized. Lucille, Earl and I will take Father by train to Pennsylvania. We'll stay with my mother's sister, Aunt Henrietta Barton. She was kind to us when Mother died long ago, though we haven't seen her since Mother's funeral when I was seventeen.

At the hotel, where many tables are laid out with food, we have a chance to see how many people have come to Father's funeral. "Wow," says George, who is at my side as we walk in, "Grandfather had a lot of friends. There must be five hundred people in here."

"Yes, George," I reply. "Your grandfather was quite famous in his day. How did you like all the stories about him today?"

"I don't think I appreciated him enough – and now he's gone."

"Indeed, son. That's how I feel as well."

"Your table is over here," someone tells me. He directs us to a long table with name tags for family members. My sisters and their husbands are seated next to me. The children are across the table. They ask why Dotty isn't here and I tell them I invited her, but she declined. As soon as the funeral service was over, she went to visit her family in Farmington.

Several servers bring our food. As I take my first bite, a shadow crosses my plate, and I look up to see Aunt Mary and Uncle Quincy. I push myself away from the table and stand up to greet them. She hugs me and holds me tight for a moment. "It's a great loss," she tells me. Quincy hugs me and says he's sorry for my loss. I watch them move to embrace my sisters. Where is all the drama that Aunty usually brings to occasions like this? Catherine and Eugene must have done a good job telling her to mind her business, though I can't imagine Eugene would have put it quite that way.

I return to my plate of half-eaten food. I feel a hand on my back and look up. George is smiling down on me. "How are you doing, Mother?" he asks.

"George, I'm fine. Thanks for asking. I've meant to tell you that it's good to have you home. I'm sorry we haven't had a chance to talk since your arrival. There's been so much to attend to that I think I've neglected you. Forgive me?"

"Mother, you haven't neglected me at all. It's a sad time and I know you've had a lot to do to make all these arrangements. No forgiving necessary."

George's sweet face is filled with concern. Something is different about him. Maybe his six months away at school has matured him. Or maybe he is just sad about the loss of his beloved Grandfather. Either way, he seems much more grown up than when he left in the fall.

"Don't worry about me, son. I'm going to be fine. Don't look so concerned." Hoping to change the subject I say, "I hope missing so much school doesn't ruin your term."

"The dean said it is a necessary absence and he will inform my professors of my misfortune. I can make it up. However, I have to leave in a few minutes. It's a long trip back. I'm sorry I'm not able to accompany you and Grandfather back East."

"Oh, I didn't expect you would, but I am pleased you are here now."

"It's a sad affair," he says. "Grandfather was old and sick. I wouldn't wish him any more pain or discomfort, but I'll miss seeing him when I come home and he's not here to share my stories. It will take me some time to get over this."

"You are right about that, George. We will all miss him."

George moves back to his seat and I turn to Lucille. "I'm ready to leave. What about you?" I ask.

"It wouldn't be polite to leave now," she answers. "We can't leave until most of the people are gone. I'm sure more people will stop by to speak to us. We need to be ready for that."

"Who makes these stupid rules?" I snap.

"Amelia, that's just the way it is, and you know it. It won't be much longer. Be patient," Lucille responds to my snide remark.

"Sorry, Lucille. I'm tired." I say nothing more. I am too tired to fight with anyone.

More people approach our table and tell us again how they admired our father. It is nice to hear. Catherine and Eugene offer to take Babe and David home. I want them to take me home as well, but I know it's better to go along with Lucille this time. Ada moves her chair closer to us. We haven't been together, just the three of us, in a long time. I'm surprised at the lack of conversation. We were never very close, but I can think of nothing to say to either one of them. Finally, the number of people chatting and milling around dwindles.

One of the servers brings over the Book of Condolences that was on the table near the entrance. Ada begins to page through it. "People are leaving very nice messages for us. You should read some of them," Ada says to Lucille and me. She turns a few pages and reads one of the entries. "Judge and Mrs. R.T. Brown from Farmington, Utah. We send our deepest condolences to the family of our dear friend and colleague, George Washington Lange." Ada reads out several other messages.

Then she touches my arm, saying, "Amelia, here's one for you." She reads, "A special condolence to Mrs. Dwight Mae Deschamps and family from Sam."

My heart skips a beat. "The only Sam I know was on the trip I took years ago with Father. You must remember how he got lost in the desert and was presumed dead. It couldn't be him, so I have no idea who this Sam could be." I can only wish.

CHAPTER 25

It's a bright, warm, late September afternoon and as I look up from my desk to the wall calendar, I note it's been seven months to the day since we buried Father. I miss him. The children miss him. I feel more tired than usual, and I've done enough work for the day. Eugene smiles at me when I say I'm leaving, waves and goes back to whatever he was doing when I interrupted him. I wanted to tell him to go home too, but I'm sure he would decline. What would the business do without him?

I meander home, looking at the trees in full bloom and wondering back over the last months. It seems only yesterday that we travelled all that way to Pennsylvania and finally laid Father to rest next to Mother. I arrived home afterward full of peace, a sad peace but glad that Father didn't have to suffer anymore.

I get to the house just as the children arrive from school. George has gone back to university and there's a definite hole in the household, but the other two keep me busy. They pull me out of my reverie and chatter about school and the day they've had. It's a nice ending to the day. David will graduate next year and then the house will be even more quiet. I feel like Babe will be with me forever but that is just the wishful thinking of a mother for her daughter.

After supper they both go off to their rooms to study. I start to clear up the supper dishes when I hear a knock on the door. It's eight p.m. Rather late for a caller. I contemplate not answering but the knocking is persistent, and I wonder why one of the children hasn't come to answer for me. Maybe a neighbor needs help. Yes, that's probably it so I open the door.

It takes a minute for me recognize the gentleman standing there and it takes a minute for him to utter his greeting.

"Hello," I hear him say. "It's me, Sam. Have you forgotten me after all these years?"

I grab the edge of the door and have the feeling I might faint. Sam steps forward as though he wants to catch me, but I step back to catch my breath. I stare at him as if frozen in time. Am I dreaming? Did I fall asleep, and this is just a crazy dream? He has accompanied me in my thoughts through all the years and all the things that happened since I last saw him in Stockton. Can this really be him? He has always been just "off stage," but to see him in the flesh and not just in memory is overwhelming.

He smiles and stands patiently.

"Is it really you?" I ask. "I... I thought you were dead." I look down at my hands, I'm shaking.

He laughs and it rings familiar in my ears. "No, Amelia, as you can see for yourself, here I am in the flesh, quite alive."

"Yes, I can see that. I..I don't know what to say," I tell him. I feel unable to move. It's like my feet are nailed to the floor. I reach out to touch the wall thinking I might faint.

He stands quiet for a moment and then says, "So, if I'm not dead, and you know who I am, will you invite me in? The neighbors might get the wrong idea if they see a strange man standing on your doorstep talking to himself."

Same old Sam and his odd sense of humor. "Oh Sam, yes of course. Do come in."

As I step back to let him pass, I hear the thumping of shoes on the stairway and realize David and Babe are coming down the stairs. They probably wonder what all the unfamiliar chatter is about. They both stop in their tracks as they realize there is a strange man standing in the foyer.

David catches my eye and wrinkles his forehead as if asking, "And who do we have here?"

"Ah, yes, uh Sam, these are my children, David and Babe. David and Babe this is Sam uh, Mr. Goutiere. Mr. Goutiere is an old friend of your father. I haven't seen him in years.

The children dutifully come forward and shake Sam's hand.

"Mr. Goutiere and I have some business to attend to and will be in the sitting room. You two can go back to your studies. You have a big day tomorrow," I tell them, trying not to sound too anxious.

They move reluctantly. "What big day?" I hear David ask Babe as they climb the stairs. "I don't have any big day. Do you?"

Sometimes I forget my children are nearly grown. I can feel their curiosity and it means I shall have to make up a better story tomorrow.

I find myself pulled toward Sam much as I was when I was a young woman. He has the same smile he did back then, sweet but now that I look closer, I see a touch of the seductive. I wouldn't have seen that in my younger more innocent days. Is it the danger in that smile that pulls me in or is it the old longing to know what could be with this man?

I lead him to the living room where we sit facing each other, he on the couch and I on a chair. I am at a loss for words at first but finally ask, "Where have you been? What happened to you in Stockton? Why didn't you let someone know where you were?" The questions come so quickly that he reaches out and puts his hand on my shoulder.

"Whoa, I can't answer that many questions all at once," he says laughing. "I'll take question number one first. I went south into Mexico after the problems in Stockton. I wasn't in the best state of mind back then and I figured I'd better get as far away from California as I could to try to figure myself out. I spent a couple of years down there. I moved in with a Mexican widow lady and as odd as it sounds, she did a good job of straightening me out."

Sam pauses and looks away. I see a grimace cross his face as though he is thinking about something painful. Before I can ask what it might be, he continues with details of what life was like in Mexico. He sounds like he was mostly happy there, but I wonder where the pain comes from. Before I can ask, he continues his story.

"She," he pauses, "Natalia, Natalia was her name," he says softly, "saw something in me that nobody else ever had, a talent for picture drawing and paints. You know it's strange. I always liked to draw, even as far back as when I first met you. I used to doodle on napkins and any odd scrap of paper I could find. A couple of times I even drew on hotel walls to pass the time. Nobody ever recognized that as a talent." He laughed and I had to laugh with him.

"I always say she helped me trade in my bottle of whiskey for a paint brush. Her husband was Indian, full blood Apache, and he died of some weird infection and left her with a bunch of half-breed kids. That was long before I showed up. She supported her kids by weaving blankets and selling them to European traders. She worked hard, but it paid off. She had quite the business going. She introduced me to her husband's family and from there on I took her advice and started painting pictures of the whole damn family."

Sam suddenly reaches into his pocket and pulls out what looks like a money clip, but instead of money he pulls off small pieces of folded up paper. As he unfolds one of them, he hands it to me. It's a small drawing of an Indian man sitting at a loom. "I drew this picture in Arizona. I intend to paint it when I get home. Like I said before, he was an Apache warrior, but he wove beautiful blankets. At least that's what he told me."

Sam shakes his head. "Sorry, I guess I lost track of the story I was telling. Sometimes I get lost in the subjects I paint. Now, where was I?"

"Why did you leave Mexico? It seems like you got along there," I answer.

Sam leans back on his chair and continues. "It could've been a good life until one day it wasn't. The Mexican Revolution changed everything, and they didn't take kindly to us white people so much anymore. So, I left. Crossed the border and headed east. I decided I better go home and make it right with my folks. I imagined they'd been searching for me for long enough. After a few months with them I bid farewell and headed out west again to do more paintings. I only do pictures of Indians like that one I showed you. The art has me wandering all across the west. I learn so much from the people I paint. They taught me how to heal myself and how to face my problems with courage. As a bonus, those pictures sell real well these days. So, I'd say I'm just an artist. Bet you'd have never thought I'd be something like that back in the Stockton days."

I smile. "True Sam. I somehow never thought of you as that." I am transfixed by Sam's story.

When he finally pauses, I ask if he'd like something to drink and he asks for tea. I chuckle to myself. That is a change. I get up to fix the tea and he follows me into the kitchen. As we wait for the water to boil, he asks me questions about my life. I tell him what tidbits I think he might be interested in but stay away from the difficult parts like Dwight's death. As I come to the end of what I think is enough about me Sam asks me a question.

"You've left out quite a bit, haven't you?" he says, that wicked smile crossing his face.

"What do you mean?" I ask afraid of what is coming.

"When I came to your father's funeral, I managed to ask some of the people standing around about you and what your status was. I got some interesting information. It seems the friends of your family didn't mind sharing what they know about you. I found out your husband died of the Spanish flu and you'd been left with three children. I also heard you are a woman running your own business. That's something to be proud of. I'm sorry for your struggles. Is there some reason you didn't want to tell me that story?"

"Sounds to me like you already know enough about me, so I don't have to tell you anymore. What you found out is true and I'm not much for talking about Dwight or his death. He was a good husband and father. What more can I say?" The words pour out of me louder and harsher than I intended, but hopefully Sam won't ask any more questions.

Sam nods as if he understands and I step aside to rescue the water that is boiling away. I pour the water through the tea strainer and into the teapot and set the teapot and cups on the table. I turn to the cupboard and reach for cookies I baked that afternoon. Funny coincidence. How would I know I'd have company this evening?

We sit facing each other sipping our tea and indulging in the sweetness of the baking. The silence grows between us. It's a nice moment but I still have a question I need answered.

"I do have another question," I tell Sam. "I need to know why you picked the time you did to show up in my life again. It's very curious."

Sam looks at me and sighs. "I saw your father's obituary in the newspaper as I was passing through Salt Lake and having dinner in one of the restaurants. It sounded like it was going to be quite an affair by the way the write-up described it. Since it was near to where I was staying, I stopped in. I thought of making my presence known right then, but then I realized it wouldn't be proper to just appear in your life at such a sad time, so I wrote a note in your book of condolences and moved on. I figured I'd give it time and on my next trip west I'd find your address and pay a visit. So here I am. And I'm glad I am."

"I'm glad you are too, Sam," I tell him.

"Are you really?" Sam says, looking straight into my eyes. "In all those years did you ever think about me – even once?"

I feel the warmth of my embarrassment spread across my face. Do I dare tell him how many times I've thought about him?

"If you only knew the truth of it, Sam. I truly thought you were dead but not one day passed in my life when you weren't on my mind and in my heart. I even thought of you on my wedding day and wondered what it would be like if it were you standing there beside me instead of Dwight. Don't get me wrong, I loved Dwight, but I remembered you and wondered. It's all very strange, isn't it?" I ask.

Sam looks at me and frowns. "What's strange about that?" he asks.

"When I think back to that trip to Stockton, I was so young and so naïve. I hardly knew you at all. In fact, I still don't really know you but like back then there was some strange attraction and as embarrassing as it is, that attraction is still there. I don't understand it but..."

Sam interjects, "But I hope you're going to say you'd like to explore that attraction because that's how I feel."

"I'm not sure that's exactly what I was going to say but I'll leave it at that. I'd like to see you again. That much I know."

"Good, I'm glad to hear that. Somehow I was afraid that when I came here tonight you'd slam the door in my face and I'd have to live with all my questions and feelings unanswered. That would have made me very sad." He stops then and asks, "Is there anything else you have been wondering about me?"

I pause for another minute. "Yes Sam, I do have one other question. What really happened to you in Stockton? Why did you disappear like you did?"

Sam looks at me without saying anything for what seems like an eternity. He finally sighs and says, "As much as I want to answer you honestly, I can't. All I can say is I am here now, and that part of my life no longer exits. If you want to get to know me better, then you must accept that I will never be able to answer that question. I think an answer would bring us both too much pain. Besides, there is a lot of it I don't remember and neither do I want to bring it all back."

I look at him and see the anguish in his face. I can't help but think I probably know most of what happened anyway. I think I agree with him when he said an answer would bring us both too much pain.

"I understand," is all I can think of to say to him.

We both look at the clock at the same time. "Midnight? How can that be? We've been talking half the night away," I tell him.

Sam smiles and stands up. "Yes, I think we've said what we needed to say and I'm glad we did. I have to be in the Denver area for the next few weeks. When I return, I want to see you again."

"And I want to see you as well," I tell him as we walk towards the front door.

Sam steps towards me and takes me in his arms. His warmth surrounds me, and it feels comfortable. After a long good-bye hug, he kisses my mouth. It's not the kiss of lust I would have imagined it might be, but it is enough for now. I watch Sam go down the porch steps and walk towards his automobile. I can't help but wonder if he will again disappear, never to return. A familiar pain creeps across my chest. The familiar pain of loneliness.

As I shut the door and turn to go upstairs, David appears at the top of the stairs. "You must have had a lot of business to discuss, Mother. It's after midnight."

I turn around and head to the kitchen. The last thing I need is to be confronted by my son. "I know what time it is, David. You should be in bed."

He is not deterred. He strolls into the kitchen after me. "What business does he want with you?" he asks. "And why in the middle of the night? I heard some of what he was talking about, and it didn't sound like business to me."

"I told you, he's an old friend of your fathers."

"No, he's not. It seems to me he's definitely an old friend of yours and frankly he's not your type."

"What in the world would you know about 'my type?'" I ask, trying to keep my anger at bay. But the tone of my voice betrays me.

David's attitude takes a sudden turn. "Look Mother, I'm just trying to protect you from any more pain than you've already had. I didn't like the looks of that guy. He..."

I interrupt him. I'm too tired to carry this conversation any further. "David, stop! I don't need your criticism right now. If you want the truth, I have long-held feelings for that man and this time, I don't intend to stop seeing him whether you like it or not. You can be happy for me or not but you should get used to it. I'm tired of being alone. Now, go to bed. I'm not going to discuss this any further tonight."

David stands blocking the kitchen door, so I am unable to make a dramatic exit and shut down this conversation. He looks at me, mouth open and red-faced. "You have feelings for him?" he asks. "How can you? God Mother, how can you even know him? He..he looks like a..a vagabond."

"He's an artist, David. An artist is not a vagabond. How can you make judgments when you don't even know him? Now, let me by so we can both go to bed." It occurs to me that my little quiet David has taken on the role of protector since George left for university. He's behaving more like an army sergeant than a protector. I don't know whether to laugh or cry.

But David stands his ground. "I want you to be happy, but this display is just shocking. You are going to be sorry if you keep this up. Mark my words."

"What display are you talking about?" I ask, confused. This is the first time I've seen Sam in many years. There is no display."

"I saw him kiss you." David says quietly. "I knew when he kissed you, you weren't talking business."

"You shouldn't spy on people, David. Spying may provide you with more information than you are ready to accept. I am tired, I am going to bed."

David steps aside and lets me pass. As I begin the long trudge up the stairs, I hear him mumble, "Sometimes you scare me to death, Mother."

Sometimes I scare myself.

CHAPTER 26

1930

I open my eyes to unfamiliar surroundings. For a split second I wonder where I am. The sound of soft breathing reminds me. I roll onto my side and watch Sam sleep. I seldom get the chance to do this. I used to be in a hurry to run home before Babe got worried. But since she moved to Sacramento, I'm less bothered by the thought of another of her lectures about what might happen if I get caught staying out all night. I always wonder who would catch me. She's the only one I care about, and she knows about Sam.

I keep telling Sam we don't have to get a hotel every time he comes to town, but he doesn't listen. I tell him it's too expensive, given these times. But he also says someone might see us or come to the door in the middle of the night and that would be bad for my reputation. I always laugh at this. Who in the world would be coming to visit me in the middle of the night? He just shakes his head and tells me, "Well, you never know." He also says he doesn't care about the money. So, we continue this way.

His eyes pop open as though he's heard my thoughts and he smiles. "Good morning, my love. How was your night?" he asks. The way he asks is suggestive.

"My night was just fine," I tell him, trying not to convey too much enthusiasm.

"Just fine?" he asks, pouting in his funny fake way. "You've broken my heart with your words, my lady. 'Fine' is not the word I'd use to describe the night."

I laugh. I can't help it. "Are you looking for a review of your performance?" I ask, my voice as provocative as I can make it. I like this silly banter.

He chuckles and asks, "What time is it anyway?"

"I don't know," I tell him, rather startled by the question.

Sam rolls over and pulls himself up to reach his pocket watch on the dresser. "Damn! It's ten o'clock. If I don't hurry, I'll miss the train. I promised the art gallery curator I'd meet him early tomorrow morning. I've got a big show coming up in Denver and I don't want to miss the opportunity."

"My goodness! It must be important if it causes you to leap out of this nice warm bed," I tell him, disappointed he's going away again after such a short visit.

He smiles at me as he grabs his clothes and starts to dress. As he does up the last of his shirt buttons, I get out of bed, and he pulls me close. He kisses me, and I feel desire rise in me again and I pull him closer.

In that instant, he lets go, steps back, and says, "I'm sorry to leave like this, Amelia. I know it seems sudden. I didn't intend to sleep so late. I thought we could at least have breakfast together, but I guess we'll have to do it next time. I must make my train."

He puts on his coat and looks around for his hat as he speaks. "Also, it might be a while before I see you again. I'm going back East after the show. My father isn't well, and my mother needs me. I'll contact you as soon as I can. I promise. I'll pay the bill on my way out." He hesitates for a moment, and I think he's going to kiss me again, but he sighs, picks up his suitcase and walks out the door.

As I begin to get dressed for the day, I can't help but think how odd this is. I understand about the show and how important that would be, but in all the times we've been together, Sam has only mentioned his parents in passing. I had the feeling he wasn't close to them because of all the trouble he put them through when they were searching for him years ago. Why hasn't he mentioned them to me earlier? On the other hand, maybe I did something to make him go. I shake my head, that can't be it. It was a perfect night. Maybe I should have told him how perfect it was. No, it must be something else. There must be something more to this story.

I finish dressing, pack my nightclothes and toiletries into my suitcase and let myself out. I use a side door to leave as I don't feel like being scrutinized by the hotel staff.

The cold January morning makes me suck in my breath as I leave the hotel. It's like a slap in the face after the warmth of the night and the bed. It's starting to snow, and I shiver. I'm not walking home in this. I decide to cross the avenue and wait for the streetcar to take me home. Sam makes me upset. I don't know why I keep doing this. He's always dashing off somewhere and then showing up again at odd times. This can't go on.

"Hey lady! Watch where you're walking!" someone yells at me as I step unconsciously into the roadway. I mouth, "Sorry." Sam will be the death of me yet.

***

A week later George calls me long distance at work. Out of the blue.

"What is it, George? Are you all right?"

I hear George take a deep breath. Then he says, "Hello, Mother. Yes, I'm fine. Don't worry, there's nothing wrong." There's a pause as he takes another breath. "I have important news to tell you." Then, again he goes quiet. I wonder if the line has gone dead.

"George? George, are you still there?" I ask.

"Yes, Mother, I'm still here. I hope you'll be happy with my news." He rushes on. "I've met a girl. A few months ago. Her name is Anna, Anna De Luca, and I've asked her to marry me and she's accepted. I'm engaged Mother, engaged. Rather, we're engaged!"

I can't believe what I'm hearing. "What did you say?" I ask, hoping it's my hearing that has gone wrong.

"You heard me, Mother. I said I'm engaged to be married and I just wanted you to be the first to know."

"Oh George, I don't know quite what to say. It's all so sudden. I... I am quite shocked."

"Don't worry, she's a very nice girl and I just know you'll love her as much as I do. That's why I wanted to tell you first."

I try to keep my calm, but I feel overwhelmed. How could he do this? I didn't even know he was seeing anyone. All I can think of to say is, "You're twenty years old. That's much too young. What are you thinking? Obviously, you're not. What about your schooling? You can't go to university and be married. How will you make a living?"

He tries to speak, but I keep going. "Where did you get this idea anyway? My god, George don't do this!" I'm ranting. I don't mean to, but I can't believe what he's saying.

"I'm going to phone you back when you're rational, Mother. Goodbye."

"When I'm rational? What about you? Don't be ridiculous. You are the irrational one. You are going to ruin your life." I keep talking though the line has gone dead. How could he be so stupid? I look up and see Eugene standing at the door looking concerned.

"What's wrong, Amelia?" Eugene asks. "Can I do anything for you? Did someone die?"

"No, of course, not," I tell him. "It's almost worse than that. Oh, Eugene, George has gotten himself into terrible trouble."

"What kind of trouble? Does he need a lawyer or something?"

"No, no, he's – he's engaged – and to a girl I haven't even met. How could he do this to me?"

Eugene looks at me and raises his eyebrows, the way he does when he doesn't understand something. "I can see why you'd be upset, Amelia, but I don't see that he is doing anything 'to' you."

I don't like the way he emphasizes "to," but I say nothing, and he continues. "I guess it's all in how you look at it. I don't think his intentions are against you. It sounds to me like he is doing this for himself and his lady friend. He wouldn't do something like this just to hurt you. Don't you know that?"

Why does Eugene have to be so analytical? "What do you mean by that? So, you think this whole thing is fine? Is it fine that he's been courting this woman for some period of time but never told me? I always tried to be a good mother."

Eugene looks uncomfortable and then says, "I didn't say it was fine, but it sounds like he has already made up his mind. I'm not certain why he wouldn't have told you he was courting someone." Eugene studies me before he continues. "Maybe George was worried about what you might say. Maybe he anticipated that you wouldn't approve."

"Eugene, I can't let him give up his university education and all that I've worked so hard for. He's twenty years old, for heaven's sake.

"If you don't mind my saying it, I think you won't be able to stop George from doing this no matter what you say or do," Eugene tells me." George has always been a reasonable young man. If he says he wants to get married, I'm certain he will have thought out all the consequences of his actions."

"I hope you're right, Eugene. I just can't believe he would do this without any warning."

"Young men in love are apt to do the unexpected and sometimes what they do is not on our timeline," Eugene adds and then smiles at me and goes back to his office.

I wish I could be as philosophical as Eugene. Perhaps he is right in this and I should just let it go. Maybe George will wake up and realize how wrong-headed this is. I know Eugene is right that George has always been so proper and particular in all his undertakings. Something else must be going on. I bet he's in some other kind of trouble.

I walk down the hall and peer into Eugene's office. "I've decided I'm going to go pay a visit to George next week. I could be gone from the office for a while."

Eugene looks up from his desk and smiles. "I wondered how long it would take you to make that decision. Just do me a favor. Don't go with too many expectations or you might be disappointed," he adds.

I frown at Eugene, a bit unsure exactly what he means by that, but it does sound like a warning. I have to find out for myself what is going on with George. All of this is just not like him at all.

I send a message to the school to let George know I'm coming, and I take the train to Arizona. It's expensive and it's a long time sitting in one spot thinking. As hard as I try and as much time as I have on the train, I still don't come up with much of a plan. I just want to talk George out of this nonsense as quickly as I can.

As I step from the train, I spot him coming towards me, smiling. At least he hasn't disappointed me in every way. He has shown up to meet me. There's still a chance.

"Mother," he says, offering me his arm, "how nice of you to visit." He smiles, but I hear the sarcasm in his voice as he stoops to kiss my cheek. He says little as he rushes me across the street to a restaurant and towards a young woman sitting at a table. This must be Anna.

As we approach, she stands up, smiling. I am struck by her beauty, though her mouth is painted with dark red lipstick. She has jet black hair, and she's dressed in a flowered dress of many colors – a bit ostentatious for my taste. What would someone like her see in George?

Before I can say anything Anna laughs. "Nice to meet you Mrs. Deschamps," she tells me, offering her hand. I nod, ignoring the attempt at a greeting. She doesn't acknowledge my snub and the smile stays on her face without a single quiver or quake. She seems very sure of herself.

"Please, sit down," she offers. "Chatting is much easier if one is comfortable, don't you think?"

I nod again, taking a seat that George pulls up for me. "What would you like to drink. Mother?" he asks. "We are just having a glass of wine."

"An iced tea would be welcome," I tell him. George heads to the bar, leaving me with Anna.

She smiles at me and says, "It's all right, Mrs. Deschamps, I understand your concern. You're afraid George will have to give up his schooling in order to support me. I would never let that happen." She lifts a glass of red wine to her bright red lips. "Don't worry. I'm fortunate enough to work in my family's perfume business. My father is generous with his money. George and I have managed to let a delightful little house just up the road from the school, so George doesn't have to live in that awful dormitory anymore. Everything is well looked after. You don't have to worry." She smiles again and pats my arm.

George returns with my iced tea. He does look happy. There's not a lot of meaningful conversation after that, though I note he refills his glass with drink more than a few times. I haven't seen that in my son before. It makes me uncomfortable. I am even more surprised when they both light up cigarettes. Why does he have to throw his life away like this?

When Anna goes to use the lavatory, George asks, "Now that you've met Anna, what do you think? She's beautiful, isn't she?"

"She is that," I respond. "George, I hope you know I just want what's best for you."

"Then be happy for me Mother. For us. That's all it takes."

"Since you've obviously made up your mind about all this, when is the wedding?" I ask.

Before he can respond, Anna returns looking fresh and smiling. As soon as she seats herself, George announces, "In answer to your question about a wedding, Mother, Anna and I were married yesterday by the Justice of the Peace. We didn't want to put everybody out by having some fancy event either for my side of the family or for Anna's."

For a second I feel like I might faint. "Married? My heavens!" I nearly choke on my words but looking at George all I can think to say is, "Well then, I suppose it's all settled. I'm not certain what else there is to say." It's hard to think of my son as a married man.

"Congratulations might be in order, Mother," George says, rolling his eyes.

"Yes, I suppose so," I tell him raising my glass of iced tea as though it's a glass of wine. It's the most positive thing I can muster at this point in time. "To be honest, I came here to talk you out of getting married, but I guess that's now a moot point. As a result, I can only hope that you both know what you're doing. You are both way too young as far as I'm concerned."

George cuts in and I hear the chill in his voice, "Age doesn't matter Mother. We love each other and that's all that matters."

"Love? Do you even know what that means?" The words are harsh and tumble out before I can stop them.

"Yes, Mrs. Deschamps," Anna suddenly breaks in. "We do know what that means and as I said before, you don't need to worry about us. We know what we are doing, and now that the good news is out, why don't you come and see where we are living. Perhaps that will ease your mind and your fears."

It's the last thing I want to do but it's the least thing I can do. If I walk away now, I may never see my son again. I can tell by the look on his face that he is testing me. He's making me choose. I sigh. I turn to Anna and say as sweetly as I can summon, "Yes, my dear. I would love to see where you are living."

The next day, I get on the train and return home. The visit to the small house where George and Anna will live did ease my fears a bit. It is a sweet little older house with two bedrooms, a kitchen and lavatory, nicely decorated. They also assured me that George can continue his studies even if he is married. It feels odd that he should be attending school while his wife is working. On the other hand, perhaps I need to change my thinking about that. Maybe I'm envious of this woman for being so modern. I just hope she isn't too modern for my son.

David meets me at the station. He's hired a motorized taxi which surprises me. He usually likes to ride in one of the open carriages prevalent in Salt Lake City these days. I say nothing to him about George until he breaks the silence by asking, "So what do you think of Anna?"

"She's not what I would expect of a son of mine."

He looks at me and I see his eyes darken. "That's not very nice, Mother," he says. I hear the chill in his voice. "You weren't there for very long, so how do you know what she's like?"

"Oh, David. I suppose you think it's fine that your brother just up and married some painted-up woman off the street and didn't even care to tell us first."

"Mother, George isn't like that. He wouldn't just up and marry somebody off the street, like you say. What do you mean by that anyway? I've heard she comes from money."

I stare at him. How does he know about this?

As we arrive at the house, David pays the taxi driver and then turns back to me as if there hasn't been any interruption. "Seems to me, he's happy. What more can we want?"

"Well, I want a lot more for a son of mine. I've met her and she just seems too, well, too sophisticated for George.

Besides, he's way too young to be married. Why wouldn't he have told me he was seeing someone?"

"I don't understand why you can't just be happy for George." David's face is quite red. Sometimes he gets so riled up about things. "Maybe George will be happier now." After a long pause he says, "Maybe people don't tell you things because they are afraid you will be upset."

David sighs. "I'm going to study in my room before supper."

He gives me a peck on the cheek. "And by the way, I'm glad you're home."

I hope it's a long time before David contemplates marriage. He has no concept of women. He doesn't see how wrong this whole thing is. He just doesn't understand.

I toss and turn for many hours that night before sleep comes.

CHAPTER 27

1933

It's been three months and I still haven't heard from Sam. I shouldn't be surprised; it's been his way. I arrive for work one morning and Eugene is chuckling to himself. "The postman has delivered a package for you," he announces. "It's addressed to "Madame Deschamps." Must be from someone who knows you well or they wouldn't know you're a woman." All these years, we've left everything as D. M. Deschamps, as if Dwight were still here – as if it wasn't a woman running the business.

"I don't think it's your birthday. Perhaps a gift from a secret admirer? It's marked fragile and it's been insured." He raises his eyebrows at me and puts the paper-wrapped package on my desk and disappears into his office.

I pick up the package. It weighs about as much as a book. The post mark that is inked on the many stamps is faint, but it looks like it says NYC – New York City. I think that maybe there's been a mistake, but the package has my name and the business address in neat script on the front. How odd. I slide the paper off and inside I find a small painting of an Indian brave, sitting in front of a loom, appearing to be weaving a blanket. I smile. The blanket was woven in one of the Navajo patterns. I know this because Sam showed me a drawing of this image awhile back and then gave me a blanket for Christmas exactly like the one in the picture. The name of the artist is in the lower corner: Sam G. He once told me that he always signs Sam G. because his name is French and it's too long and complicated to use as an art signature.

I feel a sense of relief. I've been worried about Sam. The whole three months I've had no idea where he was. I'd started to think he'd given up on me. Now thank heavens, I know that's not true. This painting is proof of that.

I turn the painting over to see if Sam's written anything on the back. Tucked into the frame is an envelope with my name on it. The note inside says:

Dearest Amelia:

I am sending you one of my favorite paintings. Favorite because it reminds me of you. I painted this when I was visiting my Indian friends in Southern Arizona some years back. Remember the blanket I gave you? It's the one in the picture.

If you contact Mr. Proutt at the Utah Museum of Fine Arts, I'm certain he can verify the value of this gift for you, should you wish to sell it at some point.

However, I hope you'll keep it close to your heart as a token of my esteem for you. Perhaps hang it on your bedroom wall and think of me. I'm still not certain when I'll see you again as my parents are taking up a great deal of my time. I do miss you.

Amour, Sam G.

Oh Sam! He sounds so uncertain about seeing me again. Of course, he'll see me again. Can't he just tell me he will see me again and soon? He has such a funny way of saying things.

I look up and see Eugene standing in the doorway. "Did you figure out whom your mysterious package is from?" he asks.

I nod. "It's from Sam Goutière," I tell him. "You know, my friend," I add, feeling a rush of embarrassment. Eugene knows about Sam, but he's not someone we talk about. I'm certain he understands the relationship as I've talked to Catherine about Sam on several occasions.

Eugene smiles and walks to my desk, picking up the painting. "He does quite spectacular work, doesn't he? He seems to have such an intimate relationship with his subjects. It's no wonder he has gained such a good reputation these last few years."

"I didn't realize you were a connoisseur of art, Eugene. I have noticed he gets recognized in the local paper from time to time for his paintings. You must have seen that as well."

Eugene nods, "I'm most certainly not an art connoisseur but I've followed his career these past few years." Eugene pauses and clears his throat. "I like what he paints – and because I know he's a friend of yours, I follow him. Have you noticed that his paintings sell for a good price? This painting has the potential to add much to your bank balance, my dear. I'm certain of it. If I were you, I'd get it appraised and insured. I think I'd put it in a safe somewhere."

Eugene returns to his office as though he's done with the conversation and has said all he intends to say. I admire the way Eugene tells me what he thinks. I wonder if that's how it would be to have a brother. Eugene's comments and the painting leave me wondering more about Sam.

I search through the wrapping for a return address. There must be a return address if he insured the package. I find nothing. I can't even write to tell him I received his gift. I rewrap the picture. I'll put it in my underwear drawer. There couldn't be anywhere safer than that for now.

***

It's a bitter cold Salt Lake morning. I've taken to walking the two-and-a-half miles to work these days to save the nickel it costs for the streetcar. Today, I wonder if it's worth it. It usually takes me fifty minutes to get to the office in the downtown from the house, but I half-run half-walk today due to the cold. I could freeze to death trying to save the cost of a loaf of bread.

I think about my renter, Mr. Jenkens. He's one of the lucky ones. Utah Power and Light kept him on even though they cut their workforce by 75 percent. They slashed his wages, but so far, he's paid his rent on time. That's enough to keep food on the table and pay for other small necessities.

Last week Eugene suggested we cut two of our workers to help us stay in a better position to pay our bills. Thank goodness for Eugene and his ability to grasp what needs to be done to keep us afloat but It's hard not to think about the people we had to tell not to come to work. We told them we'd bring them back as soon as things get better. Eugene picked the workers who had the least skills, but they are family men which made the task even harder. The fact is, one in three people have no work. President Roosevelt had to rescue the banks. People are right when they call it the Depression.

A horse-drawn cart on the road in front of me stops and the driver jumps down. He reaches into the wagon and pulls out two canvas bags. I make out the letters UFE on each bag. He deposits them on the porch of a little house, knocks on the door, and returns to the wagon without waiting for an answer. I know UFE stands for Utah Food Exchange. I've heard that the Mormon Church looks after its people during hardships, but I've never seen it happen. That's a lot of flour and sugar for one family. I sigh. It's almost worth converting for the benefits I might receive. I shake my head and continue walking. My father would roll over in his grave if he thought I could even contemplate such a thing.

As I approach the office, a dozen or more scruffy men are lined up on the street waiting for someone who needs day labor to offer them a few hours of work.

"Hey lady, got a dime for a coffee?" One of them calls out. He has an unkempt beard and matted hair.

"Yeah, you look like you can give us some dough for some Joe!" Another one shouts an obscenity. Then he blocks my way, standing in front of the door with his arms crossed. I try to enter but the others move to stand elbow to elbow with their arms crossed.

"Oh, the little lady wants to go in, does she?" says a gruff older man. "If you want to pass, you have to give us a little something for our efforts," says another, licking his lips in a crude manner.

"I'll give you something for your efforts," I retort. These men remind me of what is wrong with the world right now, and I blurt, "Leave these premises immediately or I'll send for the constables."

Silence, but no one moves. "Did you hear what I said? This is my office and I intend to enter so just step aside."

The men look down and shuffle their feet. The man in front of me turns sideways and lets me pass. "Thank you." I tell him.

I walk into the safety of the office, and shut and lock the door behind me. Eugene, approaches from his office just as I enter. "Did you hear what those men were saying? I had to threaten to call the constables when they wouldn't let me enter my own office."

Eugene tries to calm me. "Most of them are just troubled souls, trying to make a living where there is no living. I don't think they mean any harm, but we need to leave them alone. On most days they are gone by the time you get here. There's probably no work today which might account for why they're still hanging around."

Shaking, I nod and try to get control of myself. The warmth of the room is comforting, and I take off my coat and gloves. "Well, not having work is no excuse for poor behavior. You sound like you're siding with those men in line. I thought you'd be the last person to approve of un-lawfulness."

Eugene frowns. "I don't approve of their behavior, but I do understand it. Before too long it might be us that's standing on the street with them."

I pause and try to match my frown with Eugene's. "I know it's been slow but after all it's the Depression. President Roosevelt says it'll soon be over. He's trying to implement new programs to help people. Even the church is saying it'll be over soon. We'll be all right. You'll see. We'll be fine."

"Amelia, I don't think we will. We are down to our last month of being able to make the payroll and we're lucky we survived this long. You know all this. We've been over the books together and you've seen what I've seen. You also know that unless there's some sort of miracle, we will have to close the doors in a few weeks."

I look into Eugene's eyes. I know what he says is true. I hate that he keeps reminding me. These times are difficult for everyone. Even with just Babe at home with me, I've had to cut back on any extras to even pay the bills. I'm grateful I haven't had to send money to David or George this year.

David got a full scholarship to Stanford, or he'd be walking the work lines himself. He's too far away from me, but at least he has enough to eat and decent living conditions. I must stay focused on what I have to be grateful for or I will fall into total despondency.

I am grateful for Ada. A few months ago, she wrote to ask if Babe would like to spend time in California after graduation. I told her I couldn't even afford to pay Babe's train fare. Ada offered to pay her fare, her tuition to secretarial school and give her a place to live. Clarence is working on some secret project for the army and that keeps them all well fed and clothed. Babe will travel there as soon as the school year finishes, and she graduates.

George and Anna sailed for South Africa last year. George got a job in the diamond mines. I haven't heard from him since.

I turn back to Eugene. "Any ideas about what we should do?" I ask.

"There are several things you might consider," he tells me. "We might offer up the business for sale and see what we can get. There are still a few wealthy, well-connected people around. We also still own the various patents and the machines, and those things could be valuable to someone with an interest. There's also the possibility that we could find ourselves a benefactor to finance us until this economy turns around." He stops and I feel his eyes on me as if he's expecting me to say something – or to understand something from what he's just said.

"Do you want to say something more?" I ask. I pull out one of the large ledgers, so I have something to read while he's talking. I have the feeling I'm not going to like whatever it is he's going to suggest.

He sighs. "I think you could ask your brother-in-law to bail us out," he says at last.

"You mean Earl?" I run my finger down the page, but I'm not reading.

"I mean Earl."

"I don't think I could do that." The topic of this discussion turns my stomach. It would be just too humiliating.

"Why not?" asks Eugene. "He's always been interested in what we do. If I recall, a few years ago he offered to buy you out or help you out. He knows a good investment when he sees one. And, he's about as rich as any man can be these days."

I look at Eugene and feel sad. He has worked hard to keep our business going.

"Maybe he would do it just because it's you," Eugene adds.

I heave a loud sigh. He's always pragmatic. "I don't think Earl likes me all that much, Eugene. And to add, he's never been my favorite character. Besides, I'd hate to even ask. He'd tell my sister and she might see it as my being unable to look after myself."

"Well, there's always your Aunt Mary.

I cough and sputter, "Aunt Mary? Eugene, I'd rather die than ask that woman for anything. You know that. Besides, from what I hear, her health is very poor these days."

"All right, then. I guess you're forced to ask Earl." He pushes himself from his chair and walks back to his office.

I suppose I must do something. The more I think about it the more pressing it seems. I do have people – employees – to consider.

Earl and Lucille never seem to lack anything, even if it is the Depression. I think every investment Earl has ever made has brought them wealth. Maybe that's God's way of making it up to them for not being able to have children.

After work I go home and sit on the idea. The longer I think about it, the more anxious I become. I talk to Babe and she encourages me to phone, saying she'll go with me to ask. I pick up the telephone and call Lucille. She invites us to come over the next evening.

Babe and I arrive at Lucille's a few minutes earlier than six. Lucille greets us with a funny little wave and then thinking better of that, strides over for a brief hug. She points us in the direction of the sitting room, and we follow her to comfortable-looking padded chairs. She looks well, and particularly attractive this evening in a long blue dress with a gold brooch. The brooch is familiar, and I stare at it.

Lucille notices my stare and glances down at the piece. "Oh," she says suddenly, a tinge of red on her cheeks. "You recognize Mother's brooch. It's one of my favorite pieces of jewelry. It matches my dress, so I just had to wear it."

That's the piece that was supposed to have gone to me, but when mother died, Lucille grabbed up several of the nicest pieces for herself, leaving me with the less-than-perfect ones. I keep my sigh to myself and steer the conversation around to Earl, only to find out that he's away – and will be for at least a month.

"A month?" I gasp.

Lucille is surprised at my reaction. "Earl says there's another war coming, and when it does, he wants our money to ride on weapons, bombs and the like. Things will get better for us here in America if there's a wide-ranging war. At least that's what Earl thinks. He says it's already begun in parts of Eastern Europe. I don't expect him back for at least a month."

War. Eugene talked about war too. I don't like all this talk of war. What should I do? If he's not back for a month, my business might be gone. If I don't speak up now, I might not get another chance.

Before I can think of how to approach Lucille with my proposition for the business, Lucille turns to Babe and asks her how she feels about going to school in California.

"I am very excited," Babe exclaims. "It is so nice of Aunt Ada to invite me. She even offered to pay for everything now that we're having such a difficult time financially."

I gasp when Babe blurts out this information. I had so hoped I could keep our difficulties a secret from Lucille. I guess it doesn't really matter at this point. I'll have to tell her if I ask her for financing.

I can tell by the expression on Lucille's face that she is surprised at Babe's revelation. "Why I thought everything was going well for you," she says. "Is there something I don't know?"

"Well yes, perhaps there is Lucille. Things are slow at the company right now. I mean, we're not starving to death or anything but well, I've come here to ask-well, I really wanted to approach Earl about this but since he isn't here, do you think he would consider becoming a partner in my business?" I try not to sound too desperate, but I sense I've failed.

"What? Why would he do that?" Lucille barks, shaking her head as if confused by the conversation. I think I've made a mistake not waiting for Earl to return.

"Lucille, I'm sorry to bother you with this. Clearly, I should have waited for Earl to return but I wasn't aware of his absence. It's just that I was thinking the other day how helpful it would be if he was in some sort of partnership with me. What if something happened to me? Who would run the business? I think I need someone to look after things in case. Well, you know what I mean, don't you?"

"I think I know what you mean, Amelia. You mean, you need financial backing. Right?"

I sigh. I nod. "I suppose you're right. Financial backing would be helpful."

If I'm not mistaken, I think I see a smirk of satisfaction pass across Lucille's face. She sits for a minute and then tells me, "Yes, Amelia, I will talk with Earl about this the next time he contacts me."

I thank my sister and hug her as we leave. It all sounds and feels a bit stilted. Babe and I leave wondering if having Earl as a partner is a good idea. What if he agrees and then takes my business away from me? I don't think he would do that, but I have never trusted either of them. Not since they threatened to take my children away from me. That was a long time ago, and this is different. Besides I don't really have any choice.

CHAPTER 28

1935

The lady in the ticket booth smiles as she hands me my train ticket to Sacramento. "Have a nice trip," she says. "Is it a holiday?"

"Not really," I tell her. "My sister and I are traveling to Stanford University. My son is graduating next week."

"Must you tell every person you meet our personal business?" Lucille hisses, turning away from the counter, but speaking loudly enough to be heard by the clerk and anyone else passing by. "Honestly, Amelia, you can be so irritating sometimes."

I frown but say nothing. I swear ever since Earl helped me with the business, she has been irritated with me. She seems unhappy these days.

"Are you feeling out of sorts?" I ask. It's going to be a long trip if she's like this all the way.

She sighs. "Earl insisted I go on this trip with you. I don't know why. God knows what he was thinking. Amelia, it isn't that I don't want to see my nephew graduate, and from such a prestigious institution, I just hate traveling."

Lucille behaves like this from time to time when she gets anxious. I steel myself to be nice to her. For a minute I resent Earl for making her come with me.

Then she adds, "Moreover, to be frank, I don't think you can afford this trip." She meets my glare with one of her own. "In fact, you should stop galivanting around. The last three times I came to your house, you weren't there, and when I ask at the shop, Eugene tells me you're out of town. Where in the world do you go so often? It's just not right. Especially when it's our money."

"I'm not sure exactly what you mean," I say, staring at her red face and hoping to deflect her interest in why she hasn't found me at home.

She folds her gloves, places them in her purse and says, "Well, I think that if my husband has to bail out your business, you should be more careful with how you spend.

I hate it when she gets all self-righteous. My first impulse is to slap her mouth. My second impulse is to turn away from her, but then I realize being anything but pleasant will make this trip impossible. So, I put on my sweetest smile and hope my voice sounds kinder than I feel. "I'm sorry you feel this way, but I think you've got things all wrong."

I pause and sigh. "Let me tell you how things really are. First of all, Babe sent me the money for my ticket. Second, I'm grateful and appreciative of all the help you and Earl have given me, but the truth is, you don't run the company. Earl's contract with me is a monthly stipend to be certain we meet the payroll. The other part he plays is to make sure I have enough clientele to keep the business going until it can be sold. If there is a war and he thinks one is inevitable, then things will pick up for sure. If we make a profit, he gets a portion of it. The business isn't bankrupt, you know. If it were, he wouldn't help me one iota. I know that and he made that clear when we started this partnership."

I pause for a second to get my breath. "And as far as never being home, I have no idea what you are talking about. I haven't been on a trip since I went to visit George several years ago."

Lucille's face is now quite red. "Oh, I didn't realize that was the agreement you have with Earl. He doesn't talk business with me as much as he should, I guess. And Eugene told me you weren't available. I guess I just assumed you were traveling."

"Well, you can stop assuming, dear Sister. I am always home."

"I know that's not true, but if you insist on saying it is, then I'll have to accept that," she says. "I don't want to spend this whole trip fighting with you."

"At last: something we agree on," I say. And we both fall silent.

The train whistle sounds and the conductor calls "Booaarrrrd!" Earl has seen to it that our luggage has been stored in the baggage car so all we have to do is climb the steps into our compartment.

Once we're seated, Lucille tries to be nice. "You must be proud of David. He's done so well. You're so lucky with your children, Amelia. I hope you know that." She dabs at her eyes with her hankie. I wonder if the real reason she's so angry about this trip is that every bit of it – visiting with Ada and all her children, seeing Babe again, watching David graduate – will remind her she has no children of her own to celebrate, to be proud of.

"Yes, I'm very proud of David, and of Babe, and even of George. Thank you for coming with me. I know Babe and David will be happy to see you. Let's not fight any more, okay? Let's just enjoy this trip." Lucille smiles and nods. I love my sister, but sometimes she can be moody.

As it turns out, neither of us has to endure the others company very much. During lunch in the dining car Lucille finds an old school friend at the table next to ours. They have much to talk about and Lucille travels the rest of the trip in her friend's compartment, returning just in time to climb into our overnight berths. I am grateful for the quiet and the opportunity to think about the days ahead of me with my children.

Clarence meets us at the station the next morning. He hires a porter to take our bags to the car and we follow them through the station to the street. Clarence has us wait until he retrieves his vehicle from the lot a few blocks away. It's a beautiful silvery gray automobile which looks brand new. He smiles as he opens the doors for us and then takes his place behind the wheel. We both comment about the looks and the luxury of this ride, and he nods in appreciation of our comments indicating that it's nearly new. He then spends the rest of the ride expounding on how magnificently it performs.

Twenty minutes later we roll up to a two-storey plantation-style house that looks like it belongs on an estate in the south rather than in the middle of Sacramento,

California. Even with five children Ada and her family have never wanted for anything. Clarence is an engineer. Not a mining engineer like George, but something to do with electronics. Ada says he's always traveling to odd places for the government. Whatever he does, they all live well these days.

Two of Ada and Clarence's five children are still at home, and as we arrive, they greet us with hugs. Babe comes running from somewhere at the back of the house and envelops us with hugs and kisses. It's good to see my daughter again. Every time I see her, she is more beautiful. As soon as the greeting is over, she excuses herself explaining that she is in the middle of a game in the back yard with some friends and will come back when it's finished.

It's too bad I've never had the chance to know my nieces and nephews. There is little to say to them after the greeting and they wander away to do whatever they were doing before we arrived.

Ada has lived away for so long I feel like a stranger to her as well. She looks well but she's even heavier than she was at Father's funeral. She waddles her way towards me and greets me with a brief hug. "Well, well. It's about time we got together, and I can't think of a better occasion than this one. You look well, though I swear you get tinier every time I see you."

"Good to see you, Sister," is all I can say without being rude and starting a fight. I remember this part of Ada from childhood. Always poking me with a stick.

Ada tours me through the bathroom on the way to showing me where I will sleep. "I want you to see my new toilet room. We've taken out the wall between the toilet and the bath. Everything is in a room together. I saw it in a magazine, and it was perfect. Modern, isn't it?" she says as she tugs on my arm.

I've never seen anyone so taken by a lavatory. The door has a garish brass handle and Ada flings it open. She insists I go in ahead of her. I'm greeted by a bright yellow bath tub with huge claw feet next to a sink of matching colour. It certainly is posh and must have cost a fortune. The yellow color reminds me of jaundice. "It's lovely and bright," I tell her.

"I find it like a sunny day," she says, laughing.

I wonder if that line came from the magazine where Ada got her idea. Regardless, her house is comfortable. I can see why Babe is happy. She says Ada doesn't make her do any household chores. She is just expected to study and have fun.

My room is lovely with flowered drapes and a handmade quilt, Ada's handiwork. She always was the artsy one. Maybe part of my irritation with her is that Lucille and I had to go to a finishing school just so Ada could have singing lessons. I never thought that was very fair.

I put on my best dress, one that I hope Ada will consider suitable for the occasion. Suddenly I hear David's voice calling from somewhere in the house. What a surprise! I thought I wouldn't see him until the ceremonies. I rush down the stairway, and in my exuberance to see him, just about knock him over.

He laughs and clutches me in a hug. "Mother, you look at least twenty years younger than when I last saw you. It seems life agrees with you."

I blush at his attention. He always knows what to say. I'd never say it out loud but he's my favorite. I've never had an ounce of trouble from him, and he is such a good-looking boy. I guess he's really not a boy anymore. "Oh David," I tell him, "you are one to flatter. I bet you say that to all the ladies."

"No, Mother. It's a phrase I save only for you."

He takes my arm and leads me to the sitting room, and it's soon clear that he has something serious to say. I hope he's not going to say he's getting married. I can take anything but that.

"Mother," he starts. "I been mulling over a decision. I want to know what you think about it. It's very important to me. I hope you will approve." He stops. I wait for him to go on, but he doesn't. He just looks at me.

"David, I can't think anything until you tell me what it is." His hesitation is making me anxious. I'm compelled to ask, "You're not getting married, are you?"

David laughs and shakes his head. "Oh, heavens, no, Mother. It's nothing like that. Well, maybe it is something like that, but it's not that."

I sigh, grateful that I don't have to worry about another woman. "So, what then?"

David fidgets. I hate it when he does that. "So, tell me!" I blurt.

"I've been offered a commission in the United States Marine Corps. It won't take effect until next September. I mean September of '36. I'd go in as a Second Lieutenant." His words come faster as he explains. "I've thought a great deal about this. What I want more than anything is to fly airplanes and the Marine Corps is the best place to get the training I need to do that. I hope you understand." He lets out his breath as if he's been holding it for a long time.

I knew David had an interest in planes, but I didn't know he was this serious. "That's another year and a half. What will you do in the meantime?"

"I enrolled in flight school. I know the Marines will train me, but I want to have a step up before I actually join up. I mean, I am joined up, but my commission doesn't start till next September."

"David, you seem nervous about this. Is this all there is to the story?"

He nods. "Yes. It's just that I want you to approve. It's important to me that you are all right with this."

"Of course, I'm all right with it but I'm a bit frightened. Your Uncle Earl keeps saying that there's another war brewing, and we'll be part of it before too long and you're signing up. It's hard for mothers to think of their sons going off to war."

"Oh, if that's all that's bothering you, then don't worry. The way politics are today, the war will end in Europe and the US won't even be involved. I know people are talking about it, but I doubt that we'll join in. It's not our fight. Keep in mind, in the event there is a war, I'll be with the best damn outfit in the world. How can I be safer than that?"

I smile at my son. I realize there'd be no stopping him even if I wanted to. He's excited about all this and I'm proud of him. I never thought I'd have a son who'd be a pilot. Let alone a Marine. "If that makes you happy, then I'll try to be happy for you."

"Thank you, Mother. That means a lot to me." He hugs me with one arm, and I lay my head on his chest for a moment.

The next day we all dress in our finery and pile into a small bus that Clarence has rented for the occasion. He has gone to such trouble to properly entertain us for this event. I am beginning to appreciate my brother-in-law more for all his acts of kindness. Perhaps I have been too quick to judge him in the past. I realize how good he is to my sister even with all her foibles. He still seems to love her very much even after all these years. A wave of envy passes over me. I remember when Dwight was like that.

The trip to Stanford takes twenty minutes and the atmosphere inside the bus is full of excitement and joy. The nephews and nieces break out into song, and everyone joins in with great gusto. David has gone on ahead to join his comrades but I'm sure he would have enjoyed the trip as much as the rest of us. Once we depart the little bus, we brave a wind to make our way to the hall where the ceremony will take place. The atmosphere of the hall stands in somber contrast to the jubilation of the bus. I guess graduation is a rather subdued occasion. It's an ending as well as a beginning. We find our way to our seats which have been reserved for us and watch David graduate. It's a

proud moment in my life but a sad one. Sad when I think
of all that Dwight is missing.

CHAPTER 29

It's been six months since Sam sent me the painting. It's the longest period of silence from him since he came back into my life. I'm starting to wonder if I'll ever see him again. A few months ago, I took his painting out of my underwear drawer and hung it on the wall over my dresser as Sam suggested in his letter. I'm not certain that was a good idea. It's now easier to look at but the truth is, looking at it makes me lonely.

I go to work most days feeing rather empty. I try to be grateful that I have something to do every day and a house and food, unlike most of the country right now. I never thought I'd see the day when there would be people lined up in the streets, waiting in block long lines to get food from local soup kitchens. Nothing is like it used to be. No parties. No young women in pretty dresses and young men vying for their attention. Aunt Mary used to have so many teas and celebrations. I never see her anymore. I sigh. That's as it should be. I can't forget or forgive what she did to my baby. But I can't help but think about the old days.

David has wired that he is now officially a Marine and has entered Flight Training in the Marine Corps. It looks more and more as though the US will enter the war. I hope David can stay out of any real conflict.

Eugene keeps the business running like a clock, though we are hanging on by our fingernails. I spend most days writing letters and doing office work. Most of what we do are make-work projects, but luckily a few of the customers we have had over the years have remained loyal and there is still a need for new buildings in the industrial areas and they always need windows. I am beginning to understand what having loyal customers means and how important they are. We don't have a full work force, but we've managed to keep on the most essential workers. I know I am blessed. How much longer this can go on is another question.

One day when I come to the office, Eugene greets me with the news I have a letter. He says, "It's from some lawyer in New York."

"New York? How do you know it's a lawyer?" I ask. "If it's from New York, it must be from Sam. He's the only person I know in New York. It must be from him."

Eugene laughs, "No, Amelia. It's a law firm. The return address says, 'Joseph S. Montgomery, Attorney.'"

I take the letter out of his hand and look at the return address. "What on earth is an attorney writing to me for?"

Eugene shrugs. "Open it. It might have something to do with the business," he says, handing me a letter opener.

I slice the envelope and open the folded letter.

"Dear Mrs. Deschamps," it starts. I read the first line. All I see is "A matter pursuant to the death of Mr. Sam Goutière." I hand the letter to Eugene. I can't breathe and

I crumble into a chair and cover my eyes with my hands. I was right. I'll never see Sam again.

Eugene takes the letter from me. "What's happened?" he asks.

"Oh Eugene, Sam is never coming back. Sam's dead. Read the letter. What am I going to do now?"

"Oh no," he responds. "Oh my. I'm so sorry."

Eugene reads the letter and tells me what it says. "Sam has left you some money, but you have to sign for it. The lawyer has enclosed a money order for the price of a train ticket. He instructs you to appear in his office in New York as soon as possible."

"I can't even think about it, Eugene. This is some kind of nightmare. How can Sam be dead? He said his parents were sick. He didn't say he was sick."

"You've had much trouble in your life, haven't you?" Eugene says, patting my arm. I want to hug him for trying to make it all better. The tone in his voice strikes at my heart.

"Yes, I have, Eugene, much trouble and a lot of death."

Eugene resumes his usual business demeanor. "This letter indicates there are several personal items of Mr. Goutière's that he has left you, and some business matter that you need to attend to in person. That's why you must go to New York. He says that you should go sooner rather than later. I'll call Catherine."

Three days later, Catherine and I are on our way to New York. When Catherine asks me about Sam, a thousand stories come pouring out. It's a flood I can't stop. Dry-eyed, I tell her all the details: the highs and lows and how I have known him for thirty years but at the same time never really knew him at all.

When I run out of stories about Sam Catherine puts her arm around me and says, "Dear Amelia, I'm sorry for all your troubles. Just have faith that things will get better. I just feel it."

How observant and kind Catherine is. I'm just grateful she is willing to make this strange trip with me. I can't imagine why Sam's lawyer couldn't deal with this by letter.

We meet the attorney, Joseph S. Montgomery, at the Biltmore Hotel in a fancy meeting room with plush chairs pulled up to a shiny wood table. Catherine and I sit down next to each other. A waiter asks if we would like something to drink while we wait. Mr. Montgomery arrives twenty minutes late accompanied by a well–dressed middle-aged woman.

"This is my assistant, Miss Baker. She will be taking notes," he says after the introductions are done. "As you know, I'm the attorney for Mr. Samuel Goutière's estate. He made this will six months ago, so I assure you there is no other will and that what he has stated in this document are his final wishes."

I feel anxious in this meeting and I feel my hands curl into tight fists. I break into Mr Mongomery's legalistic speech and ask the only question I really want an answer to, "How did Mr. Goutière die? I didn't know he was ill. He always seemed healthy."

Even though we are the only ones in the room, Mr. Montgomery lowers his voice as though he doesn't want anyone to hear what he has to say. "He had an accident," he says, his voice condescending and abrupt.

I gasp and reach out for Catherine's hand. "What accident?" I ask.

"I don't have that answer," he snaps. "All I know is that poor Samuel died much too young."

"What about his parents? They would know how he died."

"No, his parents are long dead."

I glance at Catherine and back at the attorney. "He – Mr. Goutière – " I stumble over his name as if I'd never heard it before. "Mr. Goutière led me to believe his parents were old and sick."

"No, I knew his parents. I assure you they are dead," Mr. Montgomery fusses with his papers. "I have been the attorney for Senator Goutière's family for many years." He sighs. "Shall we proceed?" Without waiting for a reply, he pushes papers across the table to me and hands me a pen. "I need your signature on these papers. You may read them if you like, but I'll tell you what they say."

He taps the paper in front of me. "This indicates that Mr. Goutière bequeaths you the sum of $70,000. And several personal items as well."

I gasp. Seventy-thousand dollars?

He waves his hand in the air as if the personal items – whatever they are, are inconsequential. "The caveat is, that you agree not to contest his will. You agree not to ask for any amount greater."

"Sir, I didn't expect to get anything from Sam."

The attorney frowns and then indicates where I should sign.

Just as I am about to sign, Catherine asks, "Why is Mr. Goutière leaving such a sum of money to Mrs. Deschamps? Is there a particular reason for such a gift?"

Mr. Montgomery looks at Catherine and then at me. He seems to be at a loss for words.

I ask, "Is there something else we should know about all this?"

"I'm not certain I am at liberty to tell you everything, but I will say that there has been a great deal of trouble around this will. In fact, in my thirty-five years of practicing law, I have never seen a case like this. Mr. Goutière's wife is very sick. You know that, do you not?" He gestures with the pen. "She has been most distressed by this will." He pauses, then continues, "By Mr. Goutière's gift to you."

"His wife? He told me that he was once married to a Mexican woman. I assumed that was over many years ago. The one time he ever spoke of her it was as though she didn't exist any longer." Why must I blurt out such facts to a total stranger? Am I losing my mind?

There is a long pause before Mr. Montgomery continues, "I assure you that Mr. Goutière's wife is not Mexican. I see you are surprised by all this. Mr. Goutière wanted to be certain that you were –" he clears his throat. "Mr. Goutière wanted you to understand you were –" Again, his voice fails him, and he clears his throat. "That you were 'respected' throughout the time you spent with him. I'm not quite sure how else to put it, madam."

Catherine puts her hand on my back to comfort me and to remind me that I'm not alone. I'm swept up in shock and anger. No wonder Sam was gone so long between visits. No wonder he never talked of marriage. He was already married. Now he's paying me off.

"Oh, and as to the personal items I mentioned before," Mr. Montgomery adds. He reaches for a leather suitcase he had placed on the floor when he came in. He speaks quickly, as if he just wants to get this business done and get out of here. "He asked me not to open this case, and I assure you, I have respected his wishes." He places the suitcase on the table and steps back from it. "Therefore, whatever is in there will be yours and his little secret."

I don't like his tone nor his attitude. Just as I am about to tell him what I think, he puts up his hand to stop me. "I've reconsidered," he says, "I think I should tell you about Mr. Goutière's accident. It was in the newspaper a few weeks back anyway. Mr. Goutière was on a hunting trip with his son. One of the other members of his group mistook him for a deer."

Catherine stands and tells him, "Thank you, Mr. Montgomery. I think Mrs. Deschamps has heard quite enough for one day." She turns towards the door, but I stay seated.

"Give me the papers," I tell Mr. Montgomery. "I'll sign them. Then, give me the check. He owes me." How ironic that he died hunting. A fear that has such history in my family.

CHAPTER 30

1941

I listen to the radio every day because of David. The radio announcer keeps saying it's a European war, not ours, and we'll stay out of it. I hope so. People are dying, the announcer says. London is burning. The newspapers are full of horrific pictures. When I talk to David, I can't help but feel he is keen to be at war. That, I don't understand.

I'm at home just thinking about what I should have for supper on Sunday, December 7, 1941, when he calls to tell me the Japanese have bombed Pearl Harbor, the US has joined the war and he is shipping out. Just like that. All in one sentence.

"I had to let you know, Mother," he says. "You'll hear it on the radio if you haven't already. His voice is hurried and anxious. "But I wanted to tell you myself." I can hear loud engines and shouting voices behind him. "A lot of us are dead, Mother." I hear the young boy he used to be as he tries to keep the fear out of his voice.

Before I can say anything but "Oh, David," he continues, "I have to go. Goodbye, Mother. I love you."

I hold the receiver in my hand for a long time after the call. I've never heard my son so rattled. He didn't even give me a chance to say goodbye. I replace the phone in its cradle. When I put the kettle on for tea, my hands are shaking. My son is going to war. I've seen the posters showing patriotic men with proud looks on their faces. I want to be a patriot, but all I see is the waste of young men who will die on both sides. The world would be different if mothers were in charge.

The next morning Eugene is struggling to get the radio to work when I arrive at the office. It crackles as he turns the dial searching for better reception. Then President Roosevelt's voice booms into the room. He declares war on the Empire of Japan.

When the speech is finished, I tell Eugene, "David is shipping out. He phoned yesterday to tell me."

Eugene looks at me with sympathy. "He'll be among the first."

Later that day, David phones the office to inform me that he won't be shipping out until later in the year. He's going to take more flight training. He doesn't say what kind of flight training. It's all top secret.

"My other news is that I'm getting married. I know that will be a shock to you, Mother, and I apologize for that, but with the war and all, Marie and I decided we want to get married."

I am stunned into silence.

"Mother, are you there? Are you alright?"

"Yes, David, I'm here. I'm just having a difficult time trying to understand why there hasn't been a mention of

– your friend – of Marie– before now. Have you known her long?"

"Yes, I've known her for more than a year. I'm sorry that you didn't get a chance to meet her before, but we've both been working, and it just never worked out that I could bring her to meet you." After a short pause he says, "I hope you'll be happy for us. We've set the date for January 14. The ceremony will be in Yuma, Arizona."

Damn this war. It's making people do all sorts of stupid things.

"Babe and George are coming and I hope you can come. I'm sure you will like Marie."

"Wouldn't it be better to wait until the war is over?" I stammer. "Who is this girl? What's her last name? And for heaven's sake, where did you meet her?" I can't stop the questions, but David interrupts.

"I met her on one of my flights, Mother. She's a stewardess. Her last name is Warren and I love her. I hope you can be happy for me."

"Oh David, It's sudden. If you'd given me some warning – a stewardess? I've heard stories about stewardesses."

"Mother," David's voice cuts in. "Marie and I are getting married on January 14. You are welcome to attend. Or not. Goodbye, Mother." I hear the clank of the phone in its cradle.

I've upset him. I didn't mean to. No, I did mean to. Maybe if he's upset, he'll stop this nonsense. Goodness, why can't my sons marry regular people? Nice church-going girls from a family I know. I hang up the phone. Thank goodness Babe has better sense than her brothers.

The next day, Lucille and Earl stop by the office, excited to tell me about their plans to go to the wedding. They ask if I want to travel with them. Lucille says that Babe has finished her secretarial training and has just started working for a large company in San Francisco. Babe told Lucille her boss is willing to let her take a few days off to attend the wedding. It is hurtful and annoying that Lucille delivers all this news to me, instead of hearing it from my own daughter.

Earl and Lucille pay for my airplane ticket. They say it's a present to David and Marie because they know it's important to him to have me at his wedding. They act as though I wouldn't have come otherwise.

What they don't know is I can well afford to buy my own tickets to just about anywhere I want to go, thanks to Sam and his "gift." It still hurts to think about the whole thing. Only Catherine and Eugene know about that little transaction. I must admit, it's made my life a lot easier. Part of me knows I deserve the money, part of me is humiliated. I put some of the money in a savings account and bought some war bonds. At least I'll have something for when I'm old and can't work.

The airplane is loud and frightening. I hold on to the arm rests so tightly that by the time we land, my hands ache, and I'm dizzy. The stairs from the plane to the ground are so steep that the passengers are forced to move down them at a turtle's pace. According to Earl, the Yuma airport is a major training site for military pilots, and it's famous because Amelia Earhart flew out of here in the 1920s.

As we reach the tarmac, I see a man in a military uniform standing at the bottom of the stairs holding a sign that reads, "Deschamps family." Earl approaches the soldier and identifies us as David's family.

The man in uniform tells us, "Captain Deschamps apologizes for his absence, but he is attending to unforeseen business. He will join you later at the Officers Club." He holds open the car door as he says, "Rooms have been booked for all of you in the military family barracks. I'll see that your bags get put in your rooms."

We are dropped off at the Officers Club. As we enter another uniformed man approaches and asks us our names. When we tell him, he says, "Ah, we're expecting you," and leads us to a large room where Babe is sitting with a beautiful, dark-haired young woman and an older gentleman with a moustache. Before they see us, I hear them laughing. They seem to be having quite a good time.

Babe comes running when she sees us. It's good to hug my daughter again. It seems like forever since I've seen her. She looks happier than I've seen her in a long time. Her dress is elegant, and her hair looks as though she has just come from some fancy beauty salon. She is stunning. Her job must be paying well.

"Oh Mother, you must come and meet some special people." She leads me to the dark-haired beauty and says, "Mother, this is Marie – soon to be a part of our family. Isn't that wonderful? Marie, this is my mother – and David's mother as well." Babe laughs as if she's told some kind of joke.

"How do you do, Mrs. Deschamps? I'm happy to meet you." Marie's red lips give her away. She's far too pretty for her own good. I can see how a man would fall for her. To me, she is very, very much a temptress.

"Yes, dear, interesting to meet you as well. When do you expect my son will be joining us?" I ask, not wanting to engage with this girl more than necessary.

"I am sure he will be joining us before too long," she answers.

"Mother," Babe interjects. "He left word he would try to make it by five so we can enjoy a nice pre-wedding supper together."

"That'll be nice. It will be good to see him. And who is this gentleman?" I ask, wanting to get these introductions over with.

"Oh, this is my friend, Kenneth Bosworth," she tells me. Kenneth Bosworth stands and takes my hand. "I'm pleased to meet you. I expected a woman much older than the one standing before me. You look like Ollie's sister, not her mother." He lets go of my hand and smiles. He is charming, in a smarmy sort of way. I shudder. Somehow, the name "Ollie" doesn't suit my Babe. I wonder who decided on that. I hope this man is just another one of Babe's passing acquaintances.

We seat ourselves and the club hostess comes to take our orders for drinks. I ask for tea, but Babe says, "Oh, Mother. Wouldn't you like a nice glass of wine in honor of this wonderful occasion? It would do you good."

"No, Babe. It doesn't agree with me. You know that." I used to have a drink when I was with Sam, but I've had nothing since he died. Drinking makes me sad, and I don't need to be any sadder than I am at this moment. It's clear there's another mismatch on the go. To make conversation, I ask Babe why this man calls her "Ollie."

"Babe was my childhood name, Mother. I've quite outgrown it," Babe says after she orders another glass of wine. "Kenneth calls me Ollie because it's short for Olive. You should know that. You named me. Therefore, I'd like it if you'd call me Ollie as well."

Kenneth orders scotch, pulls out a cigar, lights it and proceeds to blow smoke wherever he wants. What an uncouth thing to do. I must talk to my daughter about her relationship with this man. He's obviously much too old for her.

David arrives at five o'clock and everyone stands to hug him. He looks handsome in his uniform. He's tanned and looking healthy. I want to be happy for him. I just don't think this is the time to get married. What if he should die in the war? Heaven forbid, what then? This woman would be a widow, and so young.

"It's good to see you, son," I tell him. "Good to see you."

"Mother," he says, sweeping me into a hug. "You look worried. Is something bothering you?" He takes a seat next to Marie "You have met Marie," he continues.

I'm not sure if this is a question or a statement, but I nod my assurance.

"I want you to get to know each other," David says with determination. "I hope you two will be friends."

I nod again and look at Marie. She smiles and looks away. I wonder what she's thinking.

Our dinner arrives. David orders more wine and the glasses--all but mine--are filled once again. Everyone seems cheerful. Under any other circumstances, it would be a nice evening, but I dread tomorrow. I just can't see my David married to this woman. She is doll-like. She hasn't said five words to me the whole meal. I can see his attraction to her, to her beauty, but I can't imagine that will last very long.

The wedding is held at noon the next day in front of a Justice of the Peace at the same Officer's Club. It takes no more than ten minutes. Marie wears an expensive-looking long dress cut quite low in the front – not exactly bride-like. She carries fresh-cut roses. After the ceremony, I hug David and give him my congratulations. What else can I do? Marie also presents herself for a hug, and I comply – though my heart isn't in it.

Everyone seems overjoyed, Babe in particular. Earl slips David an envelope, which I assume contains money. I have nothing to give them. It never occurred to me to bring a gift. Perhaps I will help them out at some other time. I'm certainly not giving them money. David has all the money he needs now that he's a commissioned officer.

The after-wedding lunch is held in a private room decorated with silver- and gold-colored linen and large bunches of white flowers. It's very elegant. Marie whispers something to Babe and hands her the wedding bouquet. "You're next, Ollie," she says loud enough that I can hear. Babe smiles and takes the bouquet. Another relationship I haven't been privy to. Kenneth calls for Scotch – and it's not yet evening. Babe and Kenneth don't look at each other. Neither one looks anxious to discuss the subject of marriage.

After lunch, I feel out of sorts and decide to escape back to my room. David says he'll escort me to my quarters. I smile at the military description. On the short walk to the barracks, he says, "You seem unhappy, Mother." I don't say anything, and David sighs and continues, "I sometimes wonder if there is anything that might make you happy."

"David, the only thing I've ever wanted in my life is for you children to be happy."

"Why is it then that when we are happy, you are not?" His eyes look straight into me. "When George got married, you stayed mad for months. It's been twelve years – and you still make it clear that you're not fond of Anna." He stops walking and turns to face me. I have to stop as well. "Here I am on the happiest day of my life – and you're behaving the same way you did when George got married."

"David, I'm shocked you think like that! Every mother wants her children to marry well. Look at poor George. He works hard. The two of them trot all over the world living in all kinds of God-forsaken places. Doing what? Nothing. Twelve years and they still don't have any children. It's no wonder, given the life they lead."

David rolls his eyes. "Mother," he towers over me. I feel as though I'm the child and he's the parent about to lecture me. "Mother, for heaven's sake! My brother makes more money than any of us will ever see in our lifetimes. He's one of the most hard-working, intelligent human beings that it'll ever be my privilege to know. He has the perfect mate to travel with. She loves seeing the world. It's not a life for children and they both know it."

I counter with "Well, they don't visit me. They're always off somewhere strange. I don't find her very friendly."

"It works both ways," David says. Then, he shrugs and changes the subject. "If you want me to be happy –" he pauses until I look at him, "then," he continues, his voice calm and firm, "I want you to do everything in your power to get along with Marie. I want her to be a part of this family."

We reach the barracks, and he opens the door to my room. "Marie is going to need you when I go off to war. I've told Babe the same thing. It's important for all of you to get along. Without family, we have nothing." He enters the room with me and closes the door behind him. "I don't want to go off to war and have this family at odds with each other. Promise me you'll do this, Mother. Please."

I smile. I love this boy. I guess he's not a boy anymore, but I can't help thinking of him like that.

"So Mother, will you promise me you'll look after her. Especially once I fly out?"

I sigh. "I will. I promise." At least, I'll try.

***

That night, Babe stays out late. I know because she and I share a room. I wake up when she comes in. She's been drinking. "Babe," I say, about to tell her I don't like to see her drinking.

"Ollie," she says. cutting me off. "Call me Ollie."

"Why should I do that?" I sit up in bed. "You've been 'Babe' all your life."

"Kenneth calls me 'Ollie,'" she answers, turning on the light. "That's what I want to be called and that's what you named me."

"I named you Olive May, not 'Ollie'. Ollie sounds like the name of some cheap entertainer."

Babe rolls her eyes.

I change the topic. "I don't understand why David couldn't have gotten married in a church, but I guess that was her decision."

"Oh, Mother, getting married in church doesn't matter that much these days. They got married the way they wanted to. That's good enough for me. Her dress was nice, don't you think?"

"I thought it was too showy," I tell her. I may as well be honest.

"Good grief, what does that mean?" Babe plops herself down on the edge of my bed. "You know Mother, you need to stop being so negative about everything. I love you, but sometimes you need to just stop judging everyone, especially for the little things. Nobody is perfect, you know."

I can't let her lecture me. "While we're on the subject of people not being perfect," I shoot back at her. "What are you doing with such an old man? At first, I thought maybe he was a paid escort for the evening. But, instead, it seems he's your –" I clamp my mouth shut before I say any more.

"My lover? Is that what you're trying to say?"

"Something like that." Sometimes she can be blunt.

Babe gets up and goes to her suitcase pulling out her nightgown. She slips out of her dress and tosses it onto a chair. The nightgown goes over her head, and she pulls it down over her body. Then she heads for her own bed, plunking herself down hard on the mattress.

"Mother, for your information," she says, her voice clear and final, "I am in love with this man. You'll have to handle that. He's fifteen years older than I am. I don't care what people say, do or anything. He's the first man I've known who has interested me in every way."

I sigh. I was afraid of that. I ask my next question as gently as I can, "Does he have any way of making a proper living?"

"Of course. He's the Western States Chief Representative for the Gallo Wine Company. It pays very well." She plumps up her pillow and slides under the covers.

Oh no! She acts like working for a wine company is a status symbol or something. I wonder how long it took her to memorize his title. "So, will you be getting married soon?"

Babe looks at me, her eyebrows raised. She hesitates before saying, "I doubt it, Mother. I doubt it. And further-more, I don't need your judgement. You are the last person on earth that should judge me for having a relationship without marriage."

I swallow hard and sigh before getting out of bed to shut out the light. I lie in the darkness for a few minutes, but I can't sleep without asking my question. "Why don't you want to marry Kenneth?"

"The idea of marrying anyone frightens me," Babe says into the darkness between us. "But even if I wanted to marry him, I couldn't," she chuckles. She leaves a long pause before she adds, "He's not in a position to marry anyone. He's still married to his second wife."

I am suddenly glad that marriage frightens her. It should. I think of Dwight. It suddenly dawns on me that I don't have any right to judge her. I think of Sam. It's a long time before I fall asleep. I visit my past through the early morning hours and decide before I fall asleep, I need to do what everyone is telling me to do; stop being so negative.

***

In late August, Babe telephones me at work to ask if she can come for a short visit.

"Well, of course you can come for a visit. This is your home, Babe." But I can't help asking, "Is something wrong?"

"No, no. Not really. You worry too much. See you in a week or so." She hangs up with a thud and I already know she's not being truthful.

Babe arrives looking worn out and unwell. I give her a hug, but she sighs and quickly pulls away. "Just tired," she says when I ask what's going on. "Just tired," she repeats.

I don't think even she believes what she's saying. I follow her as she carries her suitcase into her old room and sets it down.

"I made up your bed with fresh sheets and your old quilt," I tell her. "It still looks like your old high school days in here. I haven't changed a thing."

Babe smiles. "Thanks, Mother. I need a rest. It's been a long trip."

"That's okay, dear. Have a little nap. We can catch up when you're feeling better. I know how tiring travel can be."

I make dinner for us, happy to have someone to cook for. I prepare her favorite meal: roast chicken, rice and roasted root vegetables. I put the food in the oven and sit down with the newspaper.

An hour later I shut the oven off and go up the stairs to see if she's awake. I open the door and peek in. She's holding onto an old cloth bear that she always loved. When she was a child, not a night went by that she didn't hug it to her in sleep. I was surprised when she left it behind when she left for California. Then, she told me it was time for her to grow up and so, laughing, she left it on her bed telling me to save it for my grandchildren.

I sit by the bed and listen to her breathing. It's strange that when our children are little, we want them to go to sleep, but when they grow up, we want them to wake up. Where did the years go?

I miss her. If the truth be known, I miss her far more than the boys. I guess that's to be expected. A mother is usually more attached to her daughter than her sons. It's a different kind of love. Babe seems to understand me better.

I sigh. Babe's eyelids flutter and then open. She sits up, startled. "Oh, Mother, you surprised me. Did I sleep too long?"

I smile at her. "No dear, not too long, but dinner is ready."

After dinner is cleared away, Babe asks if we can have coffee in the sitting room.

"Of course," I tell her, moving to pour the coffee.

As we settle in, she begins, "I have something to tell you, Mother, and you're not going to like it. I feel I should tell you in person or not tell you at all." She laughs, but there is a nervousness about it. "Which would be impossible." When I try to speak, she waves her hand to indicate she's not finished. "But I wouldn't do that because I don't want to have secrets. We have way too many secrets in our family already."

"I'm beginning to think you are right about that," I interject. "Way too many secrets."

Babe takes a breath, nods and says, "Kenneth and I are going to be married."

Oh God, I should have guessed. Why else would she come all this way just to visit?

"Look, Mother, I know this doesn't make you happy. In some ways it doesn't make me very happy either." She looks at me, unsure about my reaction. "But, there's more to the story. I'm going to have a baby."

I gasp. This cannot be happening.

"I know it's a shock," she explains, and then takes another deep breath. "It was also a shock to us."

I want to lash out at my daughter. How could she be so foolish? I open my mouth to speak but Babe keeps talking.

"I love Kenneth. But he told me from the beginning of our relationship that he'd already tried marriage and he wasn't about to try it again. That has always suited me just fine. I never thought I wanted to be married anyway.

When Kenneth found out about the baby, he first said it was impossible. I told him it was true. The doctor had confirmed it. Then Kenneth sat down with me and said I needed to know the whole truth about him. That truth was that he has been married twice before he met me. Since he never had any children with either wife, he assumed he was sterile."

I look at Babe and all I see is my poor daughter duped by this evil man. Anger pours over me. "What are you going to do? I'm certain you don't want to marry a man who has been married twice already. What is wrong with him? How do you know he's not an axe murderer or something more dreadful?"

"Oh mother, don't be dramatic. He's not an axe murderer. He comes from a good family. His father is a lawyer. It's a good family, I assure you. He has two brothers. He had a rather wild youth – but that doesn't make him a bad man."

The term "bad man" hits me hard. A picture of Dwight snaps into my mind. I remember thinking that Dwight was a bad man when I first learned he had syphilis. It all comes clear. I am being far too judgemental about all of this again.

It's like there is a voice in my ear. "Amelia," it says, "stop being so negative about everything. Help your daughter through this just like others have helped you." It has to be my mother speaking.

"Well, if you've made up your mind about marrying this man then what are your plans?

When is the baby due? You aren't showing very much."

"I'm about four months."

"Then you better get married right away. I'll help make the arrangements. We can have a small affair, and just invite family. If you get married right away, no one will think anything of it and – "

"I can't do that," Babe blurts.

"What do you mean you can't do that? Why not?"

Babe pauses, then scrunches up her nose and frowns. "His divorce won't be final until September 15."

"Well then my dear, we shall have to have a wedding the day after that."

CHAPTER 31

1946

On March 5, 1946, two uniformed military officers enter the office. By the time I look up from my work, Eugene is already standing by my chair. They tell me that David died on the tarmac of the airport at Cherry Point, North Carolina. He was in the tail of his aircraft checking a problem as they came in for a landing. As the plane touched down, the tail broke loose and smashed into the ground. They don't know why that happened. What was left of the aircraft skidded to a stop at the end of the runway. The rest of the flight crew survived.

All I can think of is the irony of it all. My dear son makes it through dozens of overseas air battles and on-land skirmishes but dies on the tarmac in his own country on his way home. It is beyond imagination. I feel as if someone has put me in a dark closet and slammed the door shut.

Eugene calls Catherine and they take me to my house. "I'll make some tea," Catherine says as Eugene takes my coat. "I'm sure we could all use some tea." She putters away, opening cabinet doors searching for things. She places the tea, a small pitcher of cream and a bowl of sugar in front of us.

The light dances off the sugar crystals. What an odd thing to notice given what's going on. It's then that I notice a large plate of oat cookies sitting on the kitchen cupboard. Catherine thinks of everything. She's even brought brightly colored napkins. It's good to have friends.

Eugene sits near me with his hand next to mine on the table. I feel grateful for this. I listen for his breathing. I find it a comfort.

"Do you want something to eat?" Catherine asks. Eugene nods yes, and I shake my head no. Catherine holds out the plate. "Eugene believes that eating cookies is the first step towards healing whatever might ail the soul."

I take a cookie and I bite into it. I must have smiled because Catherine smiles and pats my hand.

"See," she says, "Eugene is always right."

"We're with you, Amelia," Eugene says.

When I say nothing, Catherine takes over. "I think it's time to phone Marie and find out what arrangements have been made."

My call to Marie is awkward and sad. We manage only single-syllable words before we are both overcome by sobbing. Finally, Marie is able to stumble through the plans that have been made. "David's commander says he will be buried with full military honors. Even though he died at Cherry Point, he'll be buried in the military cemetery at Rosecrans, Point Loma in San Diego, California."

"How are the children doing?" I ask. It's a stupid question. They are young. They will never remember their father. But I can't think of anything else to say. I'm trying, David. I'm trying.

I hear Marie sigh at the end of the phone line. "It's going to be hard raising them without David" she says, sadness seeping through her words. "Rachel isn't two yet, and Rory's four. Will they even remember him in a few months?"

I take in a deep breath. "We will both have to work hard to make certain he's not forgotten to them," I tell her. I hope my words are at least a little helpful. "Is there anything I can do for you before I come to California?"

"Yes, please let your family know about the arrangements. I can't face talking to people right now," she tells me, her voice breaking.

"Yes, I can do that," I tell her as sincerely as I can. Doesn't she understand that I don't want to talk to anyone either? I end the call by telling her to take care of herself and those wonderful little children and that I will see her next week. Oh God, how will I ever make that trip?

Through the last few years, I've tried to keep in touch with Marie. She and the children have come to visit a few times and at least they know who their grandmother is. I wish I was better at staying close to them but somehow the distance between us seems to hamper our time together. I still have trouble with Marie. I want to like her, but I feel awkward when she talks to me. I feel like I have nothing in common with her. Now that David is gone there is even less to discuss. I sigh. It's odd how life is full of wants and shoulds.

I put the phone back in its cradle. With Catherine's help, I make a list of all the calls that must be made. Lucille, Babe, George, Ada... I stop at Ada. Catherine looks over my shoulder at the list.

"Your friends?" she prompts me.

"My friends?" I repeat back to her. I don't have that many friends – none close enough that I would phone to tell them David is dead. "There's nobody that will travel to the funeral," I say.

Catherine looks up from writing. "Amelia, I think we should publish an obituary in the Tribune. That's the best way to notify people these days. Those people that care will send condolences."

My phone call to Lucille brings her and Earl and a large bouquet of mums to my door. They act as though Catherine and Eugene are my servants or barely worthy of a polite hello. I can feel the condescension in the few words Lucille speaks to Catherine. It's almost like she is jealous of my friendship with Catherine or perhaps she doesn't understand how close I am with both Eugene and Catherine. I don't feel like fighting Lucille. While Catherine would give me more solace, I give in and let Lucille take over. Catherine and Eugene end their visit. I apologize to Catherine as she leans in to give me a goodbye hug.

She whispers, "It's all right, we know your sister."

I nod and tell them we'll get together later.

Babe phones from Susanville, California where she, Kenneth and my four-year-old granddaughter have been living for a year. Babe already knows about David. Marie called her first. "Do you want Kenneth to come and get you for the funeral?" she asks.

"No, that's not necessary. Lucille and Earl will bring me. We're leaving tomorrow. Ada and Clarence will meet us there. I think she's bringing her entire brood."

"Well, Kenneth is setting everything up, so Marie doesn't have so much to do. I'm so proud of him," Babe tells me. "He said he would come and get you if you wanted him to. He said that without any suggestion from me."

Babe also tells me that Kenneth has a brother in San Diego. She offers to make hotel arrangements for us, but I remind her that Earl is a hotel owner himself and he's already booked rooms for us through his connections.

The trip to San Diego is peaceful. I try to sleep, but instead I spend the hours thinking about what I've lost. Happy memories of David when he was small flit through my mind. He was such a good boy. Never any trouble. It seems like yesterday that he left home and disappeared into his own life. Even after he left home, he'd phone often. He is – was different from George.

What is Marie going to do with those two little children? She's very beautiful. She's sure to find herself a rich husband. How am I going to get through the next few days? How am I going to get through the next few years?

My only memories of the funeral are watching Marie being handed a folded flag at the end of the military ceremony and me flinching when three loud shots are fired into the air, almost scaring me to death. That's when I fainted.

I'm surprised to wake up in a hospital. I open my eyes to Lucille standing over me with a determined look on her face. "Amelia, Earl and I are taking you home to Salt Lake. Do you hear me? You can't lie here any longer. It's not healthy."

I pull myself up on my elbows and look at her. She's so out of focus. "Where am I? I feel like I'm drugged."

"You are drugged," Lucille says, her voice softening. "You've been here for two days. The doctors gave you something to sleep." She sits down next to my bed. "Why didn't you tell us you weren't sleeping or eating?" she says. But she doesn't give me any time to answer her questions. "You need to look after yourself."

I try to think. I honestly don't remember not sleeping or eating.

Lucille helps me into my clothes. I am unsteady on my feet, and the room seems to turn in the opposite direction of my head. She puts my shoes on my feet and brings me my coat. "Let's go," she says. "Let's get you out of here while we can."

Lucille acts like there is some big rush but I don't understand what she means about getting me out of here while she can. Sometimes she makes no sense at all.

The flight back to Salt Lake seems to take forever. It does give me a chance to sort through all that has happened. I think of all the people that have died. It feels like everyone I've been close to has suffered some odd demise. My three baby sisters died of whooping cough, my mother, of some unknown disease, my father, of cancer, Dwight, of the un-mentionable plague, my baby, by the hand of my trusted "sort-of aunt," and now David, in an airplane crash. I wonder why I am still here. Someone once told me we have lessons to learn with every tragedy, with every loss. It's an odd concept but perhaps it's true. What would be my lesson?

Lucille interrupts my thoughts by asking how I am doing.

"Just thinking and wondering," I tell her.

"About what?" she asks.

"About the lessons one learns from tragedy and death."

Lucille sighs and I see a faint smile cross her lips. "That's a heavy subject at a time like this, but it's a good thing to think about. For the longest time after Mother died, I missed her, and I called on her whenever things got too crazy or sad. I always thought she answered me. Sometimes her voice would be as clear as a bell, but her advice was always what I didn't want to hear. Odd, isn't it? Then one day out of the blue I figured out that it wasn't really Mother that answered me but my own self that replied. I guess you could say Mother's death provided me with an opportunity to rely on my own wisdom instead of someone outside myself. Does that sound too strange to you?"

"That's pretty profound coming from you, Lucille. I'm surprised you would think something like that."

"What, you don't think I have deep thoughts? You know, Sister, if you would stop thinking that the world and everyone in it is conspiring against you and that you are the only person with deep thoughts and wisdom, you might be a lot happier. I always feel like you don't know me at all. I know I irritate you most of the time when we are together, but I have always admired your ability to get through anything. No matter what the problem you are always one step ahead in finding the proper way out. The way you stood up to the whole family when we thought we knew what was best for you. That's when I went from finding you intensely irritating to admiring your ability to look after yourself. You are the strongest woman I know. I love you and I'm proud to call you sister."

I turn and hug my sister. I must be dreaming, or perhaps still drugged. I've never heard her talk like that before. It triggers my tears, and she hands me a handkerchief.

***

It's taken me several weeks to recover from the trip and the funeral. I suppose I'll never recover from the loss of David though I am feeling the need to return to work. Poor Eugene. He has been looking after everything at work and he tries to keep me informed of all the major issues that come up. Through all his efforts the business has begun to pick up and our earnings are mostly favorable.

I arrive for my first day back at work and find Eugene smiling from ear to ear. "So happy to have you back," he tells me, reaching for a hug. It's a bit much as Eugene is not one for an embrace and is not usually given to such outward exuberance about anything. It isn't that he doesn't feel that way, but he doesn't usually show it. It feels like something is amiss.

As I take off my coat and move to the rack to hang it up, I catch movement and talking in the lunchroom. Wondering what is going on, I turn to Eugene to ask him about it, but he has disappeared. Turning back to the lunchroom I open the door and much to my surprise find the room filled with staff and balloons and a long table filled with sweets of all kinds. This is supposed to be a business, I tell myself. What in the world is going on?

I stand facing all the people and the room goes suddenly very quiet. Eugene appears and leads the group in applause. I am stunned. It's a party. And it appears to be a party for me.

Eugene holds up his hands for the group to be quiet again. He clears his throat and pauses for a moment. He begins his little speech by telling me how everyone missed me while I was away. He tells me how they all want me to know I am appreciated.

I am without words. I am invited to sit at the head of the table and food is brought to me along with juice and cups of tea. Each member of the staff brings me a card and each of the cards says something lovely about what me or the business means to them. I can barely read any of them for the tears of gratitude. It makes all the years I have spent here worth every moment. Dear Eugene, what a thoughtful thing to plan and to do. I am blessed. The party lasts for an hour, but this memory will last a lot longer.

It's good to be back at work. I am wondering how long it will be before I will have to think about selling the business. I'm in my sixties, and before I know it, I'll be eligible to collect a retirement pension recently brought about by the government. I'm not sure I ever want to stop working, but it's something to think about.

CHAPTER 32

I got a call from Lucille today saying she wanted to have dinner with me and that she has something to tell me. Lucille and I have gotten closer since our little talk at David's funeral. That was a year ago now. I am happy to have her in my life. We have been dining together every two or three weeks at one of her favorite restaurants. I just realized I haven't seen her for a month. I wonder what she's been busy doing. She seems mellower and less irritating than she did in her younger years. Maybe I'm the one that is less irritating. It's funny how as we get older, we can see the past more clearly.

I arrive at Lucille's to find her quite agitated and haggard-looking, as if she hasn't slept in quite a while. She takes my coat and we adjourn to the sitting room. Lucille's house is filled to the brim with antiques and lovely tapestries. I'd almost forgotten what a fascination she has with old china and doilies. God, the doilies. I don't know where she gets them but there always seems to be a new collection every time I visit. I guess we all have our impulses.

Once seated I note how troubled she is as she squirms in her seat and folds and unfolds her hands. "Lucille, you're upset," I tell her. "What's wrong?"

I am shocked when she bursts into tears. Lucille is not one to cry very often. She is muttering something but I can't make out the words. I let her calm down before I ask, "What is this about, Lucille? I can barely understand what you're saying, and you seem so angry. Please tell me what this is about."

"Oh Amelia," she exclaims, "My Earl is going to leave me."

"What?" This I can't believe. Earl would never leave her. "That's not possible Lucille; Earl would never do that."

"Oh, I, I don't mean leave, I mean leave as in die. Earl is going to die!" She bursts into tears again.

Now I'm totally confused.

"Lucille, where is Earl right now?" I assume he's working or traveling or something.

"He's in the hospital. I've been spending time with him there. He went in three days ago with what they said was a mild infection, but now they say it's more than that and I have to stay away until they figure it out. He might be infectious."

"Why didn't you call me sooner? I would have come and helped you."

"I didn't want to bother you. You're always so busy with work and everything."

"But I'm not too busy to help you, Lucille. Don't you know that by now?"

She ignores my question. "I don't know what I'm going to do if Earl dies. I can't live without him."

"Are you sure he's going to die. Who told you this?" This is too sudden. I can't believe it.

"The doctor said they didn't think they could save him."

A few days later, Earl is released from the hospital. I am shocked when I see him. He looks old and fragile. His color reminds me of Father, just before he died, gray with a tinge of yellow. I don't have a good feeling about this, but I try to stay positive for the sake of Lucille. She has hired a nurse to look after Earl's physical needs, but she sits in a chair by his side hour after hour.

I try to visit every other day after work as often as I can, but I always find the same scenario: Lucille sitting by his side or holding his hand. He sleeps. I know in the month that this has been going on that she hasn't taken a break from the house. I wonder if she's eating anything. I should say something but I'm not sure what.

One afternoon when I stop by, I note as I enter that the entire house smells like a hospital. Can this go on much longer? I find Lucille rolled up in a ball on the couch in the living room staring at the ceiling. I say her name, but she looks at me vacantly. I ask the nurse that is tending to Earl if something is wrong with Lucille.

She tells me, "The doctor was here and gave her a shot of something to let her sleep. Frankly, I think she is as sick as her husband. She's a strange one. I understand she is upset at his condition, but her behavior is not natural. Perhaps you should speak to the doctor if you have a chance. It's not my place to say anything more.

"No, it's not your place to say such things," is all I can think to say but I don't. It's hard to get good help these days.

Before I leave, I coax Lucille to go to her own bed and I tuck her in. She is really drugged. I am hopeful that she will wake up refreshed and better able to attend to Earl. The first thing I do when I return home is phone to ask the doctor his opinion about Earl.

"I am afraid the prognosis is very poor. I would give him another month or so. He suffers from a severe heart condition for which there is nothing that can be done. I am worried about his wife as well. She is very fragile and doesn't seem to understand what is happening. She keeps telling me he just has a simple infection. I don't know where she gets that idea. Perhaps it keeps her from believing he will die. She keeps telling me she doesn't want to live if her husband dies. I hope she doesn't mean that, but I think she is in danger of committing suicide and should be watched carefully."

Suicide? That's not my sister. She would never do a thing like that. At least I don't think she would.

The next day at work I talk to Eugene about the situation. I always seem to return to my dear friend when things turn sideways. He always has some wisdom to help me make my own decisions.

After hearing my tale of woe, he suggests I sit with Lucille as much as I can and perhaps that will give me an opportunity to find out the best way to help her. I was afraid he might say something like that. I can remember sitting with Father when he was dying. I only did it a few times because Dotty was always there, but I did it enough to know it's not something I'm very good at. I find it morbid. Sitting around waiting for someone to die is a terrible waste of time. I'd rather walk away and let them die in their own time. It dawns on me then that perhaps Lucille is waiting for Earl to die, but I wouldn't be waiting for Lucille to die so I could look at it as a mercy sitting. A sitting necessary to find out the best way to bring Lucille back to some kind of reality.

I spend the next two weeks sitting with Lucille while she sits with Earl. I go there only after work for a few hours in the evening, but that is too long for me. Lucille offers little by way of conversation. She doesn't want to discuss what will happen when Earl passes and after a few days of my questions or attempts at finding out what she wants from me, she takes to leaving Earl's side and going elsewhere in the house. Sometimes she has a bath, sometimes she reads a book or writes in a journal. She could do these things when I'm not here. Besides there is always the nurse to attend to Earls needs, but she chooses to leave when I arrive. Finally, I ask her why she won't talk to me.

"I don't need you here," she finally tells me. She's right about that. My attempts at help have failed. Neither she nor I know what she wants so maybe my absence is really what she needs right now.

I phone Lucille every couple of days for the next few months, but I get very little information. She always says the same thing, "Earl is coming along." When I ask her what that means, she says, "Just what I said, he's coming along." I want to ask what he's coming to, but I don't.

I get the dreaded call at the office in the middle of the day. It's the nurse that looks after Earl informing me that Earl has passed and that I should send someone to look after Lucille. Evidently, Lucille is refusing to get out of bed.

As it turns out, my sister eventually agrees to get out of bed. What she refuses to do is walk. In the week after Earl's death, she demands a wheelchair and tells me her legs no longer work. I insist she go to the doctor, which she does. I don't know what the doctor tells her, but he tells me privately that the paralysis is psychological, and he's seen it particularly in women who have suffered some great trauma in a short period of time. He also tells me it is a temporary condition. I heave a sigh of relief.

There is much to do to plan the funeral for Earl. He made a great deal of money in his life and thus we anticipate that the funeral will be a large one. With a funeral to plan, Lucille become more lucid and stops accepting any drugs. She seems eager to offer suggestions and writes eulogies for various speakers she wants at the funeral. On the day before the funeral, I ask Lucille if she intends to be in a wheelchair for the event.

"You are so mean, Amelia. You act as though I can help it that my legs don't work. You think I can just decide I can walk when I can't. You don't understand. I'll never walk. I know that and I accept it. Damn it, why can't you?"

Lucille's yelling when she says all that, and she's balled up her fists and she's pounding them on the arms of her chair. I take a step back and let her spend all she has on whatever words she wants to use. I've never heard my sister swear before. Pity overtakes me. There's a strange kind of sickness in all of this. I suddenly believe her when she says she'll never walk again. I don't understand it, but I believe it.

We were right about the funeral. It is enormous. It packs the church which seats five hundred. It feels like hours before we reach the cemetery to bury Earl. Hundreds of people make a large circle around the grave. Lucille doesn't cry through any of it. I push her chair through the crowds of people and listen as they whisper among themselves about the terrible tragedy of the death of a good man and the accident of his poor wife who has been left paralyzed. I wonder where they got the idea that Lucille had an accident but I'm not going to ask anyone about it. It's easier to let it go as the reality would be even more difficult to explain.

The positive thing about all this is that is brings Babe home. It is good to see her and Kenneth. They left my granddaughter behind with a friend. Babe is just a few days from saying goodbye to Kenneth who is setting off for the Philippine Islands and a new job with the US government. He's become a weapons logistics expert in the past few years. George is still in South Africa, too far for him to travel and of course, Marie. She sent her regrets and her condolences to Lucille but said she was unable to attend. It would have been nice to see the children. Ada and Clarence arrive after all the work preparing for the funeral is done. You'd think Ada would at least offer to help. Her concern is immediately focused on the wheelchair. I think it's a shock to her as Lucille has not told her anything about it. As soon as Ada sees me, she says she will stay a few days after the funeral to have a family meeting about Lucille. We agree to discuss it the next day.

We get through the reception though I am exhausted. In the reception line, Lucille looks none the worse for wear.

She speaks to each person as they approach and seems to relish the contact. Her energy is high, and she chatters away as if she has nothing but time. Many ask her about the wheelchair, and some even say they are sorry about her accident. She nods at them and says, "Yes, it is quite unfortunate." No attempt is made to dispel the misinformation. Most of the guests are talked out by the time they reach me, so I don't have to offer much conversation nor explanation. The whole thing is bizarre to say the least.

Babe, Kenneth, Ada, Clarence, and I meet the next day to discuss Lucille. I can't help but think back to the meeting the family had about me when Dwight passed away. It's almost like we've come full circle, only it's a different life being debated. I can't help but think we should have invited Lucille.

Ada opens the conversation by asking, "What are we going to do about Lucille? She can't live in that big house and stay in that miserable wheelchair. What is the story of that anyway? I keep hearing stories about some accident, but nobody told me about any accident." She stops and looks around expecting an answer to all her questions.

I sigh loudly and everyone turns to me. "All right, I'll try to answer. First of all, I think Lucille should be part of this conversation. It's her life and you did this to me once and I didn't appreciate it. On the other hand, as long as we are here, I can tell you that I've spoken to the doctor, and he assures me that the wheelchair is temporary and just a product of the shock of Earl dying that caused her paralysis. There was no accident, and I don't know why she persists in telling that fairy tale."

"Perhaps it's easier than telling people she's crazy," Ada interjects.

"Ada, our sister is not crazy. She's heartbroken and who knows how you would act if Clarence were to die. Everyone reacts differently to such news."

"Well, I know I wouldn't curl up and demand a wheelchair. That's just insane behavior."

"Maybe to you it is but it's her reaction. How can we judge her?"

Babe asks, "So how is she managing now? Doesn't she need help to go to the bathroom and bathe? Who's doing that?"

"She hired a nurse. God knows she can afford it. The good thing is she has plenty of money to hire anything she wants. I'm certain she is sitting on a fortune," I tell them.

"If that's the case then who's looking after her accounts? How do you know she's rich?" Clarence asks. The men have been surprisingly quiet through all this conversation. Maybe times are changing.

"I know because she told me, and she has Eugene looking after all her affairs along with a lawyer. Eugene says not to worry about her financial situation. She has enough money to live on for several lifetimes."

"Well, then I guess this meeting is closed. We don't seem to have much to offer her if she can hire people to look after her. It just seems strange that she would rattle around in that big house of hers. I would think it would be lonely," Ada remarks.

I nod. "I agree. I think it would be lonely. I think I'm going to visit her tomorrow and see what I can find out about her plans for the future. Maybe she'll open up once she's had some time to think. I'll let you know what I find out."

Ada tells me they are leaving tomorrow as they see no reason to stay any longer. I tell her to be sure to come for breakfast in the morning so we can say goodbye. She agrees.

After breakfast which ends up being with the same people as the night before, we say goodbye to Ada and Clarence and Babe tells me they are also leaving as Kenneth must prepare for his trip and his new job. It's been nice having Babe with me in the house for this whole ordeal.

As Babe and Kenneth are headed out the door, Kenneth says, "As soon as I get settled on the military base in Manilla, I'll be sending for Ollie. Once she's there, we'll be sending for you. I hope you'll feel welcome to come for a visit. I think the Philippines will be an interesting place in the next few years."

What a nice thing for him to say. I can see a big change in Kenneth. Living with my daughter, he is turning into a decent human being. Perhaps there is hope for him after all.

Ada and Clarence are the next to leave. They will go back to their luxurious life in California. Ada and I still have our differences, but I will put them to rest. They are far enough away that I don't really have to think about them much. It's too bad I couldn't feel closer. She is my sister after all. Somethings are not meant to be.

The next day I go to visit Lucille to see if I can find out what she wants to do with the rest of her life. The maid answers the door and says Lucille is in the library. I find her writing cards.

"How nice to see you, Amelia. I'm writing thank-you cards to all the people that sent flowers for Earl," she tells me. "What can I do for you today?"

I look for a touch of warmth in her words, but I find little. "You don't seem that happy to see me. Have I offended you in some way?"

She smiles at my question and says, "No, not really. It's not that you've offended me, but you've disappointed me. I thought you of all people, would understand my situation. Now all of a sudden everyone is trying to decide my life for me and I'm not liking it. I hear you met last night to talk about me and what I should do and where I should live."

I wonder who told her that. "I stood up for you whether you know that or not. I thought you should have been there for the discussion, but it didn't turn out that way. Nobody made any decision about your life. We just wondered about a lot of things. Besides, maybe now you know how I felt way back when."

"Yes, well, I guess I do understand how you felt back then, but I still think we meant it to be in your own interests. My situation is different. I am able to look after myself and you really were not. End of discussion. We are too old to be fighting about what was and what wasn't, so let's just call a truce and let me tell you what's what."

I stare at my sister. Her decisiveness is unexpected and the fierceness of it is unnerving. She was always aggressive with her personal opinions but so passive to most of the events in her life and so dependent on Earl for everything. I haven't seen this side of my sister, ever.

Lucille takes a breath and then says, "I have decided to sell the house and move into the Hotel Utah. They have been very accommodating. I have spent yesterday examining various rooms that would accommodate my wheelchair and have made arrangements with the staff to have my meals prepared and brought to my room every day. They have also agreed to be certain I have transportation at my beck and call. To tell the truth, Amelia, Earl made these arrangements before he died. As you know he is, was, part owner of the hotel." She then interjects and laughs, "I guess now I am part owner. He made them sign a contract that said I can use a room of my choosing for as long as I live. So, now I have everything in place to look after me for years to come. None of you need worry about me. I am set for life and I assure you I have plenty of money to see me through."

"Well, it looks like you have everything figured out," I tell her after her long explanation. I sigh, "I know we've hashed this over before, but I need to bring it up one more time. I still don't understand what is going on with the wheelchair. Certainly, you don't need it. I've told you before, the doctors have even said there is no physical reason why you can't walk. I'm sorry but I don't understand."

She looks at me and her eyes fill with tears. "What you don't understand is that I can't walk, and I never will. No matter what the doctor or anyone says, I cannot walk. I don't want your speculation about this, just know that I am better off in a wheelchair than I would be without."

I don't have any words to contradict her. She has obviously made up her mind about her own life. Perhaps she thinks that by being in a wheelchair she is assured of being taken care of for the rest of her life. I don't know. I guess she is free to make that decision. I find it interesting how differently she and I have chosen to cope with our tragedies. Each in our own way.

I walk up to my sister in her chair and bend down to take her in my arms for a hug. She responds and we sit like this awkwardly for several minutes. I love her. I don't understand her, but I love her. Finally, I get up and before I leave, I tell her, "I intend to come to your hotel room once a week from now on, for a decent meal and a game of cards."

Her eyes light up and she whispers, "And I'll hold you to that."

CHAPTER 33

1949

My office telephone rings, and I pick it up. "Mother," Babe says, "Are you sitting down?"

I hate conversations that start like this. All I can think of is somebody is pregnant or somebody is dead. It's been a quiet day, so I decide to play her game. "Yes, dear, you've called the office telephone so obviously I'm sitting down. It's an office, do you think I'm up dancing?"

"Oh Mother, I can tell you're in one of your moods today," she responds, laughing. "I have great news. I received a cable from Kenneth today and he says he has been able to get into a great house on the Army base and he is ready for me and Nancy to join him. I'm so excited. The tickets for our passage on the ship should be arriving soon."

"That's wonderful, dear," I tell her with as much enthusiasm as I can muster. I am wary of her traveling so far away to such a remote place and so close to the end of the war.

"No Mother, you don't understand the whole thing. Kenneth has arranged for you to go with me. He got permission from the commanding officer in Manilla to include you in our family. I am so happy. I can't believe he did this all on his own. He said I'll need help with Nancy and what better help than my own mother?"

When I don't respond immediately, she adds, "Please don't say no, Mother, please. I need you. Really I do."

"But Babe, what about the business, and the house and poor Lucille? Can she survive without me visiting? You've gotten along by yourself quite nicely in California these past few months while Kenneth has been gone. Why do you think you can't do that in the Philippines?"

She pauses as if thinking about what I've said and then continues. "I suppose I can get along without you if you'd rather not go, but it would be so wonderful if you would share this adventure with us. Besides, now that Kenneth has such an important job, I'm going to be expected to help him host parties for all the dignitaries and officers on the base. I'll need someone to help me do that and help look after Nancy. Besides, you really should think about retiring. Sell the business and come traveling with us. It would do you good. It will open your eyes to see other parts of the world. I just know you'd love it."

"Well, I don't know. Leaving will take a lot of planning. I need some time to think about this." I sigh and pause. "When would I have to be ready to leave?" I ask.

"Three weeks from today," she tells me.

"Three weeks? That's not very long to do what I'd have to do."

"Mother, just do it. I know you can. You can do anything when you want to. I hope you want to do this for me and my family. And before I forget, you'll need to get a passport and some vaccinations."

She's sounding impatient and I'm feeling pushed. It feels like somebody is always planning my life for me. Yes, I want to join her, but it all sounds very complicated. I hate anything related to vaccinations and she knows that, but she must really want me to do this. If I turn her down, I wonder what she will think of me. Getting a passport can't be that difficult. Just thinking about all this makes my heart beat faster. I sigh and try to relax. Maybe it is time to retire. I love the business, but I also love my daughter and she sounds like she needs me. It feels like a long time since anyone has really needed me.

"I'll let you know in a few days what I've decided," I tell her trying to conjure up a positive tone to my voice. "I promise."

We end the conversation with Babe putting Nancy on the line to babble a few funny three-year-old words that sound like "going on a ship gamma." I chuckle. It would be nice to have time with them.

I decide to let the idea of leaving sit in my head until tomorrow when I feel more like talking to Eugene about it. I'm sure he'll have some ideas as to what I should do. I'd like to go, but there is so much to consider.

Just before closing time the next day, I approach Eugene with Babe's request for me to join her overseas. I explain the situation as best I can, and the explanation turns into a plea for help in sorting it all out.

At first Eugene doesn't say much. As usual in serious situations he just listens attentively and frequently nods.

When I am talked out, he says in his all-knowing way, "What a wonderful opportunity for you. I think you should go. If you don't spend some time with your family, when will you? They could be gone for a long time and as you've pointed out, your daughter obviously needs you."

"But what about the business?" I ask.

"I've been thinking about the business for quite a while," Eugene responds. "I think I should like to buy it outright, if we can come to some understanding."

"What?" I am shocked. Eugene wants to buy the business? Can he even afford to do that? "Well, I...I don't think you have to go that far. I'll be back eventually. You can just continue to run it like you always do. Couldn't you?"

"No, Amelia, I can't. I've been thinking about offering you a buyout for a long time now. If you are going off on this adventure, I would like you to have a good clean exit from the company. That way I can make what decisions I need to make without worrying about you and what you might think."

Eugene can be so diplomatic. If he told the truth, it's Eugene that makes most of the business decisions around here. He always consults me, but I let his wisdom guide me most of the time. It strikes me that if I must sell my business there isn't anyone I'd rather sell it to than Eugene. I know it would be in good hands.

Over the next few days Eugene and I come to terms over the sale. It goes smoothly and he offers me a fair price. I am eligible for a government pension and with what Eugene has offered and my secret stash from Sam, I should have enough to keep me modestly for the rest of my life. I will keep the house and the renters. They have agreed to look after the place for a small cut in their rent. I probably won't be gone longer than two years which is the length of the contract Kenneth has with the Army.

Lucille is happy for me and says she will hold the cards until I return. She is always surrounded by hotel staff and outside friends. I am sure she won't miss me that much. I still wish she would get up and walk.

***

I don't think either of us thought it would be five years before I would return to Salt Lake City. Kenneth's contract was for two years, but he was immediately sent to Yokohama, Japan after the Philippine contract was over. I wanted to see Japan, so I sailed with them and stayed another three years.

Eugene was right to buy the business. Without me there, he could do whatever he wanted with the business.

What he did do was sell the business. He notified me by mail shortly before I was going to Japan and told me the news. I was surprised, but knowing Eugene, I imagine he got a good price. I couldn't help but wonder if that was his plan the whole time. He never was a devious person, but it did cause me to wonder.

I phone Eugene when I return, and he sounds happy to hear from me. He invites me to supper the next day. I find it strange that in all the correspondence I've had with him in the past year or so he hasn't once mentioned Catherine. Before that, his letters were full of newsy tidbits about her goings and comings. I ask about her in all my letters, but lately he ignores the question. Now that I'm invited to his house, perhaps I will find out the answer to my question. Perhaps it's just an oversight.

The man that answers the door is not the man I left when I sold him the business. Eugene has lost weight and his hair has turned gray. He seems fragile as he shows me into the house. He's still as neat and clean-looking as always, but he seems an old man though he's only a few years older than me. The sight of him shocks me as I would have anticipated that Eugene would always be straight as an arrow and oozing health and vigor. I know we are both growing old, but I just didn't think he would grow this old this quickly.

I look around for Catherine, but she hasn't come to greet me. "Eugene, where's Catherine? Is she still dressing?" I ask wondering what is going on.

"Come into the kitchen, Amelia; I've prepared a nice supper for us," he says, ignoring my question.

I follow him through the house and into the kitchen. The house still looks better than Eugene. Eugene pulls out a chair and motions for me to sit down.

He pauses in his usual way when he is thinking difficult thoughts, sits in the chair opposite me and then says, "Catherine is not here right now. She's had an unfortunate event." He pauses again and begins to ruminate as though he had something in his mouth that was distasteful.

I let him pause for as long as I can stand it and then I blurt, "Eugene, tell me. Where's Catherine?"

"Stroke, she had a stroke and I had to put her in a home." I feel Eugene's grief. I recognize it as I've felt it before in my own life. I want to hug him but knowing Eugene, I resist this urge.

"I'm so sorry, Eugene. What can I do?" is all I can think of to say.

Eugene shakes his head. "Nothing. There is nothing anyone can do. I visit her every day and try to be a comfort. I'm not sure she knows who I am."

"Are you sure there is nothing that can be done?" I ask, hoping for something positive.

He shakes his head again and then gets up to attend to the stove.

He returns to the table with two plates of lovely looking food. "I didn't know you cook." I tell him.

"I've become quite proficient at it since Catherine isn't here. Before Catherine I'd cook for myself, but she was so good at it I lost my ability where that is concerned. I used to watch her cook for me, so I picked up a few ideas about food from what she did. I cannot tell you how much I miss her, Amelia. It's times like this I wish I had held on to the business. At least I would have something else to think about. Then I think, if I still had the business, I couldn't spend time at the facility with Catherine."

It's interesting how he says "the facility" instead of hospital or home. Facility. How Eugene it is. "It must be very difficult for you." I offer

"No Amelia. I think it must be very difficult for Catherine. I can't imagine being locked in a body and unable to speak or know people. How terrifying."

"I don't know what to say, Eugene. There are no words for such a thing. How unkind the world is sometimes."

"Indeed." He looks at me with eyes that remind me of a sad puppy. "I knew you would understand. You've been through so much yourself."

I'm not sure I've ever loved anyone as much as Eugene loved Catherine. I think his must be a very different experience than mine. Perhaps only my loss of David comes close. "Everyone's experience of loss is different," I tell him. "I cannot feel what you feel, but I am here for you if you need someone to lean on. You have helped me through many things in my life throughout the years. You're a good friend Eugene. Remember that."

"Would you mind coming to visit Catherine on my next visit? Maybe the sound of another voice will help her recognize something."

"Of course, I will be happy to."

A few days later Eugene picks me up in his automobile and we visit Catherine. What I see in the bed is no longer Catherine, but a pile of bones with a head of stringy hair and a white face with skin pulled tight. Her eyes stare ahead but they are empty. I realize then that Catherine is no longer with us. It's just a matter of time. I understand why Eugene wanted company. The home itself smells of rubbing alcohol and urine. It reminds me of death itself.

I go with Eugene for a few more visits. I can understand why Eugene no longer wants to sit and hold her hand. I think if it were me, I would not go at all, but I want to be of help. Fortunately for both of us, Catherine dies in the middle of the night two weeks later. It's a blessing but I wouldn't say that to Eugene.

I help him plan a small funeral for her. Eugene insists on getting up in front of the church to say something about Catherine. I hold my breath as I cannot imagine having the strength to do such a thing. Being the person Eugene is, he carries it off perfectly, extolling the wonderful things he loved so much about his wonderful wife. He is the epitome of strength and my esteem for him rises with every word. Catherine would be so proud.

I see Eugene a few times after the funeral. He cooks supper and we talk about Catherine. Every visit I have with him I see an improvement both in how he looks and how he acts. Each visit he gets a little taller and I see a few smiles at appropriate times. I am happy for my friend. The last visit we have is when he tells me he is leaving Salt Lake and moving to New York. He has a sister there and she has invited him to come and live with her. Funny, I never knew he had a sister, but that fact would not be something Eugene would talk about until it was necessary. That is so Eugene. I tell him I'm happy for him, but I will miss our dinners.

On my way home I can't help but think how this is just another example of how things will never be the same. That phrase takes me back to all the times I've said it to myself. Maybe that's just how life is.

CHAPTER 34

December 1968

Well, believe it or not the last twenty years of my life have been spent traveling between my home in Salt Lake City, Utah, and the many exotic places in the world that my son-in-law was contracted to. It was a good way to spend my later years: a few months in Salt Lake and a year or two in some other place. I kept my house right up until five years ago. I didn't mind selling it when I did as I couldn't take care of it any longer and besides, I had a better offer. I was invited to live permanently with Babe and Kenneth. Babe said it was Kenneth's idea.

A few months ago, I moved again. I imagine it will be the last move of my life as I have received a cancer diagnosis. At this age there isn't much that can be done. Evidently, I've had this cancer for more than twenty years. No symptoms, nothing, just an obnoxious lump that kept getting bigger. Since Doc died years ago, I haven't been to visit a doctor for anything. Babe made me go. I still think it serves no purpose. We all have to die of something. What does it matter what the reason is or what its name is. Life is not forever for anyone.

Babe put me in a very nice place: The Catalina Home for the Aged. I should have known that Babe wouldn't put me in a dumpy place. What would people say if she did that? I sense she feels guilty as it is by making me come here. I would rather stay at her house, but I'm too difficult to look after. I remember what it was like with Father when he got sick. Back then we had servants to help. She has only Kenneth and he is hopeless when it comes to looking after anyone.

Yesterday, Babe and Nancy and her little ones came for a visit. It was my birthday and they brought presents. I talked to Babe about George and how much I'd like to see him before I die, but Babe just smiled and shook her head. I know he can't visit me. He drinks. He drinks too much. Sometimes I can't understand what he says when he phones. It's too bad. I had such hopes for him. I'll have to phone him before too long, if for no reason other than to say good-bye. Babe always assures me George loves me, but I wonder about that. Perhaps if I'd been more supportive of his choice of a wife he wouldn't have taken to drink. Too late for those regrets.

Babe and Nancy and I talk about how much we miss David and I tell them I regret not knowing his children the way I should have. Babe doesn't say anything, but I know she feels the same.

Babe asks me about Dwight, but my answers are brief. There are several things I would never tell her or anyone while I am still alive. One is about Dwight and the other about Aunt Mary and the baby. Of all the people that died in my life, I didn't mourn Aunt Mary, but I also didn't betray her to anyone for what she did. Perhaps that should be my biggest regret.

Maybe sometime in the future, after I'm gone, my granddaughter will write my story. She loves writing and says she would like to write for a living. Before I left Babe's house for the last time, I gathered pictures, a few badly written stories, and my diary. I put them in an envelope to be given to Nancy when I die. I hope I have left enough clues that will help her find the truth of my life.

Thinking about people that have died, Lucille comes to mind. I was sad when she passed. I still miss our card games. Ada, on the other hand is still going strong. She phones at Christma,s but that's the only time I hear from her. She has so much family. I remember thinking how she would never marry, but I think she ended up the most normal person in our family. Odd. She's still boring.

Just before Babe and Nancy leave, Babe tells me she loves me and that I've been a good mother. I thank her for that. I don't believe her, but I know I tried. I tell her she was a good daughter. I hug her tight and Nancy too. Nancy says the whole family will be back in the morning and will bring me Christmas.

The door swings shut softly, and I can't help but think how ironic it would be if I were to die on Christmas Eve.

EPILOGUE

The irony of it all is that Granny did die on Christmas Eve. I think it was her version of punishment as I don't think the last months of her life were to her liking, shut up in the old folk's home and put there by my mother. I think she felt her daughter got the best of her in the end. Dying on Christmas Eve made it very inconvenient for her entire family and I think that last act would have given her some sense of control over the world in which she found herself.

I hope that what I have found out will give her descendants some clue about one of their ancestors. I know I found a lot of myself in her. She would probably shudder at the episodes of her life I have shared so publicly, but I think all those episodes made her more human to me than she otherwise had been. She was a difficult complex woman, selfish in so many ways, but strong, ambitious, and amazingly resilient in other ways. I'm not sure she had a very happy life, but I know she had an interesting one. I think she was born ahead of her time and maybe that is the real burden she carried.

ACKNOWLEDGMENTS

It takes more than just one person alone to bring a book to life. I have been particularly blessed with many who helped make this all possible and I send them each an equal amount of love and appreciation for all their support throughout the ten years it took to give birth to this work.

Thank you to my long-suffering writers' group (Carl, Kristy, and James) who were so honest with their comments both written and spoken. They put up with my slowness in making corrections and listened to my excuses as to why my way was better even when it wasn't. I can still see the relief in their eyes when I acknowledged they were right. I hope we can still enjoy our yearly Greek dinner even after this project is over.

A thank you to Elaine Cust and Carl Hahn who edited my manuscript over and over and over again. I appreciate your persistence and support.

Thank you to those friends and fellow writers (Fran Kimmel, Sharon Gladman, Gina Reed) who took the time to read my manuscript in various stages of completion and offered such good ideas and encouragement.

BIOGRAPHY

Susan Glasier was born in the United States but has lived in Canada for fifty years. Susan received a bachelor's degree in Agricultural Sciences from the University of Arizona in 1970 and a Master of Educational Administration from the University of Alberta in 1982. She worked at Olds College both as an instructor and curriculum developer in Olds, Alberta for twenty years. She ran her own business for two years then worked as an Executive Assistant for Prairie Turf Grass Research Center at Olds College for six years before retiring in 2006.

She is a member of the Writer's Guild of Alberta. Her first book was Bend Like the Willow, Tale of an Arab Promise, a memoir based on her six-year marriage to an Algerian. She is also published in Women's Words: An Anthology published by the University of Alberta. She now lives with her husband, Robert, in Red Deer, Alberta. Between them they have four children, twelve grandchildren and nine great-grandchildren.

And finally, a ton of appreciation to my dear grand-daughter, Alyssa Scammell, who read the story of her great, great grandmother and pointed out how things that happened so long ago still live in the lives of our family members today. Sometimes a look into the past makes you realize where your strength comes from and gives you the determination to heal the present.

I also must add a ton of gratitude to my husband Robert. He was always there to tell me to keep going even when I wanted to give up. How blessed I am.